YOUNG PEOPLE WITH COGNITIVE DISABILITY IN TRANSITION TO ADULTHOOD

This book presents the lived experiences of young people with cognitive disability and their struggles as they transition to adulthood. Whether you are a young person yourself looking to transition to adulthood, a parent, or a professional supporting a young person, this book will help you understand the systemic failures that have caused abuse, exploitation, neglect, and violence. But it will also outline the inner and outer resources that have enabled young people to maintain their self-belief and overcome adversity. Despite the fact society is failing these young people, the young people in this book speak of belief and have hope for the future. Drawing upon the United Nations human rights framework, this book provides a narrative for empowerment and reform. It involves the input of co-researchers with disability and includes Easy English summaries in each chapter to ensure its accessibility to young people with cognitive disability.

KATHY ELLEM is a scholar, social worker, and disability advocate. Her interest in the disability sector has stemmed from her personal experience as a parent of a young man with cognitive disability. She values working inclusively with people with cognitive disability in research and social work practice.

PAUL HARPUR is a professor with the TC Beirne School of Law, the University of Queensland, an associate with the Harvard Law School Project on Disability, and ARC Future Fellow, Paralympian, Fulbright Scholar, and a Member of the Order of Australia 'for service to people with disability'.

FOTINI HARDY is a social worker, scholar and researcher. Hardy's interest in the disability sector stems from her experiences with the disability rights movement in the 1980s, sparking her ongoing commitment for a more just society that recognises the human rights of everyone.

MICHAEL ASHLEY STEIN is the co-founder and Executive Director of the Harvard Law School Project on Disability, and a Visiting Professor at Harvard Law School since 2005. He is considered one of the world's leading disability law and policy experts.

ANN FUDGE SCHORMANS is a critical disability scholar and researcher. Her teaching and research are informed by many years of social work practice, her experiences parenting two daughters with intellectual disability, and her engagements with people with intellectual disability in inclusive research and knowledge production.

YOUNG PEOPLE WITH COGNITIVE DISABILITY IN TRANSITION TO ADULTHOOD

Stories of Survival, Aspiration, and Systemic Failures

KATHY ELLEM
University of Queensland
PAUL HARPUR
University of Queensland
FOTINI HARDY
MICHAEL ASHLEY STEIN
Harvard Law School
ANN FUDGE SCHORMANS
McMaster University

CAMBRIDGE
UNIVERSITY PRESS

CAMBRIDGE
UNIVERSITY PRESS

Shaftesbury Road, Cambridge CB2 8EA, United Kingdom

One Liberty Plaza, 20th Floor, New York, NY 10006, USA

477 Williamstown Road, Port Melbourne, VIC 3207, Australia

314–321, 3rd Floor, Plot 3, Splendor Forum, Jasola District Centre, New Delhi – 110025, India

103 Penang Road, #05-06/07, Visioncrest Commercial, Singapore 238467

Cambridge University Press is part of Cambridge University Press & Assessment, a department of the University of Cambridge.

We share the University's mission to contribute to society through the pursuit of education, learning and research at the highest international levels of excellence.

www.cambridge.org
Information on this title: www.cambridge.org/9781009408707

DOI: 10.1017/9781009408721

When citing this work, please include a reference to the DOI 10.1017/9781009408721

First published 2025

A catalogue record for this publication is available from the British Library

A Cataloging-in-Publication data record for this book is available from the Library of Congress

ISBN 978-1-009-40870-7 Hardback

This book is dedicated to Professor Jill Wilson, a wonderful mentor and a caring friend who believed in fighting for a better world for people with cognitive disability.

One day, you too, will be strong enough to get out of the darkness like I did.
I Believe in you! You just have to be BRAVE, STRONG, and FIGHT for what is RIGHT! and when that time does come, hold your head up and SMILE, because no one else but YOU know what you've been through. Be proud that you've got a voice.
– Rosie Smith

Contents

Figures

Tables

Preface

By Willie Prince and Kyah Peirce with help from Kathy Ellem

> We are writing this as co-researchers on this project and collectively as people living with a disability. Our lives have been impacted by violence and we want to use this co-researching opportunity to help create a more inclusive and safe society. There's a lot of trauma . . . [a] lot of things going on, and not just in one area of the person's life, but in lots of areas.
>
> Willie

This book recognises that young people are our future and that no young person should experience violence. Young people with cognitive disability are a group that are at increased risk of violence, including sexual assault; physical, emotional, and financial abuse; and neglect. If we are to end abuse and violence against young people with cognitive disability, we need to listen and understand the voice of young people themselves. We also need to listen to the communities in which young people belong.

This book aims to change the way people think and act around young people with cognitive disability. It includes the stories of young people and their families about what it was like for the young person to become an adult and how they managed that change. Service providers from different organisations also shared what it was like for young people. By sharing these stories, it is hoped that doors will open for young people both in Australia and internationally, where previously these doors were closed. The book is written to raise awareness and help young people.

The young people in this book come from many different backgrounds. Whatever young people's culture or life experience, they shared the common experience of having a disability. Our society needs to help people from different cultures and experiences to coexist with each other. People with disability from different backgrounds can work together to make change.

As co-researchers in this project, we made the informed decision to come together on the project, although we all had different life experiences. Doing research was new to us, but with help we were able to provide advice, give our opinions, and work together as a group. We spoke as one voice, not individual voices. As a group voice we were stronger.

As co-researchers, we learnt about the many ways in which organisations fail young people with cognitive disability, when they are meant to support them. These organisations don't listen to young people. They think that young people understand what they say, when they might not. They need to help young people understand also. These organisations need training. As people with disability, we can provide that training to them.

This book is not the only project we have been involved in to end abuse against people with cognitive disability. Each of us is a leader in our own right and we continue to fight against injustice towards people with disability. Our presence can help others who have survived violence and abuse.

We hope this book will help you, as reader, to embrace our young people as we do. If you are a family member, this book might show you ways to keep your young person safe. Everyone needs to help young people to make their own decisions and join the fight for change in services, government, and community! Do more research! The issues facing young people with cognitive disability need to be shared on TV and social media. Violence is not okay. Take the time to understand what is going on for young people! Let them know that it is their own body, and they have a right to say yes or no. Encourage young people with cognitive disability to speak up, stand on their own feet, and be strong!

Acknowledgements

From the outset, undertaking this research and writing the book has been underpinned by the principle of 'nothing about us without us'. We start by recognising and thanking the participants who shared their life stories for this project. These are the young people with cognitive disability, their families, supporters, and professionals who help empower them. Without their bravery in taking the time to relive traumatic events, this book would not have been possible. Through telling their stories, they have illustrated how society has failed youth with cognitive disability when they transition to adulthood. It is now up to practitioners, policymakers, and community members to craft a more inclusive society, a society where abuse, exploitation, neglect of, and violence towards young people with cognitive disability is replaced with empowerment, equality, and a mutually shared sense of belonging and being valued.

The research informing this book was co-designed with people with a disability who were actively involved throughout as decision makers, advisors, and researchers. Thank you to Kyah, Willie, Rosie, Ebony, and Olivia for your generosity in sharing your experiences and wisdom. We extend our gratitude to Gillian O'Brien and staff from WWILD – Sexual Violence Prevention Association who supported co-researchers in this project. We are also indebted to the many research assistants who interviewed participants for this research. A full list of members of the research team is provided below.

The authors of this research acknowledge the contribution of the Aboriginal and/or Torres Strait Islander people who participated in the research and thank them for providing their stories and insights. We pay respect to their Elders, past, present, and emerging, and to the lands where they are from.

We also express our appreciation to the following people for their contributions to the research: Scott Berens, Professor Rick Bigwood, Audrey Brown, Carmen Buttery, Marion Carrett, Professor Leanne

Dowse, Dr John Drayton, Professor Karen Healy, Professor Tracy Humphrey, Dr Robyne Le Brocque, Professor Sandie McCarthy, Dr Noritta Morseu-Diop, Morrie O'Connor, Associate Professor Maree Petersen, Dr Jemma Venables, Professor Jill Wilson, and the very helpful and supportive staff at Cambridge University Press.

Last, we would like to acknowledge the love and support of our respective partners and spouses, and the understanding from our children when we were absent working on this project. Thank you.

Research Team

The University of Queensland
Dr Kathy Ellem
Professor Paul Harpur
Dr Fotini Hardy
Dr Adrienne McGhee
Madeline Kadel
Leilani Garland
Heidi Gerton
Rachel Watson
Chris Hampson
Mitree Vongphakdi
Harvard University
Professor Michael Ashley Stein
McMaster University
Professor Ann Fudge Schormans
WWILD – Sexual Violence Prevention Association
Rosie Smith
Olivia Eiser
Kyah Peirce
Ebony Street
Willie Prince
Gillian O'Brien and staff

CHAPTER 1

Introduction

Accessible Summary

- This chapter explains what this book is about.
- Becoming an adult is different for everybody.
- Young people with cognitive disability can find it hard to get the right supports to become an adult.
- Many young people can experience violence and abuse.
- This book tells the stories of young people with cognitive disability from different backgrounds.
- Family members and practitioners also talk about stories of young people with cognitive disability.

1.1 Introduction

The transition to adulthood for any young person can be a time marked with both opportunities and challenges. Successful adulthood, according to a normative Western perspective, is often seen as achieving independence, such as attaining full-time employment, financial independence, and a home of one's own (Ravenscroft et al., 2017). However, defining adulthood according to these narrow terms serves to exclude many young people who are not always afforded the personal or social resources to achieve such markers of independence. Young people with cognitive disability are one group whose needs and experiences are often overlooked by society.

This introductory chapter is divided into three sections. Section 1.2 introduces the paradigm and purpose of this book. This section describes the aims of this book and the disability human rights paradigm that has guided the entire project. The disability human rights frame is then explored. The Convention on the Rights of Persons with Disabilities (CRPD) (United Nations, 2006), being the first United Nations (UN) specialised disability human rights convention, states that old approaches of exclusion and rights denials are unacceptable, and that new norms of inclusion and equality are now required (United Nations, 2006, Article 3). Section 1.3 defines and clarifies key concepts used throughout this book. In addition to defining key terms, this part defines key concepts, such as youth transition and the analytical framework used to understand the transition to adulthood for young people with cognitive disability. Further, Section 1.3 includes analysis of the circumstances surrounding youth transition for Aboriginal and/or Torres Strait Islander young people with cognitive disability, young people with cognitive disability from culturally and linguistically diverse backgrounds, and LGBTIQA+ young people with cognitive disability. Finally, Section 1.4 includes a road map on how the content is presented across this book.

1.2 The Paradigm and Purpose of This Book

This section first sets out the aims of this book. People with lived experience of cognitive disability are central to the research design, implementation, and writing process for this book. The CRPD has swept in a new disability human rights paradigm that empowers young people with cognitive disability. CRPD jurisprudence illustrates the global nature of the research presented in this book.

Aims of This Book

This book arose out of a concern to expand the landscape of youth transition research. Through making those with lived experiences co-researchers, this book explores the diverse experiences of young people with cognitive disability, bringing into sharp focus the ways in which young people with cognitive disability have been subjected to violence, abuse, and neglect in their transitions to adulthood. While this book gives voice to young people's views and the views of those who support them, it also highlights the part that services, systems, and communities play in either supporting or stifling young people's aspirations for a fulfilling adult life. This book examines the dark side to emerging adulthood and to the ways in which others have failed this group of young people. The young people with cognitive disability in this book have overcome adversity and demonstrated resilience. The reader is challenged to think about what change is needed within individuals, relationships, and communities to afford young people with cognitive disability the life they deserve, free from abuse and exploitation.

International disability jurisprudence and scholarship are used throughout this book to illustrate the common challenges across jurisdictions. To unpack the challenges confronting young people with cognitive disability transitioning to adulthood, this book presents the findings of an Australian study undertaken between 2020 and 2021. The primary research presented in this book had the following aims:

- To present an understanding of the nature and experiences of violence against, as well as abuse, neglect, and exploitation of, young people with cognitive disability.
- To consider the factors that increase the risk of, or prevent, violence against young people with cognitive disability.
- To examine safeguarding measures that mitigate violence against young people with cognitive disability.
- To consider experiences related to a young person's gender, sexuality, and cultural identity – in particular, the experiences of First Nations Australian young people with cognitive disability, young people with cognitive disability from culturally and linguistically diverse communities, and young people with cognitive disability who identify as LGBTIQA+.

In Their Own Words: Nothing about Us without Us

Research on persons with disability should be led by those with lived experience of disability. The method that underpins this book is analysed in more detail in Chapter 3; however, the underpinning importance of the disability human rights informed inclusive method requires attention requires specific attention at this point. As analysed in Chapter 3 of this book, the UN Convention on the Rights of Persons with Disabilities has swept in a paradigm that requires that research on persons with disability must genuinely involve them at all stages of the research process and at all levels. This creates rights and ethical obligations on all involved in the research process to ensure the voices of those researched are also represented in the research design, implementation, and leadership of research.

Reflecting the 'nothing about us without us' paradigm towards research, the majority of the researchers have a disability and/or have children with a cognitive disability. Considering the focus in this book on young people with a cognitive disability, the research presented in this book has adopted a design, data collection, and analysis that involved collaboration with four co-researchers with intellectual disability and physical disability. The stories of nineteen young people with cognitive disability transitioning to adulthood show the diversity found in youth transitions and have applicability to jurisdictions beyond Australia. The young people included in this study were young people with intellectual disability, autism, and acquired brain injury. Many young people also had mental health concerns. Some young people were parents; others had transitioned out of state care; others identified as LGBTIQA+; and several young people were Aboriginal and/or Torres Strait Islander young people. Three young people had complex communicative support needs and their story was told by their mother or father. Young people spoke of a myriad of changes that occurred for them during emerging adulthood – for example, changes in much needed medical support, disruptions in family relationships, departing systems such as child protection and youth justice systems where the young person was an involuntary client, and cycling in and out of short-term employment.

Given that services and systems are influential in the lives of young people with cognitive disability, this book also includes the accounts of twenty-seven practitioners from disability support agencies, mental health services, domestic and family violence services, legal and advocacy services, and Aboriginal and/or Torres Strait Islander community health services. Practitioners were able to add further detail on how services and systems operate in relation to young people with cognitive disability. This includes the ways in which formal supports can both impede and facilitate a young person's transition to adulthood, and a sober assessment of how well these services and systems protect this group of young people from abuse.

The CRPD and Young People with Cognitive Disability

Introducing the CRPD

The CRPD is the first disability-specific UN human rights treaty and has created a tipping point in how states and other actors approach disability laws, policies, and practices (Harpur & Stein, 2022A). Furthermore, the CRPD is driving disability rights reform agendas across the globe. Illustratively, the Australian Disability Royal Commission[1] Final Report

[1] The Disability Royal Commission, officially known as the Royal Commission into Violence, Abuse, Neglect and Exploitation of People with Disability, was established in April 2019 to investigate violence and abuse against people with disability.

adopted the CRPD and the disability human rights paradigm as a frame to guide its operation and recommendations (DRC, 2023, 11).

The way in which the international human rights regime has approached the rights of young people with cognitive disability has profoundly shifted following the adoption of the CRPD. The modern international human rights regime provided persons with disability little to no specific protection prior to the CRPD. Illustratively, the so-called International Bill of Rights, adopted by the United Nations at the end of World War II, including the Universal Declaration of Human Rights; the International Covenant on Economic, Social and Cultural Rights; and the International Covenant on Civil and Political Rights, provides protection to persons with disability as part of humanity, yet provides no specific disability protections (Harpur & Stein, 2018). The only United Nations attribute-specific human rights treaty to expressly include protection for persons with disability, prior to the CRPD, was the Convention on the Rights of the Child (Harpur & Stein, 2019). Article 23 of the Convention on the Rights of the Child provides children with disability protection during their primary education but is otherwise silent on the rights of persons with disability.

To redress the omission of disability-specific human rights protections in the United Nations human rights treaties, the United Nations General Assembly adopted a resolution to establish an Ad Hoc Committee to draft a disability convention (Harpur & Stein, 2022). Ultimately, in December 2006 the CRPD convention drafted by the Ad Hoc Committee was adopted by the United Nations General Assembly and shortly received sufficient ratifications to commence operation.

The CRPD includes a sweeping disability human rights regime, which aims to transition society from dominant and disempowering laws, policies, and practices to a new world where ability diversity is celebrated and disability inclusion realized (Stein & Lord, 2007). In part the CRPD advances this transformational agenda through its comprehensive rights catalogue. The CRPD includes disability-specific rights that spread across all aspects of humanity, including rights to equality and non-discrimination, to privacy, to health, to education, to work, to family, to participating in culture, and to participating in and holding public office, as well as related transition rights (Bantekas, Stein, & Anastasiou, 2018). The way in which the CRPD rights empower young people with cognitive disability in their transitions will be analysed in each chapter to help inform this book.

The CRPD Illustrates the Global Challenges Confronting Young People Transitioning to Adulthood

Although much of the research in this book is sourced from primary research performed in Australia, an analysis of the CRPD, and the jurisprudence arising from this convention, illustrates the global nature of the challenges addressed in this book. Although the substantive rights relevant to this book will be analysed in subsequent chapters, the global implications of this book can be demonstrated by analysing the CRPD and related jurisprudence. This section will draw from the United Nations body that governs and interprets the CRPD, the Committee on the Convention on the Rights of Persons with Disabilities (CRPD Committee) (CRPD Article 34). As part of its mandate, to report on states' compliance with the convention, the CRPD includes a governance framework to inform and monitor convention compliance by state parties (CRPD Articles 35–37). Part of this governance framework includes the CRPD Committee providing interpretative guidance on articles through the issuing of General Comments (United Nations Committee on the Rights of Persons with Disabilities 2014, 2014A, 2016, 2016A, 2017, 2018, 2018A, 2022). These General Comments will be referred to throughout this book.

Additionally, the CRPD governance framework requires state parties to provide reports and cooperate with the CRPD Committee. Through this process, the CRPD Committee produces periodic Concluding Observations on state parties to the CRPD. In addition to directly informing the primary research (United Nations Committee on the Rights of Persons with Disabilities, 2019, 2019A), these Concluding Observations can be used to illustrate how the issues raised in this book concerning young people with a cognitive disability are experienced in common with other jurisdictions. Therefore, this section will include a representative selection of Concluding Observations from across the globe. In the below sample the CRPD Committee refers to persons with cognitive disability with various labels, including autism, intellectual disability, and psychosocial disability. For consistency, this section will use the term 'cognitive disability'.

This book deals with the challenges people with cognitive disability encounter in transitioning to adulthood. The CRPD Committee has specifically addressed challenges encountered by persons with a disability in transitioning through various domains of life. Illustratively, in the Concluding Observation on Mexico, the CRPD raised a concern about the high dropout level of children with disability from the education system after age fifteen (United Nations Committee on the Rights of Persons with Disabilities, 2022A, Para. 54(c)). Relatedly, in the Concluding Observation on Germany, the CRPD Committee raised concerns about the high number of people with a disability in sheltered workshops and the slow rate of transitioning from such work arrangements to the open labour market (United Nations Committee on the Rights of Persons with Disabilities, 2023, Para. 61(a)).

In addition to addressing transition concerns, the CRPD Committee has addressed many specific challenges confronting young people with cognitive disability analysed throughout this book. This can be evidenced with respect to how intersectionality increases vulnerabilities for young people with cognitive disability (United Nations Committee on the Rights of Persons with Disabilities, 2016, Para. 47). The CRPD specifically addresses intersectionality in its articles on age and on women (Articles 6 and 7). In addition to CRPD Articles 6 and 7, the CRPD Committee has expanded upon the heightened vulnerability caused by intersectionality in a number of areas, which can be connected to age or gender, such as in the Concluding Observation on Hungary, addressing Roma children (United Nations Committee on the Rights of Persons with Disabilities, 2022B, 48(f)), or the Concluding Observation on New Zealand, addressing Māori children (United Nations Committee on the Rights of Persons with Disabilities, 2022C, 47(c)). In other examples, the vulnerabilities associated with intersectionality are not linked to Articles 6 or 7. This has occurred, for example, with respect to minority cultural status, such as being from an ethnic minority in Georgia (United Nations Committee on the Rights of Persons with Disabilities, 2023A, Para. 49(c)), or having indigenous or Afro-Peruvian status in Peru (United Nations Committee on the Rights of Persons with Disabilities, 2012, Para. 36).

The CRPD Committee has specifically addressed concerns against people with cognitive disability in a range of areas of life. Illustratively, the CRPD Committee has raised concerns about the violence confronting people with a cognitive disability in the Concluding Observations on India, Japan, Malawi, and Austria (United Nations Committee on the Rights of Persons with Disabilities, 2019A, 2022D, 2023B, 2023H). Violence is often more prevalent when persons with disability are subjected to institutionalisation (United Nations Committee on the Rights of Persons with Disabilities, 2017, Para. 82), and has been addressed when reporting on state parties, such as the Concluding Observation on India (United Nations Committee on the Rights of Persons with Disabilities, 2019A, Para. 32(c)). The reporting on violence can also draw from research published in the state party, for example, the CRPD Committee supports its concerns about the high rates of violence against people with cognitive disability in Austria, by citing 2019 research published by the state party Federal Ministry of Employment, Social Affairs, Health and Consumer Protection (United Nations Committee on the Rights of Persons with Disabilities, 2023H, Para. 39).

Violence against people with cognitive disability has many causes. In Japan, for example, prejudice and violence against people with cognitive disability is connected with eugenic principles (United Nations Committee on the Rights of Persons with Disabilities, 2022D, Para. 19). Equally harmful, in Malawi, for example, the CRPD Committee observed that disability stereotypes and prejudices relating to people with cognitive disability, including those that portray them as in need of protection or as mystical or abnormal, underpin harmful practices according to the CRPD Committee, such as confinement, abductions, forced sterilizations, and killings (United Nations Committee on the Rights of Persons with Disabilities, 2023B, Para. 17). The discounting of people with cognitive disability is also connected with failures to recognise and engage with organizations of persons with cognitive disability – a challenge noted in the CRPD Committee's Concluding Observations on Myanmar, Djibouti, the Lao People's Democratic Republic, and Israel (United Nations Committee on the Rights of Persons with Disabilities, 2019G, Para. 64(c); 2021, Para. 60(c); 2022G, Para. 63(c); 2023E, Para. 9(b)).

Despite the prevalence of violence against people with cognitive disability, the CRPD Committee has identified that state parties are failing to appropriately intervene. For example, the CRPD Committee's Concluding Observation on China raises concerns, inter alia, regarding people with a cognitive disability when they engage with the justice system as complainant and defendant, in areas including procedural accommodation, the lack of accessible information and communication in the context of legal procedures, and the inaccessibility of buildings (United Nations Committee on the Rights of Persons with Disabilities, 2022E, Para. 30). The CRPD Committee has raised similar concerns pertaining to laws and policies' failures to prevent, investigate, and punish violence against people with a cognitive disability in Concluding Observations on Ecuador, Venezuela, and Mongolia (United Nations Committee on the Rights of Persons with Disabilities, 2019B, Para. 30(a); 2022L, Para. 30(a); 2023C, Para. 31).

In addition to the justice system, social security provides an additional avenue of protection for people with cognitive disability. In Concluding

Observations, such as that on Slovenia, the CRPD Committee has noted that people with a cognitive disability live in poverty (United Nations Committee on the Rights of Persons with Disabilities, 2018B, Para. 47). The CRPD Committee has observed that the poverty of people with cognitive disability is not addressed due to budgetary, policy, and regulatory social security responses (United Nations Committee on the Rights of Persons with Disabilities, 2019C, Para. 45). Impoverishment and states' failures have contributed to degrading treatment. This is illustrated by the CRPD Committee's Concluding Observation on Malawi, where concerns were raised about children with cognitive disability who are 'subjected to begging, including by their guardians and in absence of a dignified opportunity for self-realization' (United Nations Committee on the Rights of Persons with Disabilities, 2023B, Para. 33(e)).

Education is a means to escape from poverty (United Nations Committee on the Rights of Persons with Disabilities, 2016A, Para. 10 (c)). But young people with cognitive disability can encounter barriers enrolling in a school. For example, the CRPD Committee noted that young people are denied access to education, in its Concluding Observations on the Lao People's Democratic Republic, who have either intellectual disability or autism; on Switzerland where they have either 'intellectual or psychosocial disabilities'; on Togo an 'intellectual impairment'; and on Great Britain and Northern Ireland, where a student is deemed 'disruptive to other classmates' (United Nations Committee on the Rights of Persons with Disabilities, 2022G, Para. 44(e); 2022H, Para. 47(c); 2023D, Para. 47; 2017B, Para. 52(c)). Even if young people with a cognitive disability are enrolled in a school, as the CRPD Committee has noted in its Concluding Observations on Hungary and Austria, this does not mean that they are provided reasonable accommodations/adjustments or supports they need to enjoy educational equality (United Nations Committee on the Rights of Persons with Disabilities, 2022B, Para. 48(e); 2023H, 55(c)). Related to the lack of supports is the lack of protection for students with cognitive disability against bullying in the CRPD Committee's Concluding Observations on Australia (United Nations Committee on the Rights of Persons with Disabilities, 2019, Para. 45(c)).

Links between a lack of education, poverty, and inadequate housing are heightened for people with cognitive disability. Illustratively, the CRPD Committee noted in its Concluding Observation on Canada, that almost 15 per cent of people with a disability lived in poverty or extreme poverty and that many persons with cognitive disability face homelessness

(United Nations Committee on the Rights of Persons with Disabilities, 2017A, Para. 49). The CRPD Committee has expressed concerns, in its Concluding Observations on South Africa and Indonesia, that where housing has been provided to people with cognitive disability, that such housing is group homes, institutionalised and unsafe (United Nations Committee on the Rights of Persons with Disabilities, 2018C, Para. 34; 2022I, Para. 44(b)). The analysis of CRPD jurisprudence in this section has illustrated the global nature of the challenges confronting young people with cognitive disability. The next section will provide key terms and explain how this book is structured.

1.3 Defining Concepts and Terms Used in This Book

This section defines key terms used throughout this book. Cognitive disability impacts on how young people transition to adulthood. This transition is complicated by intersectional vulnerabilities. The heightened impact of intersectionality is especially apparent for young people with cognitive disability who are Aboriginal and/or Torres Strait Islanders. Young people from cultural or linguistically diverse communities experience different heightened vulnerabilities. Similarly, young people who are LGBTIQA+ also experience heightened vulnerabilities.

Important Terms Used in This Book

Intentional Inconsistency: In Their Own Words

The ability of people with cognitive disability to speak in their own voices means that there are situations in this book where the language will appear inconsistent. For illustration, even though the authors prefer the umbrella term 'cognitive disability', where a participant uses a different term to describe themselves, then the preferences of young people with cognitive disability will be respected.

Person-First Language

There are global differences in the way in which language is used for disability. This book is written in 'person-first' language to describe persons with disability, as this was the majority preference of those with lived experience in the study. 'Persons with disability' is used as a generic term to align with the CRPD. 'Young people with cognitive disability' is the term adopted in discussions about the participants in this study. The merit of this approach to language is that it recognises the personhood of young people apart from any conditions or labels, focusing on the person's skills, abilities, and strengths (West et al., 2015).

Cognitive Disability

This study utilises the term 'cognitive disability' as an umbrella term to describe several conditions, that is, intellectual disability, acquired brain injury, and autism spectrum disorder. These separate conditions are explained below as a point of reference for the reader, noting that clinical descriptors of conditions can provide general understandings of the functional impact of a person's impairment and, in this case, can be an important consideration when examining the experiences of transition. However, it is also vital to note that young people with such labels are a heterogeneous group, and therefore clinical definitions may be poor indicators of young people's experiences. Indeed, many of the young people in this study did not identify with these labels, and their experiences of disability are not adequately summarised by these diagnostic categories.

Intellectual Disability

According to the American Association on Intellectual and Developmental Disabilities, 'intellectual disability' is a term used to describe significant limitations both in intellectual functioning and in adaptive behaviour as expressed in conceptual, social, and practical adaptive skills, with the age of onset prior to twenty-two years (Schalock et al., 2021, p. 439). The World Health Organisation's (2022) International Statistical Classification of Diseases (and related health problems) (ICD-11) further divides intellectual disability into degrees of severity, namely, 'mild', 'moderate', 'severe', and 'profound' disorders of intellectual development. Another category of intellectual disability that is not documented in diagnostic manuals, yet nonetheless refers to a group of people who experience significant social, emotional, and psychological vulnerabilities, is 'borderline' intellectual disability (Wieland & Zitman, 2016).

Acquired Brain Injury

The term 'acquired brain injury' (ABI) refers to any damage to the brain that happened after birth (Australian Institute of Health and Welfare, 2007). The causes of ABI are varied, and can include abusive head trauma, accidents, lack of oxygen, stroke, and degenerative neurological disease. A person's cognitive, physical, emotional, and independent functioning can be impacted by having an ABI (Legano et al., 2021).

Autism Spectrum Disorder
The term 'autism spectrum disorder' has been described in the *Diagnostic and Statistical Manual of Mental Disorders: DSM-5-TR* as a condition 'characterized by persistent deficits in social communication and social interaction across multiple contexts, including deficits in social reciprocity, nonverbal communicative behaviours used for social interaction, and skills in developing, maintaining and understanding relationships' (American Psychiatric Association, 2022). A diagnosis of autism spectrum disorder also requires the presence of repetitive, restricted patterns of behaviour, activities, or interests. Diagnoses such as Asperger's syndrome and pervasive developmental disorders have been subsumed under the broad category of autism, but many people continue to use these terms out of personal preference. Other young people prefer to consider autism in social terms of human rights and identity, rather than as a deficit-focused medical term (Kapp, 2020). The neurodiverse movement advocates for people whose sensory and cognitive experiences fall outside the norm, that is, people who are neurodivergent (Gratton, 2021).

Violence
Acts of abuse, neglect, and exploitation of and violence to young people with cognitive disability represent extreme examples of prejudice, discrimination, and marginalisation that can and do occur on a daily basis (Richardson et al., 2016). While these acts occur at an individual level and must be addressed on a person-to-person basis, they are also indicative of broader societal values and beliefs that permeate relationships, communities, services, and institutions (Goodley & Runswick-Cole, 2011).

The authors in this book were conscious that some language which refers to acts of abuse can serve to minimise or silence the experiences of young people with cognitive disability who are victims of such acts (Healy, 2020; Thorneycroft & Asquith, 2015). Consequently, the term 'violence' has been used as an overarching concept to describe the many different types of abuse experienced by young people. Violence, it is felt, best encapsulates the oppressive material, structural, systemic, and cultural conditions young people with cognitive disability encounter, as well as the practices that are committed against the person. Violence is used not only to describe extreme acts of violation of human rights, but also so-called smaller acts of abuse and neglect against young people with cognitive disability. In some respects, it is those 'smaller' acts that are at greater risk of becoming normalised by those who have the authority and power to change them. As will be seen throughout this book, these 'smaller' acts of violence can set the scene for further criminal behaviour (Burch, 2021).

Defining Transition to Adulthood

The path to adulthood for all young people in contemporary Western societies is often defined as an opportunity for young people to become autonomous and to exercise their right to citizenship (Bekken, 2022). As previously mentioned, the traditional markers of 'successful' transitions, such as finding full-time work, achieving financial independence, marriage, and parenthood, reflect cultural values about adulthood, but fail to account for the complexity of youth experiences (Pearson et al., 2021). These cultural values imposed on youth transition construct young people as individual actors who are aiming to meet an ideal version of adulthood, rather than understanding who young people are and how they feel in the present (Pearson et al., 2021).

A more accurate descriptor of youth transition used in this book is one in which there is a change in role or status. This change can potentially occur over many different contexts and involves moving between or within a variety of social structures (Strnadová & Cumming, 2016). For any young person, becoming an adult is not a step-by-step, linear process, nor does the transition necessarily have a predetermined end (Smith & Dowse, 2019). Applying a uniform and simplistic framework for understanding change in young people is therefore problematic, and especially so for young people with cognitive disability, who are likely to face multiple and interlocking disadvantage throughout their life (Ellem et al., 2019).

The 'most normal' way of becoming an adult is often out of reach for young people with cognitive disability (Bekken, 2022). Social expectations around independence can fail to consider young people with cognitive disability who may be dependent on others for daily personal care (Jacobs et al., 2020), who may have difficulties setting goals and organising activities (Schalock et al., 2021), who may require support with social interaction (American Psychiatric Association, 2013), and who may have co-occurring medical and psychiatric conditions that can create barriers to community inclusion (Wisner-Carlson et al., 2020). These individual difficulties, related to a young person's impairment, are compounded by structural inequalities in society, which position young people with cognitive disability as defective and incomplete in achieving the ideals of adulthood (Midjo & Aune, 2018). This group of young people may therefore be excluded from receipt of transition supports.

Approaching Youth Transition through an Intersectional Lens

Having a cognitive disability can be considered as one social identity among many others that can impact on youth transition (McLaughlin, 2023). Intersectionality, a theoretical framework first coined by Crenshaw (1989) and foregrounded by African American feminist scholars, examines the simultaneous lived experience of multiple facets of social identity (Thill, 2019). According to this theory, identity categories such as those related to gender, sexuality, ability, ethnicity, and culture are interconnected, creating overlapping and interdependent systems of discrimination and disadvantage (Hill Collins & Bilge, 2016). By using intersectionality as an analytical tool for understanding youth transition in this book, the experiences of young people with cognitive disability of youth transition no longer just relate to their disability, but also to other social identities. This study also considered Aboriginal and/or Torres Strait Islander young people with cognitive disability, young people with cognitive disability from culturally and linguistically diverse backgrounds, and LGBTIQA+ young people with cognitive disability.

Transition Experiences of Aboriginal and/or Torres Strait Islander Young People with Cognitive Disability

The relationship between youth transition and social disadvantage is very apparent for Aboriginal and/or Torres Strait Islander young people with cognitive disability, yet little is known in Australia about how many Indigenous young people have a cognitive disability nor how this group fares in transition. An Australian Institute of Health and Welfare (AIHW) analysis of self-reported data on disability from the 2014–2015 National Aboriginal and Torres Strait Islander Social Survey (NATSISS) found that, while the majority of Indigenous young people did not have a disability, 20 per cent (or 13,500) young people reported having an intellectual disability (AIHW, 2018). This proportion of young people with intellectual disability warrants further attention.

Many Aboriginal and/or Torres Strait Islander young people with cognitive disability may never have had their disability appropriately diagnosed or recognised and may never have received any support from disability services (McCausland & Dowse, 2020). Aboriginal and/or Torres Strait Islander young people with cognitive disability may be unable or unwilling to identify with a having a disability, as such diagnostic labels may seem culturally or socially inappropriate. Those who do receive disability support may experience interactions with service providers that lack cultural awareness and sensitivity (Green et al., 2018).

There are likely to be multiple structural and practical barriers to Aboriginal and/or Torres Strait Islander young people with cognitive disability in receiving the services and supports they need as they transition to adulthood (McCausland & Dowse, 2020). The effect of intergenerational trauma, racism, and socioeconomic disadvantage can impact on adult transition, and this group of young people may have poor access to education, income, shelter, and food security (AIHW, 2018). Aboriginal and/or Torres Strait Islander young people are over-represented in child protection and criminal justice systems; are disproportionately exposed to risk factors such as grief, loss, and discrimination; have higher rates of suicide and risk of suicide than other groups of Australian young people; and are at greater risk of abuse, neglect, and exploitation (Cuervo et al., 2015).

Transition Experiences of Culturally and Linguistically Diverse Young People with Cognitive Disability

Another group of young people with cognitive disability who can experience added barriers and challenges in transitioning to adulthood are culturally and linguistically diverse young people with cognitive disability. 'Culturally and linguistically diverse' is used here to refer to a diverse group of young people that includes migrants, refugees, or multicultural young people (Wyn et al., 2018).

The act of migration presents challenges for any young person, requiring adaptation to a new environment, language, and culture, as well as having to negotiate changes in growth and development as the young person matures into adulthood (Khawaja & Carr, 2020). Departing one's country of origin also involves leaving established support networks behind and experiencing associated grief and loss (Jorgensen et al., 2021). Culturally and linguistically diverse young people with cognitive disability may also experience intergenerational conflict with their family members as they settle into the new country and seek to navigate two cultures, that of their country of origin and that of the host country (Khawaja & Ramirez, 2019). For young people with cognitive disability who are refugees, past experiences of displacement, war, torture, and persecution can also shape their settlement processes, and adversely impact on their physical and psychological health and their ability to fully participate in society on an equal basis with others (Stein & Lord, 2012; Federation of Ethnic Communities' Councils of Australia et al., 2019).

Culturally and linguistically diverse young people with cognitive disability have been described as a hidden population (Burns, 2020), and many authors have documented common experiences of social isolation for this group of young people (King, Edwards, Correa-Velez, Darracott, et al., 2016). There may be intense feelings of shame, guilt, and stigma within the young person's family regarding cognitive disability (Amparo Advocacy, 2016), and the family may feel unsupported emotionally and socially from their country-of-origin community in Australia (King, Edwards, Correa-Velez, Hair, et al., 2016). In addition, a family may be distrustful of, or lack awareness of, formal supports and services regarding disability (Jorgensen et al., 2021; Zhou, 2016).

Advocacy services for culturally and linguistically diverse people with disability view Australia's immigration law and policy as discriminatory to migrants with disability (National Ethnic Disability Alliance, 2023). An assessment of Australia's compliance with the CRPD by the CRPD committee raised concerns about the *Migration Act (1958)* (Cth) and the health requirement in *Migration Regulations (1994)* (Cth) that allow immigration authorities to refuse entry to refugees and migrants on the basis of their disability and its perceived economic cost (Committee on the Rights of Persons with Disabilities, 2019). It was recommended that these laws be amended, that the ten-year qualifying period for migrants to access the Disability Support Pension be removed, and that refugees with disability are not transferred to the neighbouring country, Papua New Guinea, or other 'regional processing countries'.

Discrimination and neglect of young people from culturally and linguistically diverse backgrounds with cognitive disability can also occur on a daily basis, in public places such as shopping centres, schools, and workplaces (Wyn et al., 2018). In addition, disability services have been known to turn away clients from culturally and linguistically diverse backgrounds on the basis that agencies do not feel they have the resources to work with people with limited English language skills (Federation of Ethnic Communities' Councils of Australia et al., 2019). The failure of the Australian community and supports and services to adequately cater to culturally and linguistically diverse young people with cognitive disability undermines their health and well-being and is likely to increase their risk of experiencing abuse and exploitation.

Transition Experiences of LGBTIQA+ Young People with Cognitive Disability

The acronym LGBTIQA+ refers to many identity categories, including lesbian, gay, bisexual, transgender, intersex, queer/questioning, asexual, and other terms. It is a collective term that people use to express their gender, sexuality, identity, and relationships. This descriptor acknowledges the diversity of people's identities and the unique ways in which people describe their histories and experiences (O'Shea et al., 2020).

Very little research has been conducted on the prevalence of LGBTIQA+ young people who have a cognitive disability in Australia. An online survey of 6,418 LGBTIQA+ young people in Australia aged between fourteen and twenty-one found that almost two-fifths of the sample reported having a disability or a long-term health condition (39%, $n =$ 2,500) (Hill et al., 2021). Participants self-identified as having neurodiversity/autism (6.6%, $n = 422$), intellectual disability (0.1%, $n = 10$), and acquired brain injury (2.1%, $n = 132$). There are limitations to these findings, being a non-representative sample, and therefore comparisons cannot be made with general population data. This highlights the importance of further research.

The task of negotiating one's identity and making sense of one's place in the world is particularly challenging for young people with cognitive disability who identify as LGBTIQA+ (Bates, 2020). A safe transition to adulthood for this group of young people is dependent upon acceptance from others, support to develop a positive self-image, and opportunities to build connections with peers (Dinwoodie et al., 2020). The process of coming out to others about one's sexuality may be a constant negotiation, where young people need to make safety-based decisions about others' responses (Toft et al., 2019).

Many young people with cognitive disability have been historically regarded as non-sexual, incapable, or uninterested in sex (Wilson et al., 2016). These social attitudes can be compounded when a young person identifies as LGBTIQA+. Disability service providers may show more support to the sexuality of heterosexual young people with cognitive disability than to LGBTIQA+ young people (Dinwoodie et al., 2020). This group of young people may struggle to belong in disability services, yet also feel unsupported in LGBTIQA+ services (Miller et al., 2021).

LGBTIQA+ young people with cognitive disability are at higher risk for depression, anxiety, substance abuse, and suicidal ideations and attempts than other groups of young people (Dinwoodie et al., 2020; Stoffelen et al., 2018). They may be subjected to bullying, abuse, and violence from both strangers and acquaintances, and subsequently internalise homophobic attitudes, seldom reporting matters to police. LGBTIQA+ young people may assume that police will be homophobic and discriminatory if they were to disclose their experiences of violence (Pickles, 2021).

1.4 Structure of This Book

Each chapter of this book is prefaced with an accessible Easy English summary. This section provides a road map to the twelve chapters in this book.

Accessible Chapter Summaries

Each chapter of this book is prefaced with an accessible Easy English summary. Easy English is a form of written communication that has been developed within Australia for the last twenty years (Basterfield, 2019). In other countries, such as the United States, United Kingdom, and Scandinavia, the term 'Easy Read' is often used to denote the same process. Easy English is targeted towards people who have limited literacy. This can include people with a cognitive disability, and therefore, the addition of this communication style is important for this book in order for it to reach young people with cognitive disability. These Easy English summaries use short sentences, everyday words, a minimum size fourteen font, and bullet points (Anderson et al., 2017). The summaries have been reviewed by co-researchers with cognitive disability to guide their development.

Chapter Road Map

This work is organised into several thematic chapters. In Chapter 2, 'Violence against Young People with Cognitive Disability', we examine what is known about the nature and extent of abuse experienced by young people with cognitive disability and consider the implications for transition to adulthood. We draw upon both Australian and international literature to look at the difficulties in ascertaining the prevalence of abuse in young people with cognitive disability, and the personal, environmental, service, and system factors that can increase the risk of abuse in this group.

In Chapter 3, 'Working in Partnership with People with Lived Experience: An Inclusive Methodology', we speak to the participatory nature of this study, and outline the research aims, the theoretical framework, and research methods involved in this study. This chapter is an honest reflection on the processes of engaging in inclusive research in an area that is highly sensitive and presents significant ethical complexities. We discuss inclusive research principles and how they relate to our work and include insights from co-researchers with disability on the study.

Chapter 4, 'Amethyst's Story', is an account of one young woman's experience of violence. Amethyst is an Aboriginal and South Sea Islander woman with cognitive disability who shared her account of domestic and family violence, sexual and physical abuse, degradation, coercive control, and exploitation. Her story sets the scene for our book and illustrates how violence cuts across multiple systems and is intimately related to ableism, racism, and gender bias. The story is explained through an ecological intersectional lens, the key theoretical framework of this book.

Chapter 5, 'The Experiences of Young People with Cognitive Disability: The Complex Road to Adulthood', shares the many barriers that young people in our study encountered in emerging adulthood. Ableism in many guises impacted on young people's struggles to assert independence, to develop meaningful relationships, and to navigate adulthood safely. The chapter also highlights the need for cultural safety and respect as well as the need to depart from heteronormative assumptions to allow some young people to explore their sexuality in their own way.

Chapter 6, 'The Many Faces of Violence', outlines violence in many forms. We reveal many incidents of abuse of young people with cognitive disability, including domestic and family violence, physical abuse, emotional and psychological abuse, neglect, exploitation, and sexual assault. While it may appear that the examples given are separate and discrete events, the violence was likely accompanied by other acts of harm. The impact of these events on the transition to adulthood can be cumulative, enduring, and disruptive, and require young people to reclaim their power from the persons and contexts that led to the abuse.

In Chapter 7, 'Young People and the National Disability Insurance Scheme: "The Standard Cookie Cutter Approach"', the reader is introduced to the ways in which service systems may set the context for abuse, neglect, and violence to occur for young people with cognitive disability. Section 7.2 discusses the ways in which the concerns of young people with cognitive disability may be problematised by service systems. The chapter describes the difficulties that can occur when fiscal and managerial considerations of services override fundamental needs of young people. Section 7.3 examines the National Disability Insurance Scheme (NDIS)[2] from the perspective of young people with cognitive disability, family members, and practitioners. Many participants report challenges in accessing the scheme and ensuring supports were appropriate. While many young people were grateful for the supports on offer, further change was needed to ensure

[2] The National Disability Insurance Scheme is a scheme of the Australian government that provides funding to eligible people with disability.

young people exercised meaningful choice and control over their lives as they transitioned into adulthood.

Chapter 8, 'Don't Give Up on Us: Young People's Experiences of Education and Employment', explores the transition from education to work for young people with cognitive disability. The desire to belong, to have friendships, and to have some certainty and direction when leaving school was evident in young people's accounts. Some young people were able to find paid work after school, but this often did not meet their aspirations. Education and employment experiences often failed to provide the stability and support young people needed to navigate young adulthood.

Chapter 9, 'Housing, Home, and Mental Well-Being: The Need for Self-Determination and Safety', discusses the complexity involved for young people with cognitive disability to access their fundamental rights for safe housing and appropriate mental health support. Many young people were denied access to appropriate, stable, and affordable housing where they could live safely and independently. Others had no choice about whom they lived with, and the combination of these further exacerbated exposure to violence for the young people. The challenges of receiving appropriate mental health support that recognised and accommodated the particular needs of the young person with cognitive disability were also highlighted.

In Chapter 10, 'Young People's Experiences of the Child Protection and Criminal Justice Systems', the complexities involved for young people with cognitive disability who come to the attention of both systems is discussed. The lack of recognition and accommodation of a young person's disability when entering the child protection and criminal justice systems resulted in experiences of abuse, neglect, exploitation, and violence, reflecting systemic level gaps. The cognitive disability of parents was seen as a defining factor in determining their 'fitness to parent', resulting in children being removed from their care. Young people's experiences of the criminal justice system were shaped by the system's lack of understanding of their cognitive disability and an absence of appropriate skills in authorities to respond effectively to this group, thus resulting in further violence and harm.

Chapter 11, 'Having Someone in Your Corner', identifies the importance of appropriate positive social supports for young people with cognitive disability. Access to support at the micro and meso levels was identified as vital to creating a sense of safety, belonging, and connection. Such supports included informal support through family and friends, but also pets, and at a formal level through organisations and services. Importantly, the young people shared that having these supports was key to enabling them to navigate the complexities of multiple systems.

In Chapter 12, 'In the Voices of Participants: What Needs to Change', we come back to the profound human rights violations that young people with cognitive disability have experienced. We focus on what it is that young people with cognitive disability, their families, and practitioner stakeholders say is needed to reduce the violence experienced. We recommend that an integrated strategy across life stages and government agencies is critical to redressing the human rights violations experienced by young people with cognitive disability transitioning to adulthood.

1.5 Conclusion

While the young people who participated in this research desire to be free from violence, they desire more than just that. They desire and are entitled to exercise all their rights and to operate as empowered and equal actors in society. The young people have struggled against profound barriers to exercise family, housing, educational, and economic rights.

This book reinforces and reiterates findings from past research and inquiries in Australia and overseas. This is a stark reminder and, the authors hope, a wakeup call of the devastating impact of current disabling discourses that underpin structures, systems, and processes. These discourses create a culture where violence can thrive and construct young people with cognitive disability as vulnerable and powerless. Australia and other countries need to address unequal power relationships between young people with cognitive disability and others. Young people are our future, and we need to afford them the opportunity to transition into the next great leaders. Laws and policies must protect them, but also empower young people with cognitive disability to become full and equal citizens in society.

CHAPTER 2

Violence against Young People with Cognitive Disability

Accessible Summary

- This chapter explores what we know about violence against young people with cognitive disability.
- It looks at what can make it more likely that young people with cognitive disability are abused.
- It's hard to really know how many young people with cognitive disability have experienced violence.
- Young people with cognitive disability can be harmed by workers or family and friends who are meant to help them.
- Abuse can happen in many places.
- Services and society need to learn how to keep young people with cognitive disability safe.
- We need to make sure young people can make decisions for themselves.

2.1 Introduction

Transitioning from youth to adulthood is challenging for everyone; however, young people with cognitive disability are more vulnerable during transition points in life due to support needs and heightened risks before and after the transition (McCauley, 2021). The extent to which young people with cognitive disability are vulnerable to violence is influenced by their diversity of life experiences, as well as the multiple contexts in which transition takes place. Young people may experience interpersonal conflicts

(Larkin et al., 2012) and have intersecting vulnerabilities, related to cultural identities, sexuality, and other factors (Davis & Gourdine, 2022; Ramasamy et al., 2021; Rees & Manthorpe, 2010).

Systems often fail persons with cognitive disability (Cantor et al., 2020). Where systems do work, then those systems can reduce exposure to violence (Pillay et al., 2021). While systems can be effective for children, youth, or adults, those systems may not provide effective support for those who need to transition between services (McCauley, 2021).

This chapter presents the findings of a scoping literature review that addressed the following questions:

- What is known from the existing literature about violence against young people with cognitive disability as they transition to adulthood?
- What does the existing literature say about the risk factors that lead to violence against young people with cognitive disability?

The review represents a summary and synthesis of relevant research from both academic and grey literature, predominately focusing on studies and reports published after 2013. This review illustrates how transitioning to adulthood for young people with cognitive disability increases vulnerability to violence. It will show how estimates of violence against people with cognitive disability are likely to be lower than actual occurrences. Further, it demonstrates how personal risk factors can increase vulnerability to violence. The research demonstrates the universal nature of the challenges young people with cognitive disability experience.

2.2 Young People with Cognitive Disability and Their Experience of Violence

The ways in which cognitive disability can affect an individual are diverse. Several authors have examined the relationship between cognitive disability and social vulnerability to violence (Fisher et al., 2016; Jawaid et al., 2012). Limitations in adaptive behaviour, often attributed to people with intellectual disability (Schalock et al., 2021), may indicate a person is unaware of potential risks in social interactions. Individuals with certain types of cognitive disability can engage in behaviours that leave them susceptible to victimisation, such as young people with foetal alcohol spectrum disorder (FASD) who may engage in high-risk behaviours, or individuals with Williams syndrome who may be overly social (Fisher et al., 2016). If a person has impaired social cognition arising from their cognitive disability, they may have difficulty interpreting social-emotional cues from others, thus leading to further susceptibility to exploitation (Jawaid et al., 2012).

Many people with cognitive disability can experience difficulties in expressive and receptive communication and memory, particularly people with severe intellectual disability (Schalock et al., 2021). This can impede young people from reporting abuse, and others may regard the young person as an unreliable witness, yet perpetrators may see the young person as an ideal victim (Wyman et al., 2019). In addition, trauma reactions to abuse that are often communicated non-verbally by a person with cognitive disability may be misinterpreted by others (Salerno-Ferraro & Schuller, 2020). Kildahl et al. (2020) report on the diagnostic overshadowing of post-traumatic stress disorder (PTSD) by professionals who work with people with cognitive disability in Norway. Diagnostic overshadowing refers to the failure to detect symptoms of trauma, instead attributing these to features of the young person's cognitive disability (Brenner et al., 2018; Wislocki & Zalta, 2023).

2.3 Intersectional Experiences of Violence among Young People with Cognitive Disability

Young Women with Cognitive Disability

Internationally, studies that have examined the risk of abuse of persons with disability often highlight the gendered nature of violence, and how females with disability are at a higher risk of physical, sexual, and emotional abuse than women without disability (Dowse et al., 2016; Plummer & Findley, 2012). There is a lack of evidence as to whether young women with cognitive disability experience more abuse than their male counterparts (Barron et al., 2019), but it is reported that women with psychological or intellectual disability experience higher rates of violence than other women with disability (Australian Bureau of Statistics, 2016). The nature of abuse experienced may reflect broader social attitudes to women with disability who may be regarded as inherently weak, incapable, and vulnerable (Arstein-Kerslake, 2019). Types of violence and abuse reported by authors include intimate partner violence (IPV) (Ludici et al., 2019), denial and discouragement of sexual and reproductive choices (Arstein-Kerslake, 2019), and removal of children by child protection authorities for parents with intellectual disability (Collings et al., 2018).

LGBTIQA+ Young People with Cognitive Disability

Chapter 1 outlined what is known from the literature on LGBTIQA+ young people with cognitive disability and their experiences of transitioning to adulthood. Researchers in the United Kingdom and the Netherlands have noted that this group of young people are at higher risk of mental ill health, problematic substance use, and suicidal ideations and attempts than other groups of young people (Dinwoodie et al., 2020; Stoffelen et al., 2018). Further research is needed to determine the extent to which LGBTIQA+ young people with cognitive disability experience violence in the context of prevailing discriminatory social attitudes. A recent analysis of national online survey data from a 2019 Australian study found that LGBTQA+ people with disability (the study did not have any intersex people who participated) experienced higher rates of abuse, violence, and neglect than LGBTQA+ people without disability (Australian Research Centre in Sex, Health and Society, & Living with Disability Research Centre, La Trobe University, 2022). It was found that LGBTQA+ people with disability who had experienced violence had higher rates of suicidal ideation and attempts than those LGBTQA+ people with disability who had not reported experiences of violence.

First Nations Australian Young People with Cognitive Disability

As mentioned in Chapter 1 of this book, First Nations Australian young people with cognitive disability are another group of young people at great risk of experiencing violence and abuse (Cuervo et al., 2015). The ongoing impacts of racism, colonisation, socioeconomic disadvantage, and intergenerational trauma increase the likelihood for interpersonal violence and abuse in First Nations communities (Australian Institute of Health and Welfare, 2018). Australian First Nations young people with cognitive disability are over-represented in child protection and criminal justice systems (Ellem & Richards, 2018; McCausland & Dowse, 2020). This over-representation in detention settings increases young people's exposure to physical violence and abuse, and in some cases deaths in custody (Human Rights Watch, 2020). Further research is warranted to examine the ways in which human rights imperatives for this group of young people have been ignored by authorities (Dowse et al., 2014). There is an urgent need to provide appropriate supports to enhance the quality of life of First Nations young people with cognitive disability and their communities (Holland et al., 2023).

Young People with Cognitive Disability from Culturally and Linguistically Diverse Backgrounds

The experiences of young people with cognitive disability from culturally and linguistically diverse backgrounds are often under-represented in research (Burns, 2020). Burns (2020, p. 305) discusses the research related to the 'global north and international migration'. There is a lack of empirical research on this group of young people, yet it is well established that these young people are likely to find it difficult to fully participate on an equal basis with others in the countries to which they migrate (Federation of Ethnic Communities' Councils of Australia et al., 2019). Globally, culturally and linguistically diverse young people with cognitive disability may be subjected to feelings of shame and stigma regarding their disability, and their families may be distrustful or lack awareness of disability supports and services (Amparo Advocacy, 2016; Burns, 2020; Jorgensen et al., 2021). The Australian Bureau of Statistics (ABS) 2016 Personal Safety Survey found that among people from culturally and linguistically diverse backgrounds in Australia, people with disability were almost 1.5 times more likely than those without disability to experience violence.

2.4 Prevalence of Abuse against Young People with Cognitive Disability

Obtaining accurate information about the prevalence of violence against people with cognitive disability is a difficult undertaking, with many methodological inconsistencies between prevalence studies, and often small non-representative sample sizes (Healy, 2020). Many studies on the prevalence of abuse of people with disabiity do not provide specific information about young people with cognitive disability.

Studies differ in their use of definitions of disability and of victimisation, and therefore results cannot be adequately compared across studies (Nixon et al., 2017). In addition, definitions of abuse may be drawn from research in general populations, and thereby fail to consider the unique forms of violence experienced by people with disabiity (Platt et al., 2017). Research studies may also involve data collection processes that unintentionally exclude people with severe cognitive disability – for example, online surveys that are inaccessible to people with communication challenges (Dammeyer & Chapman, 2018; Khalifeh et al., 2013).

It is important to note that national and international estimates of violence against people with cognitive disability are likely to be lower than actual occurrences (Mikton et al., 2014; Robinson et al., 2021). There are several factors that can influence this, including the failure of service providers and systems to recognise and record episodes of abuse (Dowse et al., 2013) and the difficulties of young people with cognitive disability to disclose abuse if they are in a dependent relationship with perpetrators (Khalifeh et al., 2013) or if they do not have the communicative means to do so (Dammeyer & Chapman, 2018). Even where young people with cognitive disability do reach out to police and other authorities, there may be little or no official action, due to prejudicial attitudes of those in power (Douglas & Harpur, 2016).

The most recent Australian studies on prevalence of abuse of persons with disability indicate that this group experience higher incidences of victimisation than the non-disabled population and are therefore at higher risk of experiencing violence. The ABS Personal Safety Survey (2016) of 715,300 adults found that 25 per cent of young people (18–29 years) with disability (165,835 young people) reported experiencing violence in the last twelve months, compared with 20 per cent of those aged 30–44 and 11 per cent of those aged 45–65 with disability. In addition, young women with disability (18–29 years) were twice as likely to report experiencing sexual violence over their lifetime than young women without disability. The survey also found that people with cognitive and psychological impairments reported higher rates of all types of violence in comparison to people with other types of impairments (Sutherland et al., 2021). These findings refer to persons living in private settings and do not include those persons with disability who reside in non-private dwellings such as care facilities or people whose communication style requires another person to speak on their behalf. It is likely also that Aboriginal and/or Torres Strait Islander people and people from a culturally and linguistically diverse background are not represented in the data (Dowse et al., 2016).

A substantial number of studies both in Australia and internationally have reported that children with disability are at a higher risk of physical, sexual, and emotional abuse and neglect than children without disability, and many of the acts of abuse occur multiple times for individuals (Maclean et al., 2017). A few of these studies make a distinction regarding impairment type and indicate that young people with cognitive disability are a high-risk group for victimisation:

- A US study that involved a logistic regression analysis of a national dataset revealed that children with intellectual disability had 2.84 times greater odds of experiencing victimization than children without disability (Brendli et al., 2021).

- Higher rates of maltreatment referrals were found involving children with autism spectrum disorder (ASD) (17.3%) than children without ASD (7.4%) in a study of 24,306 children born in 2008 in Tennessee in the United States (Fisher et al., 2019).
- A population-based record-linkage study of all children born in Western Australia between 1990 and 2010 found that children with disability represented 25.9 per cent of children with a maltreatment allegation, even though children with disability made up only 10.4 per cent of the population. Children with intellectual disability, mental/behavioural problems, and conduct disorder had an increased risk of a maltreatment allegation (Maclean et al., 2017).

2.5 Risk Factors for Abuse of Young People with Cognitive Disability

The predictors of abuse against young people with cognitive disability cannot be understood as single, discrete factors (Curtiss & Kammes, 2020). Any act of a violence is likely to be embedded in a number of experiences related to a person's place they occupy in society (Dowse et al., 2013). The analysis of findings in this book adopts an intersectional ecological framework for understanding abuse, violence, and neglect in the lives of young people. This approach considers cross-cutting issues such as social prejudices, lack of education, poor healthcare, poverty, social isolation, and service and system failures and how these issues interact in complex ways and contribute to the marginalisation and disempowerment of young people with cognitive disability (Siebers, 2013). There is merit, however, in defining particular risk factors that render young people vulnerable to harm. The following section, while not exhaustive, has organised these factors according to Sobsey's (1994) seminal text *Violence and Abuse in the Lives of People with Disabilities*, where risk factors were categorised into two broad groups: personal and demographic, and institutional, environmental, and service risk factors.

Personal Risk Factors

Personal risk factors take into consideration demographic variables of young people with cognitive disability who have been victims of abuse and neglect (Sobsey, 1994). The following discussion draws on the international and Australian body of research.

Care and Behavioural Support Needs

A young person with cognitive disability may be dependent on adults for their basic needs. This may involve specialised forms of care and exposure to myriad forms of touch from others on a daily basis. It may be that disability workers and professional staff oversee the young person's toileting and personal hygiene, and in turn, the young person becomes acclimatised to this degree of intimacy with many different caregivers (Robinson, 2012). The young person may learn passivity and compliance with caregivers, particularly in contexts where caregivers respond to young people's behaviour in controlling ways. Compliant, passive responses from young people make it easier for perpetrators to gain close contact to and control of the young person (Beckene et al., 2020).

Sometimes a young person with cognitive disability may present with behaviours that place high emotional, physical, economic, and social demands on families and others who care for the person, and there is little outside support for the family (Peer & Hillman, 2014). For example, a young person with foetal alcohol spectrum disorder (FASD) may lack focus, be impulsive, and have poor judgement. These behaviours can be extremely frustrating for the young person's caregiver and potentially lead to an increased risk of physical abuse (Legano et al., 2021).

Previous Experiences of Abuse

Young people with cognitive disability are often unprotected and live in unsafe situations (Robinson & Graham, 2021). In addition, young people with cognitive disability who have experienced abuse have a higher probability of repeated victimization (Reiter et al., 2007). Repetition of abuse can occur when those around the young person fail to recognise behaviours that indicate a young person is traumatised, depressed, or suicidal. It may be that the odd or challenging behaviour is attributed to the young person's disability (e.g., mutilation, eye-poking, and sexual inhibition), rather than an indicator of abuse occurring (Barron et al., 2019). A young person's limited verbal skills can also prevent the reporting of abuse (Beckene et al., 2020).

Social Isolation

Unfortunately, many young people with cognitive disability may experience social isolation and chronic loneliness, which can lead to seeking connection with others who may exploit them (Gilmore & Cuskelly, 2014). The young person may have a lack of awareness of social norms of friendship and make unsound judgements of character and situations, and an exploitative relationship based on domination and control can eventuate (Forster & Pearson, 2020; McCarthy, 2017).

It is important to note that common experiences of young people with cognitive disability who identify as LGBTIQA+, come from a culturally and linguistically diverse background, or who are First Nations Australian young people involve disconnection to communities of support. A young person with cognitive disability may also have limited opportunities to develop intimate, sexual relationships with others. This aspect of their life can be restricted and, in some instances, completely denied by people and services who support the young person (Ginn, 2021). Misconceptions about the sexuality of this group of young people can lead to discriminatory attitudes and the denial of sexual health and relationship education, and can affect a young person's identity development and satisfaction in life (Schmidt et al., 2021). Paradoxically, if a young person is over-protected and has little experience of intimate relationships, this in turn can increase their vulnerability to experiencing sexual assault, as a lack of sexual knowledge, experiences, and protection skills can impair the young person's ability to recognise an experience as abusive (Eastgate et al., 2012).

Visibility of the Young Person's Disability

Some authors have suggested that visual indicators of disability can lead to increased risk of victimization (Scherer & Reyns, 2019). Visual indicators can include physical features attributable to a genetic syndrome, the use of mobility aids and hearing technologies, and communicative differences such as stuttering, which can become readily apparent in brief encounters with a person. In a US study that examined the association between visible disability and the risk of victimization, Scherer and Reyns (2019) noted a higher risk of abuse among persons with visible disability than those without because of perceived powerlessness of such people. The visibility of the disability may represent a situational opportunity for offenders who regard persons with disability as especially attractive targets (Wilcox et al., 2014).

Invisibility of the Young Person's Disability

Abuse and violence can also occur when a young person's disability is not identifiable to the perpetrator. Invisibility may refer to a failure to fully understand the limitations and challenges associated with a young person's disability. For example, parents may have unrealistic expectations of their child with cognitive disability and interpret intellectual or communication problems as stubbornness or refusal to respond to verbal requests. This may lead to inappropriate physical punishment of the young person (Legano et al., 2021).

A young person's cognitive disability can also be invisible to services and systems. Perhaps the most common example of this may be in the encounters with criminal justice authorities of young people with cognitive disability, where accommodations are not made in police interviews due to a lack of recognition of the young person's impairment (Ellem & Richards, 2018). Of course, even when known, youth justice systems struggle to appropriately respond to cognitive disability and neurodiversity (McVilly et al., 2022).

Environmental, Service, and Institutional Risk Factors

While certain individual factors may increase the risk of abuse of young people with cognitive disability, the nature of violence is multi-faceted and takes place within environmental, social, and cultural contexts (Goodley & Runswick-Cole, 2011). Abuse can occur in any setting. Table 2.1 lists several potential locations where abuse can occur.

It is less clear from the existing literature explored here which contexts have a higher proportion of incidences of abuse. A study of referrals relating to the abuse of people with intellectual disability in the United Kingdom found there was a slightly higher number of referrals of abuse recorded in residential care than in a person's own home, and less referrals of abuse from day care and in public places (Beadle-Brown et al., 2010). Whether these findings would be similar in other contexts is uncertain. The following section briefly examines the nature of abuse and neglect

Table 2.1 *Location of violence against young people with cognitive disability (Frohmader et al., 2015; Marques Garcia Ozemala et al., 2019)*

- Social settings such as family or other personal relationships
- Residential settings such as the home or apartment, foster home
- Service or institutional settings such as group homes, supported residential facilities, boarding houses/hostels, residential aged care facilities, hospitals, prisons, respite facilities, schools
- Public spaces
- Online environments

within the family, in online environments, and within service settings, including institutional settings and personalised arrangements.

Families with Complex Support Needs

Young people with cognitive disability may be more vulnerable to abuse if they are supported within families where there is a constellation of disadvantage (Maclean et al., 2017). Family members may experience poor health and well-being, poverty, inadequate housing, intergenerational trauma, mental health concerns, and problematic substance use, which can impact negatively on their ability to provide adequate care (Corr et al., 2019). In addition, young people with cognitive disability may require extensive physical, emotional, and financial supports that may result in caregiver stress (Lightfoot, 2014). Sufficient outside supports are needed for families under stress in order to prevent abuse and neglect and to avoid a young person with cognitive disability being forcibly removed from relatives, or families relinquishing care (Ellem et al., 2016) .

Online Environments

Online environments shift how violence is experienced by young people with cognitive disability. Positively, social media can help persons with cognitive disability to find and maintain friendships in ways that are not possible with human-to-human contact (van Schalkwyk et al., 2017). Unfortunately, online environments and social media can also expose young people to disability hate crimes (Hall, 2019). This can occur through cyber-bullying (Jenaro et al., 2018), trolling, and flaming (Sherry, 2010). Flaming involves discursive hostility, where the speaker's intent is perceived or experienced as hostile.

The online environment can act as both a protective factor and risk factor to young people with cognitive disability who seek intimate, sexual relationships. The internet may create opportunity for intimacy that a young person with cognitive disability may never have experienced, since many persons with cognitive disability have historically had their sexual rights denied (Brown, 1994). Social media may enable young people with cognitive disability time and space to get to know potential partners long before agreeing to meeting them in person (Darragh et al., 2017). This may reduce the probability that the potential partner will be abusive. However, the internet may also pose a risk of sexual solicitation of some young people with cognitive disability if the young person is not supported to navigate online environments safely and successfully (Buijs et al., 2017; Lines et al., 2021). A recent report produced on behalf of the eSafety Commissioner for the Australian Government also noted how perpetrators of abuse could solicit, post, and distribute images of women with cognitive disability without their permission (Harris & Woodlock, 2021).

Online abuse can have damaging impacts upon young people with cognitive disability (Oksanen et al., 2014). Other examples of the ways in which online communication and other technology can be used by perpetrators include technology-facilitated stalking using GPS devices, scamming and requests for money, and gaining the trust of young people with cognitive disability and thereby gaining access and control of accounts, devices, and personal information (Harris & Woodlock, 2021).

Congregated and Institutional Settings

Some service settings are regarded as posing greater risks of abuse to young people with cognitive disability or just failing their need (Gibbs, 2022). The Australian Senate inquiry *Violence, Abuse, and Neglect against People with Disability in Institutional and Residential Settings* (Senate Community Affairs Reference Committee, 2015) highlighted the risks associated with service models based on institutional and congregate housing, which exist internationally. These service contexts place persons with disability together in one location, where staff resources and support are shared to achieve economy of scale. Historically, such arrangements were often isolated settings, with overcrowding and incompatibility between residents (Hutchison & Kroese, 2015). In response to growing demand from disability rights activists, deinstitutionalisation followed – a movement that became well advanced in Scandinavian countries, the United States, Canada, the United Kingdom, and Australia (Mansell et al., 2010). While conditions and practices in residential settings have improved, many young people with cognitive disability in many jurisdictions may be placed in out-of-home care arrangements under statutory child protection orders or detained in youth justice facilities. Institutionalised practices also occur in many contemporary services and are not merely defined by the size of the service (Bigby et al., 2012). Mansell et al. (2010) found that despite the shift to smaller group homes for persons with disability, these remained 'micro-institutions' with the potential to perpetuate and 'transplant many of the features of institutions' and thus opportunities for abuse (Mansell et al., 2010, p. 105). This was further reinforced by the definition of what constitutes an institution proposed by People First of Canada that stated, 'An institution is not defined merely by its size' (Mansell et al., 2010, p. 105).

These facilities have been heavily criticised by both international and Australian academics, justice practitioners, and child advocates for human rights violations, punitive practices, and degrading treatment of young people, particularly First Nations young people and young people with cognitive disability (Mansell et al., 2010; O'Brien & Fitz-Gibbon, 2018). This was further supported by the recent final report of the Australian Royal Commission into Violence, Abuse, Neglect and Exploitation of People with Disability (DRC, 2023G). Internationally, it is recognised that the use of control and restraint of young people, the significant power imbalances between young people and staff, and the inadequate training with regard to complex behaviours are all factors that can lead to violence and abuse of young people with cognitive disability (Mirfin-Veitch & Conder, 2017).

Attitudes of Service Providers

Where there is a lack of a strong philosophy of care and social devaluation of service users in any service arrangement, there is a greater risk of maltreatment and violence toward young people with cognitive disability (Hutchison & Kroese, 2015). Managerial indifference to abusive behaviour or maltreatment can lead to poor safeguarding of persons with disability (Ottmann et al., 2017). Disability staff may be reluctant to report instances of abuse because of fears of the impact on service users, the family-professional relationship, and work colleagues (Mitchell et al., 1999). Young people with cognitive disability may also be excluded from decisions about how to ensure safe services through paternalistic support agencies; or, conversely, an agency may become defensive about abuse allegations raised and cover up such reports or downgrade the severity of incidents (Ottmann et al., 2017). In such situations there is potential for incidences of abuse to reoccur.

A balance also needs to be achieved in service agencies so that young people with cognitive disability can experience choice and autonomy in their lives, as well as appropriate safeguards from agencies (Fyson & Kitson, 2010). This group of young people need equal opportunities as other young people to participate in their communities and explore emerging adulthood on their own terms. Too often, young people with cognitive disability may be relegated to only socialising with others in the confines of the program they attend (Thomas & Wolfensberger, 1999).

Service providers can assist young people with cognitive disability to engage in positive risk-taking, where young people can assert more control over their lives and take risks, but have support to manage such risks. This approach recognises how the service environment can either further disable or enable young people with cognitive disability to live full lives (Seale et al., 2013).

Inadequate Operational Procedures

In addition to attitudinal barriers, services may have poor processes that fail to safeguard young people with cognitive disability. These processes can include poor staff recruitment protocols, inadequate reporting guidelines, and a lack of transparency in providing support (Hollomotz, 2012). Those who provide support, whether it is paid commercial support (Baidawi et al., 2020) or from family (Gibson, 2020), can also be those who perpetrate the violence. Management practice is influential in motivating or hindering staff from reporting abuse and neglect. Effective supervision has been found to be critical in ensuring staff members have the knowledge and resources to respond to incidents of abuse (Ottmann et al., 2017).

Poor Staff Training and Skills

In their Australian study of violence against women and girls with disability, Dowse et al., (2013) found that many professionals lacked the capacity to address concerns about violence. Capacity-building and effective training in assistive communication are important strategies to prevent and respond to abuse of young people with cognitive disability (Johnson & Yee, 2020). This is especially the case for young people who demonstrate behaviours that challenge others (Ottmann et al., 2017). Failure to respond adequately to complex behaviours may result in the use of inappropriate restrictive practices and human rights violations (Legano et al., 2021).

Violence in the Context of Personalisation

Contemporary research into violence against young people with cognitive disability must take into consideration the recent trends in personalisation of disability services. This is particularly the case in the Australian context, with the advent of the National Disability Insurance Scheme (NDIS), which has personalised services to persons with disability on a large scale. The NDIS has transformed the vast majority of supports to persons with disability to personalised arrangements, determined by a participant's level of need and self-defined goals (Carey et al., 2018). Whether major policy shifts to personalisation have any impact on the prevalence of abuse in disability services has become an emerging, yet still under-researched theme in the literature (Ismail et al., 2017).

It has been argued that enhanced choice in supports for persons with disability can promote safeguarding, by improving a person's autonomy and decision-making around care, and moving away from ineffective and institutional systems of control (Duffy & Gillespie, 2009). A clear evidence base for such claims has not been established in the studies included in this review, although some UK studies found there were fewer reports of abuse or poor-quality care from participants who used direct payments to employ support workers than from other service contexts (Stevens et al., 2018), or no significant relationship between the levels of uptake of personalised budgets and the number of abuse allegations made (Ismail et al., 2017). As is the case with other research on the prevalence of abuse, it is difficult to determine if the findings of these studies are a result of under-reporting (Stevens et al., 2018).

Internationally, some authors have also raised concerns that personalised supports may increase the risk of abuse and exploitation to persons with disability, particularly when a person has impaired decision-making capacity, such as young people with cognitive disability (Manthorpe et al., 2011). For young people with cognitive disability and family members who directly employ support workers, there is a need to ensure that support staff are adequately trained and able to manage any risks that can arise in the care situation (Schwehr, 2010). Research on professionals' perspectives of personalisation in the United Kingdom found that practitioners often expressed concerns about the potential for abuse when persons with disability employed unregulated support workers (Stevens et al., 2018). These concerns have not been substantiated by the literature in this review. However, there may be a preference for unregulated support workers by persons with disability and families (Ismail et al., 2017). A study of parents of children with disability who used direct payments in Northern Ireland found that many parents were concerned about the delays in getting paid carers into the home and anxious about the risk of harm to their children if they employed support workers who were not relatives or friends of the family (McNeill & Wilson, 2017).

Perhaps what may be more useful in these ongoing debates about personalisation is to consider ways in which safeguarding concerns can be addressed without compromising participants' choice and control.

A small qualitative study from the United Kingdom pointed to the need to provide information and resources to participants in personalisation schemes regarding quality and safety in support (Aspinal et al., 2019). The authors interviewed twelve people who used personal budgets and had recently been the focus of a safeguarding investigation. It was found that not all participants could discern when they were starting to become at risk of abuse and neglect or when such an incident took place. It was concluded that participants in personalisation schemes need – in addition to information about navigating social care systems – sound professional advice on how to recognise acts of abuse and/or neglect, as well as an understanding of what constitutes quality care (Aspinal et al., 2019). These needs are particularly relevant to young people with cognitive disability who may be new to self-direction and may also require assistance in identifying healthy, supportive social relationships (Aspinal et al., 2019; Fisher et al., 2020).

Violence in the Australian Context

Of significance, this research was undertaken during a time of examination of the treatment of people with disability in relation to violence and abuse in Australia. The Commonwealth of Australia established the Disability Royal Commission (DRC) in 2019 (DRC, 2023B). The final Disability Royal Commission report was released late in 2023, at the time of writing this book. Comprising twelve volumes, the report covered all disabilities and most domains impacting on persons with disability across their lives (DRC, 2023A, 2023B, 2023C, 2023D, 2023E, 2023F, 2023G, 2023H, 2023I, 2023J, 2023K, 2023L). The importance of giving persons with a disability a voice in disability reforms was emphasised expressly with the first volume recounting a selection of the more than 9,000 people with disability who gave their stories to the Commission (2023A) along with a specific volume focusing on the experiences of Aboriginal and/or Torres Strait Islanders with a disability (2023I). The report highlighted the importance of a human rights lens, which has been missing in Australia (2023D), evidenced by the failures of the overall disability services system including intersecting systems such as housing, education, employment, and the criminal justice and child protection systems (DRC, 2023C, 2023F, 2023G, 2023J). The DRC provided a unique opportunity for Australia to undertake a thorough review of the experiences and current practices and systems in place and how Australia has fared in meeting – or, as was the case, failing to meet – its human rights obligations. The report has highlighted the ongoing challenges at a structural and systemic level that continue to perpetuate discrimination, exclusion, violence, and inequity for persons living with disability. Recommendations included mechanisms for inclusive governance and steps beyond the DRC (DRC, 2023E, 2023L).

An area the DRC Report referenced as requiring additional research attention is the experiences of young people with cognitive disability transitioning to adulthood, specifically, the needs of people with cognitive disability with regard to employment, homelessness support, co-designed decision-making processes regarding policies and practices, attaining financial independence, expanding capabilities of the health and workforce, and screening and assessment of children and young people in the criminal justice system (DRC, 2023F, 2023G, 2023H). Although the attention and recommendations in the DRC are positive, implementing these and other recommendations to enhance the lives of people with cognitive disability will require more in-depth research attention. This book complements this work with its in-depth focus on young people with cognitive disability.

2.6 Conclusion

Our review of the national and international literature points to services, systems, legislation, and society not meeting their obligations to people with disability. It also became evident that the issues experienced by young people with cognitive disability are universal, pointing to the ways in which this failure to meet the overall human rights obligations has implications on their transition to adulthood.

It is known that laws do not treat all categories and variations of disabilities equally. Socially constructed hierarchies of impairments result in persons with physical and sensory disability receiving preferential treatment when compared with those persons with cognitive disability (Harpur, 2020; Harpur et al., 2017). Professionals and organisational practices may also infantilise young people with cognitive disability, for example, by providing segregated educational settings and failing to prepare young people for independence (Franklin & Smeaton, 2017). Alternatively, services and systems may take a blanket approach to self-determination in young people, offering individualised models of service delivery, such as the NDIS in Australia, where young people are expected to articulate their aspirations for adulthood and thus direct the supports on offer. However, as indicated, this fails to consider the extra supports needed by young people with profound cognitive disability (King, 2020) or those needs of young people with cognitive disability who have experienced adverse life events, such as child protection involvement, poverty, and homelessness (Ellem et al., 2020). Further, even where support is provided, it is often provided in a fragmented and complex way by multiple state and private agencies (Chung, 2018).

Similarly, other factors, such as a young person's cultural and gender identities, may be ignored (Bekken, 2020). Services, systems, and legislation may therefore either over-protect or neglect young people with cognitive disability, placing the onus for achieving adulthood on the individual young person and/or their family. The nature of transition, the disruptive and damaging aspects of abuse and neglect, and service, systems, and societal responses to these matters are the focus of this report. Chapter 3 outlines the methodological approach and key research questions in the study.

CHAPTER 3

Working in Partnership with People with Lived Experience
An Inclusive Methodology

Accessible Summary

- This chapter explains how the researchers talked to young people with cognitive disability, their families, and practitioners.
- The researchers included people with disability on the research team.
- The researchers wanted to know what was happening for young people with cognitive disability.
- They wanted to know about the world in which young people with cognitive disability lived.
- There was a lot to be learnt about working well with people with disability in research.
- It's important that people with cognitive disability have a voice in the research that is about them.

3.1 Introduction

Any research approach to understanding youth transition for young people with cognitive disability requires a thoughtful methodology. This methodology must be inclusive of the diverse experiences of young people and sensitive to the substantive ethical issues that may arise in discussions involving violence and abuse. In four sections, this chapter explains how the researchers worked with young people with cognitive disability, their families, and practitioners to find out what it was like for young people to become adults.

Section 3.2 outlines the research questions and aims and reminds the reader of key concepts related to this study. Section 3.3 discusses how youth transition and experiences of violence are understood through an intersectional ecological systems framework. Drawing upon the work of Crenshaw (1989) and Bronfenbrenner (1986), the authors argue for a holistic understanding of transition experiences of young people with cognitive disability. An intersectional ecological systems framework considers the influence of diverse identities, as well as social, cultural, economic, and structural forces on young people's experiences (Levine & Breshears, 2019). It requires a societal response to acts of violence against young people with cognitive disability and advocates for collective responsibility to ensuring the well-being of all young people.

Section 3.4 discusses the need to prioritise the voices of young people with cognitive disability, elaborating on the mandate for inclusion from the CRPD. This section explores principles underpinning the work of co-researchers with cognitive disability, as well as summarising the content of the workshops undertaken with this group.

Section 3.5 outlines the method. This includes in-depth discussion on how interviews were conducted and ethical concerns addressed in this highly sensitive study.

3.2 Key Aims, Questions, and Concepts

The study underpinning this book addressed the following research aims:

- To present an understanding of the nature and experiences of violence against young people with cognitive disability
- To consider the factors that increase the risk of, or prevent against, violence towards young people with cognitive disability
- To examine safeguarding measures that mitigate against violence towards young people with cognitive disability
- To consider experiences related to a young person's gender, sexuality, and cultural identity – in particular, the experiences of First Nations Australian young people with cognitive disability, young people with cognitive disability from culturally and linguistically diverse communities, and young people with cognitive disability who identify as LGBTIQA+.

The primary research question for the study was:

What are the experiences of violence for young people with cognitive disability as they transition to adulthood?

The secondary research questions for the study were:

How do young people with cognitive disability who embody multiple intersections of identity experience violence as they transition to adulthood?

What are the risk factors that lead to experiences of violence for young people with cognitive disability transitioning to adulthood?

What are the protective factors that prevent experiences of violence for young people with cognitive disability transitioning to adulthood?

For the purposes of this research, a young person with cognitive disability was defined as fifteen to twenty-five years old, but the research also included interviews with young people with cognitive disability up to thirty years of age for their retrospective accounts of transitioning to adulthood.

We adopted a broad understanding of 'violence' and take violence to include the definitions listed in Table 3.1.

Transition to adulthood has been understood as a change in role or status, potentially occurring over many different contexts (Strnadová et al., 2016). This concept of transitioning from youth to adulthood has intentionally been left broad, encompassing both normative transitions, such as leaving full-time schooling and gaining employment, and more complex and multi-dimensional transitions, which may not ordinarily be

Table 3.1 *Understandings of violence against young people with cognitive disability*

Violence and Abuse	Neglect	Exploitation
Violence and abuse cover a range of behaviours towards people with a disability. These could include assault, sexual assault, constraints, restrictive practices (physical and chemical), forced treatments, forced interventions, humiliation and harassment, financial and economic abuse, and significant violations of privacy and dignity on a systemic or individual basis.	Neglect includes physical or emotional neglect, passive neglect, or wilful deprivation. Neglect can be a single significant incident or a systemic issue that involves depriving a person with disability of the basic necessities of life such as food, drink, shelter, access, mobility, clothing, education, medical care, and treatment.	Exploitation is when a person takes advantage of someone else. This could include improper use of another person or the improper use of or withholding of another person's assets, labour, employment, or resources, including taking physical, sexual, financial, or economic advantage.

viewed as normative, such as gender transitions and relationship transitions (Dowse et al., 2014).

3.3 An Intersectional Ecological Systems Understanding

In order to capture the complexity involved for young people with cognitive disability who have experienced abuse, neglect, exploitation, and discrimination, it was important to consider the person in their environment and the impact of multi-level systems on their lives. Thus, an intersectional ecological systems perspective has been used as the frame of reference for analysis of the data and includes considering all the potential identities that an individual holds, the interactions of these identities with one another, the systemic contexts within which these identities are situated, and the potential interactions of such systems (Levine & Breshears, 2019).

An intersectional ecological framework moves beyond narrow explanations of abuse and exploitation of young people with cognitive disability. There is a need to shift the focus from individual vulnerability of young people as the key risk factor to the social, cultural, economic, and structural forces impacting on their lives (Hollomotz, 2009). By examining the broader influences on abuse and discrimination there is room for change and for including society in that process (Levine & Breshears, 2019). Abuse of young people with cognitive disability is no longer a 'wicked problem' that cannot be addressed. As Thompson (2006, p. 15) contends, '[t]here is no middle ground; intervention either adds to oppression (or at least condones it) or goes some small way towards easing or breaking such oppression.' Change in one system, however minor, may lead to subsequent changes in other systems and thereby assist in better outcomes for young people with cognitive disability.

With the goal of advocating for social justice activism, an intersectional-ecological approach to discrimination affords a deeper discussion of complicated nuances present in the narratives and discourses regarding multiple minority identities (Velez & Spencer, 2018). As such it provides a conceptual framework that takes into consideration the multiple and intersecting layers and identities of people and systems, and seeks to address abuse, neglect, and violence within and across each of these layers.

The framework for this study recognises ability status, race, gender, sexuality, and culture, along with other vulnerabilities, as intersecting dimensions of how society is structured. These dimensions 'are not separate, additive, dimensions of social stratification but are mutually defining and

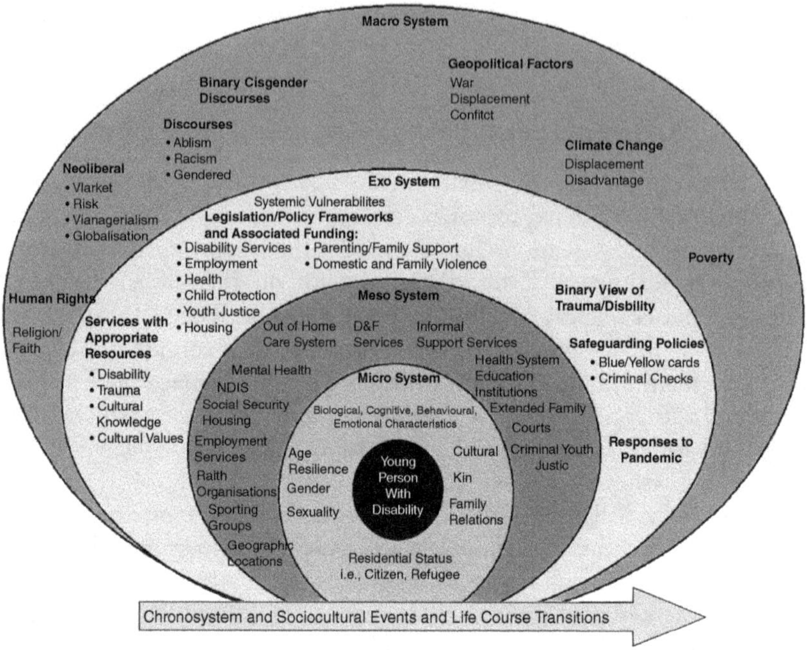

Figure 3.1 Intersectional ecological systems framework for understanding the experiences of young people with cognitive disability

reinforce one another in a myriad of ways' (Warner and Brown 2011 in Levine & Breshears, 2019, p. 148). An intersectional ecological approach recognises the privileges and oppression that people hold due to how identities are socially constructed (Crenshaw, 1989). It challenges the impact of structure and power on the lives of young people with cognitive disability and interrogates the beliefs and discourses that lead to violence and abuse.

The ecological systems framework developed by Bronfenbrenner recognises the intersection and interaction between the different levels of systems that impact on an individual (Nelson & Lund, 2017). Figure 3.1 illustrates these different levels and their application to young people with cognitive disability.

The nested layers consist of the following, recognising the influence and interactions are bi-directional.

Micro System

The micro system is a complex system at the level where, as human beings, we spend most of our time, and therefore this system has a great deal of influence on the person. This includes the person's relationship with their partner and their relationship with their immediate family. Extended family and kinship have influence either directly (micro system) or indirectly (via the meso system). Included are institutions or systems directly affecting the individual; it can be single or immediate settings where the individual engages in interpersonal interactions, the home, school, and other direct settings (Algood et al., 2011). The focus is on the experience of that person, and, as such, abuse, neglect, exploitation, and discrimination are direct. The micro system can provide an informal safety support network for a person, or alternatively can be a source of insecurity, fear, uncertainty, abuse, and neglect. However, any interaction within the micro system is influenced by the broader discourses that perpetuate discrimination, violence, and othering.

Meso System

The meso system involves the interaction between two or more settings the person participates in, for example, home, education, and social life. Included here are formal and informal interactions with others (Levine & Breshears, 2019). People's reactions to a young person, including their attitudes, values, beliefs, and culture can be observed within the meso system, and for young people who are marginalised within society, these attitudes can result in direct discrimination (Buljevac et al., 2022). An example of this is the experiences of young people with cognitive disability experiencing bullying or discrimination in schools.

Exo System

The exo system consists of the cultural institutions and structures that are underpinned by the policy and legislative framework of society. The individual is not an active participant in this system; however, they are impacted by the events around them. This can include indirect impact of the workplace or legal system and the consistency and level of support provided. Geographic location impacts individuals in terms of access to services, supports, affordable transportation to services, gaps in social support networks, and limited disability-specific services. These factors highlight how exo system factors can further perpetuate discrimination and oppression with the individual not being able to influence the distribution of power or resources (Harwick et al., 2020).

Macro System

The macro system includes the culture in which we live. Social inequality, oppression, and injustice are perpetuated through hegemonic discourses that drive a given culture (Curtiss & Kammes, 2020). Crenshaw (1989) discusses the phenomenon where multiple identities further complicate the level of injustice – for example, a woman of colour who is also lesbian – referred to as 'injustice squared'. Examples include cultural beliefs that condone and enable sexual violence and beliefs that stigmatise the sexuality of young people with cognitive disability (Curtiss & Kammes, 2020). Culture also influences service delivery. Key macro discourses that are relevant include ablism, racism, gendered discourse, neoliberal ideology, and dominant whiteness and colonisation discourses.

Chrono System

The chrono system provides the critical element of time to understanding the experiences of young people with cognitive disability, recognising that transitions through the life course and sociohistorical events are contextual and time-specific. For example, the 1980s disability rights movement and deinstitutionalisation brought about major changes to all persons with disability in Australia and internationally (Curtiss & Kammes, 2020). Events are shaped by and shape the broader culture of the macro system. The chrono system also demonstrates that neurotypical developmental milestones are not applicable to all young people, and that the physical, emotional, psychological, and social development of young people with cognitive disability must be considered on an individual basis (Ellem, Smith, Baidawi, McGhee, & Dowse, 2020).

An ecological systems framework recognises how changes in one level can impact others, so to achieve meaningful change that addresses the inequalities that young people with cognitive disability experience requires shifts in multiple systems (Harwick et al., 2020). As Hollomotz (2009) argues, an ecological systems framework can provide important insights into how to prevent future abuse, neglect, and exploitation by considering the intersecting systems that influence and, indeed, create environments where risk factors continue to prevail. Core to this is removing the primary focus on the individual in terms of the person's 'vulnerabilities, attributes', and so on, to considering how as a society, we create the constructions of vulnerabilities through persistent disabling and excluding discourses. Risk as a concept does not simply originate from the individual, but rather is made up of complex social processes and intersections, which must be understood if ongoing harm is to be addressed (Hollomotz, 2009).

3.4 Prioritising the Voices of Young People with Cognitive Disability

The CRPD has transformed how persons with disability are involved in decision making in society. The aphorism of 'nothing about us without us' was central to the drafting of the CRPD (Harpur, 2017). This participatory dynamic has shifted practices and created expectations that persons with disability will be visible and included in public and private decision-making processes (Harpur & Szucs, 2023).

The strong involvement of persons with disability in all aspects of the CRPD extends to the convention's research agenda. The need to engage persons with disability in data gathering and performing research is implicit in all articles in the CRPD. For example, the CRPD includes data gathering and research obligations in its general obligations, in Article 4, and through over-arching data gathering obligation in Article 31. The General Obligations in Article 4 require research to achieve the desired policy and regulatory outcomes, as well as including express research obligations to undertake or promote research and development of universally designed goods, services, equipment, and facilities, and to undertake or promote research and development of the availability and use of new technologies, including information and communications technology, mobility aids, devices, and assistive technologies, giving priority to technologies at an affordable cost (CRPD Article 4(1) (f) and (g)). Relatedly, Article 31 outlines the responsibilities of state parties in ensuring that research is accessible to people with disability (Salmon et al., 2018). The CRPD Committee has explained how these data-gathering and research obligations are required to realize rights in General Comments and in Concluding Observations on States (United Nations Committee on the Rights of Persons with Disabilities, 2016, Para. 62(b); 2016A, Para. 66; 2018, Para. 34; 2022J, Para. 59; 2022, Para 59). Illustratively, in General Comment No. 7, the CRPD Committee explained, in discharging their data collection and research obligations to formulate and implement proper policies to give effect to the Convention, that 'Persons with all kinds of disabilities should be consulted and involved, through their DPOs [disabled persons' organizations] . . ., in the process of data and information collection and the interpretation thereof' (United Nations Committee on the Rights of Persons with Disabilities, 2018A, Para. 68).

The academic research team in this study was guided by the CRPD's commitment to involving people with disability in all aspects of research. We sought to legitimise and promote the knowledge and expertise of young people with cognitive disability by giving primacy to their voices in the research, and by being guided by, and working with, co-researchers with lived experience of cognitive disability.

The research team adapted principles from W-Dare fact sheet for disability inclusion (Gill-Atkinson et al., 2018) to guide our research processes and ensure that persons with disability were fully included. These principles are listed in Table 3.2 alongside the actions taken in this project to embody these values.

The co-researchers in this study were Rosie Smith, Olivia Eiser, Kyah Peirce, Ebony Street, and Willie Prince. Co-researchers were supported by Gillian O'Brien and staff from WWILD – Sexual Violence Prevention Association. Co-researchers attended up to four workshops at the Association. The dedication and commitment of paid support staff to assist co-researchers in attending these workshops is to be commended. Co-researchers also willingly engaged in telephone and email conversations and individual meetings with the University of Queensland research team in between these workshops to provide feedback on the research process and further insights for the overall study.

Co-researcher Workshops: Content and Insights

The first co-researcher workshop was conducted in January 2021. The focus of this workshop was for co-researchers to get to know each other, to explain about research in general terms and specifically about this project, to talk about the role of co-researcher and what this would involve, and to ask co-researchers their initial ideas about the research project. Given the sensitive nature of the research, some ground rules were agreed upon within the workshop regarding confidentiality, having a safe space for co-researchers to engage or withdraw from activities in the session, and to invite people to ask questions when needed. A key challenge in this workshop and in subsequent workshops was clarifying with co-researchers that we were not asking them to share their own stories about abuse and violence for inclusion in the study. This involved a careful conversation with people that affirmed the importance of their own histories, but how their role in this study was to be in the 'pilot seat' and to help others to find the same courage they had shown in sharing their story.

Table 3.2 *Inclusion principles as they related to this study*

Principle	Actions taken
Research aims and objectives Research must provide tangible benefits to persons with disability, and work toward greater inclusion of persons with disability in research.	• The focus of this research project was to empower young people with cognitive disability and to find better ways to safeguard, prevent, and respond to the violence, abuse, neglect, and exploitation in their lives. • By focusing primarily on this group of young people, the project enabled their voices and perspectives to become heard in a public forum. • The research team adopted a developmental approach to working with co-researchers with disability. This involved conducting workshops that outlined what research is, what being a co-researcher involved, and how being a co-researcher was different from being a research participant. It is hoped that the skills that co-researchers developed in this study can be utilised in other research projects affecting the lives of young people with cognitive disability.
Program design Persons with disability should be involved in identifying the research problem and methods for conducting the research.	• The research problem was identified from a consultation with key stakeholders, including persons with disability. • The tight timeframe for the project and the ethical complexities involving talking to young people with cognitive disability about abuse meant that the research team needed to develop the research design and gain ethical clearance prior to engaging with co-researchers with disability. • Asking young people with cognitive disability to identify research methods assumes that these young people have previous experiences of conducting research. This was not the case for our group of co-researchers. While clearly this was a constraint in achieving this program design principle, the co-researchers in this project provided valuable advice on what to consider when interviewing young people, input into the language used in the interview guide, and suggestions regarding recruitment strategies.
Participation Ensure that persons with disability are included as active participants throughout the research as decision makers, advisors, researchers, etc.	• As previously mentioned, the co-researchers with disability in our project helped identify issues and needs of young people with cognitive disability experiencing abuse and exploitation, assisted in distribution of information about the research, and identified avenues for recruitment of young people. They have also participated in some analysis of the data and contributed ideas to the formulation of this book. • Given that co-researchers themselves had experiences of abuse, neglect, and exploitation, a decision was

Table 3.2 (*cont.*)

Principle	Actions taken
	made by the team not to involve them in conducting interviews with other young people, due to the potential for re-traumatisation. It was decided that interviews were best conducted by experienced practitioners who had been trained in identifying and responding to trauma in young people. Co-researchers with disability advised these practitioners about what they regarded as important when interviewing young people.
Ethics Researchers must apply processes of ethics approval that ensure that persons with disability are included in research as active and willing participants. This includes harm minimisation, ownership, and informed consent.	• This research was cleared by the University of Queensland Human Research Ethics Committee (Project Number: 2020/HE002805). • Multiple strategies were used to ensure that young people with cognitive disability can provide voluntary informed consent (see Section 3.5 on method). • The research team ensured that young people with cognitive disability and family members were not harmed by participating in this research. The interview guides for participants followed a protocol for responding to reports of abuse in interviews, and each interviewer contacted participants after they were interviewed to check in on their well-being. • Similarly, great care was taken to de-identify and store sensitive data related to young people's and family members' experiences in a secure, confidential database, University of Queensland Research Data Manager.
Disability awareness Researchers and other stakeholders are aware of disability and its implications, and of the importance of including persons with disability in research. Research is conducted in a culture of inclusion.	• Including persons with disability in research is seen as a priority to the research team as attested by each investigator's professional and lived experiences: ◦ Dr Kathy Ellem has been a scholar, social worker, advocate, and ally in the field of disability for over two decades. As a social worker she has practiced in both government and non-government sectors, working with children, young people, and their families in disability and child protection services. Her interest in the disability sector and subsequently disability research has stemmed from her personal experience as a parent of a young man with cognitive disability. ◦ Professor Paul Harpur is a person with a disability, a guide dog user, former dual Paralympian, and an internationally and domestically acclaimed disability rights scholar. He leads a four-year Australian Research Council Future Fellowship

Table 3.2 (*cont.*)

Principle	Actions taken
	(FT210100335), at the University of Queensland, which aims to support universities to become disability champions of change, is an Associate of the Harvard Law School Project on Disability, and has worked to advance the rights in the CRPD internationally and within Australia. ◦ Professor Ann Fudge Schormans is a practicing social worker for many years. She has worked with people labelled/with intellectual disability in the community living and child welfare sectors. Her current and recent research projects employ inclusive, co-researcher methodologies and knowledge production. She is also a parent of a young woman with cognitive disability. ◦ Professor Michael Ashley Stein is a person with disability, executive director of the Harvard Law School Project on Disability, and one of the world's leading experts on disability law and policy. Professor Stein participated in the drafting of the UN Convention on the Rights of Persons with Disabilities. ◦ Dr Fotini Hardy is a practising social worker and scholar who has worked in health, academia, aged care, disability, child, and family practice. Her interest in the disability sector has been long-standing, including supporting symposiums, research, projects, and voluntary roles. Hardy is the aunt of a young man with cognitive disability. • The research team aimed to create a shared community of practice in research which all stakeholders had a role in research processes by: ◦ Involving 'hard-to-reach' groups, namely, young people with cognitive disability and a First Nations Australian person with disability as research team members ◦ Remunerating co-researchers for their work on the project ◦ Ensuring co-researchers had appropriate resources and supports to participate in the work, e.g., taking care in the timing of workshops, providing transport and catering, and adapting workshop material into Easy English ◦ Involving co-researchers in decision making at different stages of the research ◦ Engaging in continual reflection about how to best work together as a team

Table 3.2 (*cont.*)

Principle	Actions taken
Strengths-based approach Utilise a 'strengths-based approach' that recognises the contribution that persons with disability can make to research and builds on their existing strengths.	• The research team regarded young people with cognitive disability as the experts on their lived experience. As such, young people were regarded as the authorities in describing their disability in their own terms, and in choosing what information they wished to share for the research. • All participants were asked directly what recommendations they would like to make to those who had the power to guide a reform agenda, and their suggestions are included in this book. • Similarly, the research team recognises the valuable insights obtained from co-researchers in this project and accordingly have worked with the co-researchers to produce a forthcoming publication on what has been learnt from working together on this project.
Comprehensive accessibility Barriers to participation in research for persons with disability are addressed. Information about the research process, research tools, and research books are provided in formats that are accessible. This project recognises the diversity within the disability community and the impact of age, gender, socioeconomic status, education, geographic location, and impairment type on the opportunities of a person with disability to participate in research.	• This research sought young people with cognitive disability from a diverse set of backgrounds. However, the data collection methods used did not enable the direct participation of young people with cognitive disability who had complex communication support needs. Members of the research team did not have sufficient experience in augmentative and alternative communication (AAC) systems, and therefore relied on the accounts of family members to include this group of young people. • While there were considerable time constraints within this research study that limited the number of meetings between academic and co-researchers with disability, it is hoped that the process has generated a desire among co-researchers to engage in future research. • Information in workshops with co-researchers was shared at a gentle pace, ensuring time for questions, clarification of research concepts, and opportunity for feedback. Material was offered in Easy English with visual cues to facilitate understanding. • Co-researchers were provided travel assistance to attend workshops and support from workers at WWILD – Sexual Violence Prevention Association if they needed to debrief about sensitive topic matter covered in these sessions. • The co-researchers came from a variety of backgrounds (names listed below). Four were young women with cognitive disability, and the group also included a First Nations man with physical disability.

Table 3.2 (*cont.*)

Principle	Actions taken
	All co-researchers were actively engaged in leadership activities within their communities.
Dissemination of research findings Persons with disability have an opportunity to contribute to the development and drafting of research outputs and are involved in their dissemination. Voices of persons with disability are visible in research findings.	• Co-researchers were invited to contribute to this book by writing the preface, assisting with accessible summaries, and developing artwork for the cover. • Each chapter in the book begins with an Easy English summary of the contents to enable access for people with cognitive disability.

Several valuable suggestions arose from this workshop and follow-up phone calls:

- In reference to First Nations Australian young people with cognitive disability, Willie shared, 'We need to be conscious about how we speak out for those who can't speak for themselves.' Willie explained that in Indigenous cultures, talking is the way of learning – the 'yarning circle'. He stressed the importance of paying respect to the person who is talking in the group, and that no one should talk over that person.
- A few co-researchers cautioned the academic researchers about inviting disability support workers to the young person's interview. There were fears that a young person would experience harm if the support worker did not like what the young person said in the interview. The academic researchers explained that a support worker would only be present if the young person expressly requested their presence, and that care would be taken to re-direct the interview if a young person started to talk about a matter that concerned the support worker.

The second co-researcher workshop was held in April 2021. The academic researchers had begun data collection with young people by this time and were keen to discuss with co-researchers how to make improvements in interviewing young people. Co-researchers provided constructive advice here, including ensuring that the interviewer invited the young person at the beginning of the research conversation to let them know if they did not understand what was being talked about. Some alternative words were suggested for 'exploitation' ('manipulating' was preferred) and for 'safe' ('comfortable' was offered). The co-researchers were not adamant on these suggestions, stating that each young person will have a different opinion about what language to use.

This second workshop was also an opportunity to brainstorm places and people researchers could approach for recruitment. Co-researchers were keen to assist in publicising the research, with some co-researchers taking participant information sheets and flyers away with them to distribute to their own networks.

The third co-researcher workshop was undertaken in July 2021. This workshop involved the most preparation for the academic research team, as it involved supporting co-researchers to engage for the first time in data analysis. Academic researchers considered how to deconstruct abstract terms such as 'analysis' and 'coding' into language that had more concrete and tangible meaning. 'Analysis' was explained as a way of understanding what was happening in young people's stories, including the 'why', 'when', and 'how'. 'Coding' was described as 'giving a name to things', such as putting the labels onto lolly or sweet jars. The academic researchers demonstrated some coding on segments of transcripts and then co-researchers were assisted to work in small groups to do the same on another short excerpt from the data.

The raw, deidentified data used in the workshop was carefully selected, focusing on positive accounts from young people as to what made them feel safe. The academic researchers deliberately avoided data that went into abuse and violence in detail, as they did not know the personal histories of co-researchers and did not wish to trigger strong emotions within the group setting. It was also important, as this was a new activity for all co-researchers, that the content being examined was relatively straightforward. This way the co-researchers could focus on the new task and develop some familiarity with the analysis process.

Co-researchers discussed several issues after engaging in the coding process. These included the role disability support workers played in helping a young person to feel safe or comfortable. Questions were asked as to how a young person knows a support worker is good or bad, and what choices young people have in terminating a disability support worker. Co-researchers also talked about the friendships that could develop with a support worker over time, and that it can be difficult for the young person to address poor practice in a worker if the worker had been supporting the young person for several years. Co-researchers gave examples of poor practice, such as taking personal calls while working, smoking on the job, or turning up late.

Co-researchers agreed with the young people's accounts that it was vital to feel safe at home. One co-researcher posed the question, 'If you don't feel safe at home, how will you feel safe anywhere?'

Gillian O'Brien, the manager of WWILD – Sexual Violence Prevention Association, as well as the co-researchers and the academic researchers, all discussed the use of telephone help lines by young people. It was noted by academic researchers that none of the young people in the study had mentioned using these services. It was commented that the act of picking up the phone and communicating to someone on the other end was likely to be daunting to a young person with cognitive disability who may have communication difficulties. Some of the co-researchers also noted that for some young people with cognitive disability the abuse becomes 'normal', and so they do not talk about it.

The final workshop was an opportunity for all the research team to reflect on the study and what was learned. Co-researchers emphasised talking as a way of learning, something that is customary in Aboriginal and/or Torres Strait Islander cultures.

Overall, the work undertaken with co-researchers was integral to the project. Co-researchers' knowledge, advice, and contributions reminded academic researchers of their moral responsibilities to truly listen to young people in this study. While the work with co-researchers was constrained by time available, it is hoped that their involvement in this study marks the beginning of further endeavours for them in the research space. Their part in this research has added to the study's authenticity.

3.5 Method

The study adhered to the guidelines of the ethical review process of the University of Queensland and the National Statement on Ethical Conduct in Human Research (Ethical Approval Number: 2020/HE002805). Any changes or additions to the research team or process were first approved by the University of Queensland Ethics Committee.

The study was undertaken in urban, regional, and rural areas of Queensland, Australia. The research team also interviewed two practitioners from regional Victoria. Recruitment for all participant groups occurred through first approaching gatekeeping organisations including disability services, employment services, homelessness sector, youth services, Aboriginal and Torres Strait Islander services, and domestic and family violence services. Professional associations and advocacy organisations were also approached.

Challenges in Recruitment

There were significant constraints on the research team in conducting the fieldwork for this study. Data collection took place during the height of the COVID-19 pandemic in Australia, where travel between states was restricted, public health measures were continually changing, and the stressors placed on organisations that support people with cognitive disability were high. Many interviews with young people were postponed due to lockdown measures. Recruitment efforts were restricted by the need to conduct interviews with young people face-to-face to ensure their voluntary, informed consent and a confidential environment in which to share sensitive information. Young people from culturally and linguistically diverse backgrounds were hard to reach, and the team at times relied on accounts from practitioners to develop understandings of the issues facing some groups of young people.

Sample

Young People

Sixteen young people participated in the research, aged between eighteen and thirty, with three additional young people aged sixteen, twenty-one, and twenty-two who had complex communication support needs and who were represented by their parents.

- Young people were asked to describe their disability in their own words. Diagnoses included intellectual disability, autism (with many young people preferring to identify as neurodiverse), physical disability, and acquired brain injury. Many young people had co-morbid mental health concerns.
- Six of the young people lived with family members, one lived on the same property, with family support on hand, with two of these young people receiving support worker assistance funded through the National Disability Insurance Scheme (NDIS). The remaining twelve were living independently with support worker assistance.
- Three of the young people were parents. Milly and Rachel had young children in their care, and Amy had three children all in the care of the statutory child protection services.
- Four participants identified as First Nations Australian young people.
- Three young people's stories were relayed by parents, where the young person with cognitive disability had complex communication support

needs. While this project did not use AAC systems to interview this group of young people directly, family member accounts included valuable insights into service and systemic issues that were abusive and discriminatory towards this group. One young person's story was shared by a practitioner.
- Many young people had chosen to have either a family member or support person present at the interview (Table 3.3).

Practitioners

Twenty-seven practitioners participated in the research, with a vast majority providing disability-specific services within the organisations they worked in. Experience levels ranged from 1.5 years through to over thirty years in working with young people with cognitive disability. Backgrounds included degrees in social work, psychology, human services, nursing, health, counselling, occupational therapy, business, and law. The majority of practitioners came from Southeast Queensland, with some participants from North Queensland and Victoria (Table 3.4).

Obtaining Informed, Voluntary Consent

All participants were required to provide their consent prior to an interview taking place. Obtaining voluntary and informed consent from young people with cognitive disability was critical for this project. There were several strategies employed by the researchers to ensure young people fully understood what their participation involved:

- Participant information sheets and consent forms were written in Easy English in plain text and pictorial formats.
- Participants had the option of providing written or verbal consent
- A screening tool or guide was also used as a reminder to interviewers to check understanding with young people.
- Where a young person was unable to provide informed consent, their assent was sought, and consent was obtained from a parent or guardian.

In-depth, Semi-structured Interviews

The primary data collection method was semi-structured, in-depth interviews:

- Individual interviews with young people with cognitive disability (some requested to have a support person present).

Table 3.3 *Participants: young people*[a]

Young people	Mode of interview	Age	Cultural background	Current living situation	Disability	Gender
Amethyst	Face to face, support worker present	29	Aboriginal and South Sea Islander	Living independently with paid support	Neurodiverse or autism, PTSD	Female
Amy	Face to face, support worker present	30	Australian	Living independently with paid support	Behavioural, labelled intellectual disability	Female
Angel	Zoom	24	Unknown	Living independently	Intellectual disability	LGBTIQA+
April	Face to face	24	Australian	Living independently with paid support	Intellectual disability	Female
Becky	Zoom	25	English/ New Zealand/ Australian	Living independently	Dyspraxia, dyslexia, ADHD, anxiety	Non-binary
Cody	Zoom	22	Australian	Living independently with paid support	Neurodiverse or autism, obsessive compulsive disorder (OCD)	Male
Cooper	Face to face	23	Australian	Living with parents with no paid support	Lesion on brain (Acquired Brain Injury)	Male
Danni	Face to face, with mother speaking on Danni's behalf	22	Australian	Living with parents with paid support	Pachygyria, a form of lissencephaly, level 3 cerebral palsy, mobility impairment, lung issues, difficulty verbalising	Female
David	Face to face with mother (young person not present)	21	Australian	Living with family with paid support	Complex communication support needs, autism, OCD, mental health issues	Male
Ben	Zoom	25	Australian	Living independently in a granny flat under parents' home	Autism, ADHD	Male

Goldie	Face to face, support worker present	22	Aboriginal/ Russian	Living independently with paid support	Autism, borderline personality disorder, complex PTSD, anxiety, and major depressive disorder	Female
Hilde	Face to face	18	German/ Australian	Living with parent with no paid support	Neurodiverse or autism	Female
Kim	Zoom with father (young person not present)	16	White Australian	Living with mother, father, and two siblings	IQSEC2 gene syndrome (atypical Rett), intellectual disability, epilepsy, anxiety disorder, dysphagia, hypotonia	Female
Milly	Face to face, support worker present	21	Australian	Living independently with paid support	Intellectual disability, Asperger's syndrome, anxiety disorder	Female pansexual
Rachel	Zoom with Gabby, manager of Sexual and domestic violence service for persons with disability	30	First Nations	Living independently with support worker in public housing. Mother of a one-month-old child	Intellectual disability, PTSD	Female
Simon	Zoom, mother Lesley present	30	English Irish	Living with parents and siblings	Down syndrome, schizophrenia	Male intersex
Sophie	Face to face, mother interviewed separately	20	Australian	Living with family with paid support	Down syndrome, anxiety disorder, autism, ADHD	Female
T	Face to face	29	Australian	Living independently with paid support	Neurodiverse or autism, fibromyalgia, personality disorder	Male
TBone	Face to face, mother present	19	Aboriginal	Living independently with paid support	Neurodiverse or autism, pervasive developmental disorder not otherwise specified (PDD-NOS), PTSD, depression	Male

[a] All names are pseudonyms primarily chosen by the young person themselves.

Table 3.4 *Participants: practitioners*

Practitioners	Gender	Age	Organisational context	Role
Dean	Male	33	Non-government disability, mental health service	Mental health support coordinator
Dylan	Male	44	Disability employment service	Director
Greg	Male	68	NDIS provider	Senior manager
G	Female	26	Transition to employment program for young people involved with Child Safety and Youth Justice	Social worker
Riley	Non-binary, trans		Specialised domestic, family violence, and sexual assault service for persons with intellectual disability	Advocate to support people to make submissions to Disability Royal Commission[a] and specialised role with LGBTIQA+ service delivery community
Matthew	Male	60+	Specialised services for persons with intellectual disability including young people coming out of Child Safety; response to homeless young people	CEO and social worker
Jan	Cisgender Female	71	Specialised domestic, family violence, and sexual assault service for persons with intellectual disability	Counsellor and educator
Leanne	Female	56	Private NDIS provider and individual disability advocacy agency	Social worker and advocate to support people to make submissions to the Disability Royal Commission
Chantal	Female	41–50	Disability advocacy agency	Social worker and advocate
Rod	Male	26	Currently community mental health support (1 month), previously specialised disability support service	Occupational therapist
Sonia	Female,	35	Family-focused	Support coordinator
Lyn	LGBTIQA +	46	disability support	Support coordinator and team leader
Brianna	Female	35	service, Sunshine Coast	Support coordinator
Beth	Female	50+	Specialised service contracted by Education Queensland to facilitate transition planning for young people in particular schools, Sunshine Coast	Transition planners
Matt	Male	50+		

Emma	Female	30	Specialised service supporting children and young people and families, Brisbane	Human services practitioner
Mary	Female	41–50	Specialist support for young people 15–25 with or without NDIS support, outreach, transition, and post care support and counselling, Brisbane	Social worker
Dan	Male	21–30	Aboriginal and Torres Strait Islander	Aboriginal youth well-being workers
John	Male	21–30	community health service, Brisbane	
Gabby	Female	31–40	Specialised domestic, family violence, and sexual assault service for persons with intellectual disability, Brisbane	Social worker, advocate, and manager
Lorraine	Female	21–30	Legal service for prisoners	Lawyer for parole matters
Keith	Male	45–50	Disability service, Townsville	Manager
Lorna	Female	51+	Advocacy service in Victoria for persons with intellectual disability, brain injury, complex communication needs, people from culturally diverse backgrounds, and LGBTIQA+ people	Advocate
Monica	Female	51+	Advocacy for persons with culturally and linguistically diverse backgrounds with disability, Brisbane	Advocate (individual and systems)
Darius	Male	40+	Advocacy for persons with disability from culturally and linguistically diverse backgrounds; multicultural support for refugees and asylum seekers Brisbane	Committee member and social worker
Annette	Female	21–30	Legal service for prisoners	Solicitor for parole matters
Barbara	Female	51+	Higher education; advocacy for persons with disability from culturally and linguistically diverse backgrounds	Academic and committee member

[a] The Disability Royal Commission is a shortened version of the Royal Commission into Violence, Abuse, Neglect and Exploitation of People with Disability. It was established in April 2019 in response to community concern about violence against people with disability in Australia.

- Individual interviews with family members/supporters.
- Individual and group interviews (maximum of three participants) with service practitioners.

Interviews with participants were no longer than one hour in duration (including breaks requested by participants).

Data collection (interviews) with all participant groups was conducted either face-to-face or undertaken using online videoconferencing technologies (Zoom). Face-to-face methods were preferred for interviews with young people to enable greater rapport building, as well as to ensure that the young person was in a private space where they could not be overheard by others. However, some young people requested videoconferencing. Public health measures related to social distancing during COVID-19 outbreaks also necessitated conducting online interviews at different stages in the data collection process.

Engagement with First Nations Australian young people, families, and practitioners required flexible approaches to data collection and the adaptation of research methods in order to honour key ethical principles of respect, beneficence, justice, research merit, integrity, and the additional values of supporting cultural safety (as outlined in Chapter 4.7 of the *National Statement on Ethical Conduct in Human Research* with respect to Aboriginal and Torres Strait Islander peoples) (National Health and Medical Research Council, 2018). Where possible, the research team engaged First Nations Australian researchers to conduct interviews.

Life Mapping

Interview guides were used to guide the interview or collaborative conversation with all participants, and visual tools, such as life maps, were used in interviews with young people to help the young person place their life events in a meaningful order (Gray & Ridden, 1999). The construction of a life map at the beginning of the interview with young people facilitated conversation of both positive and negative events in the young person's life. Life mapping is a research method that enables young people with cognitive disability to tell their stories of abuse, violence, neglect, and exploitation during their transitions to adulthood. Life mapping has been successfully used in studies with persons with cognitive disability previously (e.g., Boodle et al., 2014). In life-mapping, the researcher focuses on building rapport with the young people and asks questions that are both brief and clear in meaning. Where the young person attended the interview with a support person, this person was able to assist the young person with telling their story, by providing extra information about the person's life. The support person only offered comment with consent from the person with cognitive disability. While a second interview was available to be scheduled to enable the young person to talk further about events in their life, this was not requested or required.

Supporting Methods: Field Notes

The extensive use of field notes by members of the research team was also considered as method in the study. Field notes are important inclusions in research where there is considerable engagement by researchers with participants-in-community (Bailey, 2018) and where that engagement contributes to the overall findings of the study.

Speaking about Abuse

The young people with cognitive disability who participated in this study were a diverse group, and there was only a small window of time to build rapport and to get to know fully how each young person communicated and what was important to that person. Some young people spoke of experiences that would indicate that discrimination, abuse, and violence may have occurred, but the young person chose not to discuss these incidents in detail, or the experience may not have been recognised as abuse by the young person as it was considered part of their everyday life. Similarly, other sensitive topics such as experiences of sexuality or racist attitudes towards a young person's cultural identity may not have been discussed directly with the researcher. It became apparent that some of the young people were not able to fully express their views in the interviews. This may have been due to the researchers' reliance on verbal communication in data collection. Some young people who verbally communicated their story had a support person or family member present in the interview. This support person often provided gentle prompting to assist the young person to tell their story. Other young people with complex communication support needs were represented by a close family member who shared their experiences of abuse. While this could not replace the first-hand experience of the young person, it did highlight the efforts family members took to safeguard their young person and the difficulties in finding appropriate and respectful services for this group of young people. Given all these complexities, the findings are likely to be only a partial representation of abuse and violence in young people's lives.

The research team had a duty of care to all participants that participation in the study did not cause unintended harm. There were several strategies to minimise the burden of participation:

- All interviews were conducted by experienced practitioners who had the skill set to respond to any potential trauma that could arise within an interview.
- The interview guides for young people and family members were designed so that participants could talk about positive aspects of their lives to begin with, before getting onto more difficult subject matter. The interviews ended by asking the participant about hopes for the future and drawing the person back to the present moment if needed.
- The interviewers arranged with young people and family members to contact them the next day after an interview to debrief and answer any concerns they may have.
- All participants were informed about what the research team's response would be if they disclosed illegal or criminal activities that had not been prosecuted. Details of this were stated in the participant information sheets and in the interview guide. The approach involved discussing the implications with the person and seeking counselling support and legal advice if needed.
- All participants were given information about relevant counselling support should they require this.
- Interviewers would often debrief with the chief investigator after an interview with a young person, to discuss any concerns that may have arisen.

It was an interesting finding in our study that all young people with cognitive disability elected to have only one interview. We had anticipated as researchers that we would need to conduct several interviews with each young person to allow them the time to discuss life events. Young people were generally very clear as to the purpose of the interview, and to a large extent knew what they wanted to say, how much they wanted to disclose, and to do this only one time. Not all young people required the use of a life map to help them construct a narrative around what happened. Some young people had previous contact with other research projects on violence and therefore were prepared to discuss experiences of abuse from the beginning of the interview. The interviewers were very much led by the young person as to how conduct the research conversation.

Data Analysis

All participant interviews were transcribed verbatim by a professional transcription service. Upon receipt of the transcript, identifying information was changed to ensure confidentiality. Young people were asked to provide a pseudonym for their account. Pseudonyms included interesting names such as Amethyst, TBone, and Goldie. Dates and places were also changed in participants' accounts.

Data analysis of young people's interviews involved constructing each participant's life story. By deliberately providing a chronological order to young people's accounts, this allowed the researchers to familiarise themselves with the data and further understand the context surrounding acts of violence and exploitation. It also shed light on the impact such acts had on young people's experiences of transition.

All interviews were analysed thematically with the assistance of NVivo 12 qualitative software. Thematic analysis is an iterative process of data reduction, organisation, and interpretation. Each transcript was systematically coded, later categorised into themes, and then further refined as the analysis progressed (Braun & Clarke, 2022). Most of the codes were generated inductively, formulated based on what participants said. At other times, the researcher would explore the data using pre-generated codes, such as using the definitions of abuse and violence adopted in this project.

Co-researchers with disability were included in the analysis of two transcripts. They provided insider cultural knowledge to help identify relevant themes and to add authenticity to the process (Strnadová et al., 2020).

Data Storage

All data for this project was stored electronically on a secure research data management (RDM) platform and/or on servers accessed by password-protected devices. Only members of the research team had access to the project data. Identifiable data, such as consent forms, was kept separately to transcripts, and audio files were deleted once the data from these files had been transcribed.

Writing about Abuse

Honouring and giving voice to the young people's experiences of all the different forms of abuse was a priority for this research; however, this involved ethical challenges. Being able to capture the sheer breadth and depth of abuse was difficult at times. It has been important to describe the different 'types' of abuse, to name such acts, and to compare and contrast between what young people experienced and what was conveyed by family members and practitioners. However, these acts of abuse do not sit as neat and separate categories. They co-exist in a complex system of discrimination and disadvantage, related not only to social responses to the young person's disability, but also to other identities related to gender, culture, and sexuality. Describing singular acts of abuse is also deceptive, in that it fails to convey the chronological progression of violence and neglect in young people's lives. It may, however, afford more privacy to young people, as excerpts from young people's stories are less identifiable to the reader than presenting their whole story. Only one full story is presented in this book (see Chapter 4) as a means of 'capturing the whole', but even then, significant detail is omitted to ensure the confidentiality of the individual.

Any research project that attempts to convey lived experience can only impart participant perspectives at one point in time. The findings reflect what a young person with cognitive disability was willing and able to share to a relative stranger, and young people placed enormous faith in the researchers to disclose such sensitive aspects of their lives. Communicative challenges for some young people meant they may not have always had the language to describe fully what happened in their lives. Sadly, some acts of abuse may also have gone unnoticed as the young person may not have recognised these acts as abusive; rather, they may have seen such events as something that was part of their everyday circumstances. As the researchers interpreted and wrote up these findings, there was a growing recognition that what was not mentioned in accounts was equally important, yet not able to be commented on in great depth.

Finally, being immersed in the stories of abuse as part of the interview and analysis process has, in itself, been challenging. Data analysis as a process of coding, categorising, and identifying themes is not value- or emotion-free. While the research team has worked with reflexivity and engaged in peer debriefing, it has been difficult not to be affected by the young people's stories. The moral outrage that the researchers have experienced in hearing these stories has been real and was a motivating factor in completing this book.

CHAPTER 4

Amethyst's Story

Accessible Summary

- This chapter tells Amethyst's story.
- Amethyst is an Aboriginal and South Sea Islander young woman with cognitive disability.
- Amethyst is not her real name.
- Amethyst was abused many times as a child and a young adult.
- Her story can tell us a lot about what needs to change for young people with cognitive disability.
- We need to understand that abuse affects a person's whole life, their family, and their world.

4.1 Introduction

This chapter is dedicated to highlighting one young person's story of violence, that of Amethyst. We feel this is a fitting way to begin the readers' understanding of the nature and extent of violence that can occur in the lives of young people with cognitive disability. This does not mean Amethyst's story is any more important than that of any other participant who shared their experiences in our research. Rather, Amethyst's story highlights the impact of the convergence of systemic level failures at every level of her life: meso, exo, macro, and chrono systems. The failures at the meso, exo, and macro levels impacted on her family's ability to keep Amethyst safe. Presented here is only a partial story; the impact on the family itself is something that has not really been covered in this book, but we recognise and acknowledge the trauma, stress, and harm this has caused for them.

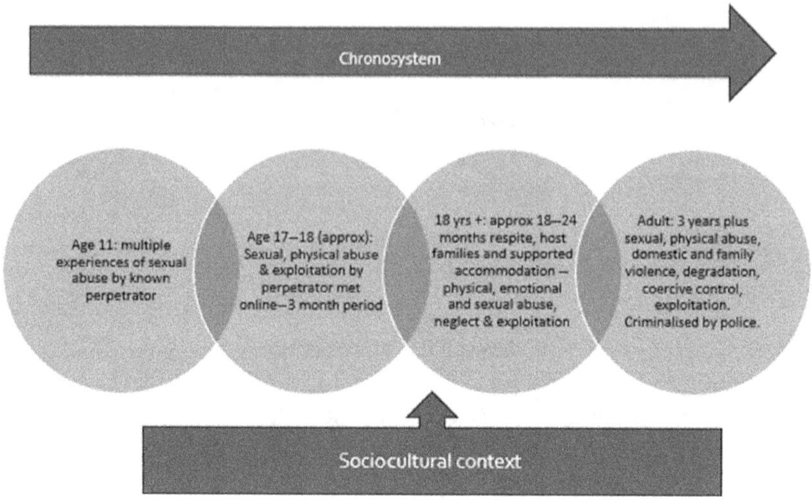

Figure 4.1 Experiences of abuse across Amethyst's life

Amethyst's story was constructed using the life map process, and an analysis was completed of the different system-level failures using an intersectional ecological framework. Figure 4.1 illustrates the extent of abuse she has experienced.

4.2 Amethyst's Birth to Teenage Years

Amethyst was born in Brisbane. She identifies as female and is of Aboriginal and South Sea Islander heritage. Amethyst is neurodiverse; she has autism, non-epileptic seizures, and post-traumatic stress disorder (PTSD). Amethyst lived with her mother, father, and two sisters until her teenage years.

Amethyst changed primary schools in year 4 due to bullying from other students, and this is where she met her best friend, who she is still friends with.

When Amethyst was aged eleven, she was sexually assaulted multiple times, and her mother supported Amethyst in telling her story to authorities and in having the perpetrator prosecuted. Amethyst was not able to access counselling support at this time due to a lack of specialist and available counselling services. This experience contributed to Amethyst developing PTSD.

Amethyst then attended a specialist high school. When Amethyst finished school, she had nowhere to go or anything to do. Her mother was working and could not leave Amethyst home alone given her past experiences. Her mother left Amethyst in the care of her father (Amethyst's grandfather), who was in his seventies and living in an aged care facility. This arrangement was considered a 'safe option'. Amethyst described this as being a 'sad time'; she was desperate to be around people her own age. Amethyst put a message on Facebook, stating, 'I will do anything to have a boyfriend.' Nathan, an adult man, responded to her message and Amethyst moved in with him. Over the three-month period that Amethyst lived with Nathan, she experienced sexual, physical, and psychological violence, as well as exploitation.

When Amethyst returned home to her mother, her behaviour became violent and Amethyst's mother found it difficult to cope. While there is no definitive information, it is possible that Amethyst experienced further PTSD symptoms as a result of the violence. Amethyst was placed by her mother in a 'respite' centre for people with disability to provide additional support. Amethyst lived there for eighteen months where she again experienced abuse and neglect by other residents who lived there with her. Amethyst was described as becoming suicidal at this time.

4.3 Early Adulthood

At about the age of twenty, Amethyst then moved in to live with a host family,[1] provided by her disability service. The host family, who were paid to care for Amethyst, financially abused her by charging her rent. The host family withheld her medication, telling her that it was 'toxic'. Further, they emotionally abused her by trying to separate her from her mother. Amethyst did not see her mother for six weeks.

At the same time, Amethyst was attending a day service that catered to people with more severe levels of cognitive disability. In this environment, Amethyst reportedly started to lose her own words and functioning. Staff from the day centre alerted Amethyst's mother about the host family and their treatment of Amethyst. When her mother found out, she and a caseworker from Disability Services Queensland[2] went and forcibly removed

[1] A host family is an arrangement where a person with a disability lives with a host family, who are in turn, funded to provide support from a formal service provider (Cocks et al., 2016).

[2] Disability Services Queensland was the state government service for people with disability prior to Australia's transition to the National Disability Insurance Scheme (NDIS). Further information about the NDIS is found in Chapter 7.

Amethyst from the host family. During this time, Amethyst was described as experiencing a 'full-blown psychotic event' for about six weeks.

During this time, Amethyst had non-epileptic seizures as a result of the stress she was experiencing and ended up spending seventeen days in hospital. Nathan, the person who had abused her earlier, was still on the scene during this time and would visit her in hospital after her mother left at night. No one realised he was visiting her and that he was continuing to abuse and exploit her financially.

At about the age of twenty-two, Amethyst was placed with another host family who also reportedly neglected and physically and psychologically abused her, resulting in her losing twenty kilograms in weight. Amethyst and her mother described the host family as running their home like a 'military operation'. They denied Amethyst her dignity and limited her freedom. When she forgot to make her bed one morning, they reportedly took her bed away and she had to sleep on the floor. Amethyst had to adhere to regimented mealtimes; failure to do so would result in her missing out on meals. This host family also reportedly financially exploited Amethyst because they were paid to care for her but only did the bare minimum. Amethyst ran away from the host family and was missing for a week. When she returned to her mother, she was taken to the police to report the abuse. During this time Nathan continued to visit her and financially abuse and exploit her. Amethyst's mother identified that he had obtained about $10,000 AUD from her over a few years.

Amethyst was then moved to her third host family where she was also exploited by being expected to babysit their children. Amethyst's mother reported that there was never any food in the house and yet the family were being paid to care for Amethyst.

Amethyst was then moved by Disability Services Queensland into a share house with another girl. The house was staffed with twenty-four-hour care. Amethyst lived there for about one year, and during this time the other young person started to steal from her, eating her food. This young person eventually moved out and another young woman moved in. The new housemate required support with personal hygiene and was described as going to the park and meeting up with men. These factors made Amethyst feel uncomfortable. After about three months living with Amethyst, the young woman sexually assaulted her when she walked in on Amethyst having a shower and grabbed her breasts. Amethyst's mother complained, and the only option was for Amethyst to move out of the supported accommodation. By doing so, she lost the formal support she received in this arrangement to live independently.

4.4 Moving into Public Housing

Amethyst then moved into a public housing one-bedroom unit with paid support for eight hours per day. Her mother expressed concerns that she would be vulnerable and be targeted living in public housing. On the day Amethyst moved in, she was targeted by a man who had just recently been released from prison for sexual abuse of a minor. Amethyst's mother described him as having the maturity of 'twelve- to fourteen-year-old.' This man targeted Amethyst and started to isolate her from her family, including her mother and other supports. This relationship was horrifically abusive. The perpetrator committed reproductive abuse by trying to get her pregnant. Amethyst had five miscarriages and one abortion, and it is not evident what medical or counselling support she received. Other forms of abuse included being physically attacked, drugged, isolated, choked, and having the hair on her head shaved off by him.

Amethyst had a job during this time for three hours per week, but the perpetrator made her quit. Amethyst had moved into his unit, and the perpetrator 'moved druggies' into her unit so he could access drugs. The people paid him rent in drugs, and during this time Amethyst continued to pay her rent. The perpetrator sold her jewellery and other belongings as part of his financial abuse and exploitation of her. The perpetrator also used Amethyst's laptop to exploit her, posting videos on YouTube of her drugged while he sexually abused her.

Amethyst remained in this relationship for three years. Her mother fought for the police to rescue her. The police reportedly ignored her pleas and disregarded a letter from the psychiatrist about her cognitive level and abilities. Her mother also experienced threats and intimidation by the perpetrator during this time. While the Vulnerable Persons Unit[3] had visited her once, no action was taken.

In early 2019 Amethyst was able to escape from the perpetrator and ran to the police station seeking safety. She then returned home to her mother. At some stage throughout this period, Amethyst had been placed under the care of the Office of the Public Guardian,[4] although the details were not clear.

[3] This refers to the Domestic, Family Violence and Vulnerable Persons Command of the Queensland Police, a unit that seeks to prevent, disrupt, investigate, and respond to domestic and family violence and other harms perpetrated to vulnerable Queenslanders.

[4] The Office of the Public Guardian Queensland is an independent statutory office that seeks to protect the rights interests and well-being of adults with impaired decision-making capacity. The Office can appoint a public guardian to make personal, health, and legal decisions on behalf of a

Amethyst returned to the relationship with the perpetrator out of fear because while living with him, he had made her draw a map of where the security cameras were in her mother's house. Amethyst was reportedly afraid for the safety of her mother as a result. Amethyst remained in this violent relationship for another month, at which point the police contacted her mother to advise that Amethyst was in the watchhouse at the police station under arrest. Amethyst spent four to five days in the watchhouse. During this time, she experienced a denial of her civic rights in terms of access to cultural support, as well as medical and counselling support. A lawyer supported the family during this time, and the perpetrator was subsequently convicted of child pornography and sexual abuse.

4.5 Amethyst's Current Situation

Amethyst has moved about seven times since then to ensure her safety as the perpetrator was due to be released on parole around the time of the research interviews. Amethyst now has twenty-four-hour support workers; however, she is frightened for their safety as well as hers. Amethyst and her mother clearly continue to feel unsafe and live in fear of the perpetrator. Police reportedly said they would not charge the perpetrator as this would interfere with their prosecution of Amethyst.

At the time of the interview, Amethyst was in a positive relationship with Lance, whom she met through a disability support service. Since returning home, Amethyst has been accessing counselling support. Amethyst also visits her family once a month as part of a 'contract' with her family, as her new partner was taking over all her time.

4.6 Analysis of Amethyst's Story Using an Intersectional Ecological Systems Approach

Amethyst's micro system consisted of her mother, father, sisters aged twenty-five and thirty-three, her 'Pop', and nieces and nephews, who have remained close and consistent supports. Her micro system has changed in terms of the relationships she has been in. When Amethyst was in her most recent abusive relationship, her micro system reduced in size to include only her abuser, as she was purposefully isolated from her family. Although Amethyst had a strong and supportive family, they were unable to protect

person with impaired decision-making capacity (www.publicguardian.qld.gov.au/about-us/our-purpose).

her from abuse and neglect while she was placed with the host families, or when she moved in with the perpetrator of the most recent abuse. During these times, Amethyst's family had little control, and the lack of oversight and support from services within the meso system meant that the abuse continued.

In terms of meso systems, this has included her schools where she experienced bullying, the aged care facility where she stayed with her grandfather, the respite centre, the day service, host families, and supported accommodation. Education, police, the criminal justice system, disability service providers, health, public housing, and specialist support services have also been part of her meso system. For the most part, her meso system has been unprotective and negative. The most positive members of this system have included her more recent support staff through the specialist counselling service and the support workers she accesses. Once she completed schooling, there was no pathway for Amethyst, highlighting important gaps in the meso, exo, and macro systems in terms of policies and funding to ensure all young people with cognitive disability have access to meaningful and appropriate post-secondary school opportunities.

Amethyst has had limited interaction with employers. Her lack of further education and experiences of abuse and trauma have also impacted on her opportunities to date.

At an exo and macro system level, the lack of recognition of her disability by the services meant to protect her, such as the police and the Vulnerable Persons Unit, demonstrates a significant systemic failure. Amethyst's cognitive disability was not recognised, acknowledged, or understood, and the different systems allowed the perpetuation of significant violence towards her. The refusal by police to charge the perpetrator with his horrific abuse and coercion of her is a significant failing. There appears to be little recognition that Amethyst was a victim of abuse and violence.

A further exo and macro systemic level failure has been the lack of protectiveness of the respite and host families who were meant to support and protect her. The fact that the abuse, neglect, and exploitation lasted for as long as it did reflects systemic-level failures.

At a macro level, the discourse of ableism and neoliberalism are apparent. Ableism is evident through the lack of recognition and acknowledgement of her disability by police, the lack of appropriate opportunities for someone leaving the school system, and the lack of safe places a young person with cognitive disability can access when the parents work. The fact that this significant level of ongoing abuse, neglect, and exploitation has been able to occur over a period of eighteen years for Amethyst is disturbing and distressing. It has denied Amethyst her fundamental human rights.

Neoliberalism, and its emphasis on the free market, is reflected through a disability provider system that privatises support services, with what appears to be limited oversight of care. The impact of neoliberalism was also evident through the focus on financial imperatives in service delivery rather than what Amethyst needed, which was safe and supportive accommodation. It was considered economically expedient to move Amethyst out of the house she was living in, because it had three bedrooms, rather than consider that at that time, Amethyst needed continuity and stability. The risks of moving a young female person with cognitive disability to public housing were not considered, and Amethyst was placed in a situation where she experienced significant violence and harm that has also resulted in her criminalisation. This could have been prevented with more person-centred and targeted support.

There have been some shifts in attitude at one level in the macro system in Australia, with the provision of some disability-specific support services for young people with cognitive disability who have experienced domestic and family violence; sexual, physical, and emotional abuse; and neglect. This has been a positive shift that has translated at the exo level in terms of provision of funding for such services. However, there is still much to do here, as these services remain very limited and are only one part of the solution in responding to these issues.

The chrono system outlines the lifelong impact of Amethyst's experiences of abuse on her physical health and her psychological well-being. Amethyst's story demonstrates how the biological age of a young person is not an accurate indicator of the person's developmental needs, yet systems pay greater attention to biological age. This view has had dire consequences for Amethyst. She was deemed to be an adult by authorities even though the evidence was that she was not – this is systemic negligence. It is recognised that there have been shifts in attitudes and service provision since Amethyst was aged eleven, moving from terminology of 'respite' to 'short-term supported accommodation' under the National Disability Insurance Scheme (NDIS). It is difficult to say if Amethyst would have stayed for so long in 'short-term' accommodation under the new system, or if the current NDIS system would be responsive enough to the crises she experienced from an early age.

Further, there is now also greater recognition of the significance of gender violence and coercive control (United Nations Human Rights

Office of the High Commissioner, 2018); and of the need for young people with cognitive disability to have access to meaningful post education support and opportunities for employment (DaWalt et al., 2021). The NDIS has similarly provided more opportunities for targeted support, as we have seen with Amethyst's current support network in her meso system. However, we continue to see the impacts of ableist discourse and a focus on funding constraints for people with disability in Australia that perpetuate ongoing neglect of people's human rights.

Amethyst's experience also can be understood in relation to her identity as a First Nations Australian young person. While the story in this chapter shared by Amethyst and her mother does not directly refer to the personal, social, economic, and political treatment of Aboriginal and/or Torres Strait Islander peoples in Australian society, nor racism or colonial attitudes, there is evidence of these dynamics in subsequent chapters in this book. Colonisation and racism have likely impacted across all systems in Amethyst's life. Service providers likely lacked cultural awareness and sensitivity when responding to Amethyst's situation (Green et al., 2018). Some of the difficulties with police officers may be indicative of long-standing tensions that Aboriginal and/or Torres Strait Islander young people have experienced with police (Baldry et al., 2013).

In conclusion, Amethyst's experiences of horrific violence indicate there are gaps in fundamental support in every level of her ecological system. Although she had a supportive family, this was not sufficient to protect her throughout her life. An intersectional lens provides an in-depth understanding of the multiple levels of oppression and violence Amethyst has experienced as a young First Nations Australian woman with cognitive disability. By sharing Amethyst's story in its entirety, our aim is to highlight the enormous impact on a person's well-being when multiple systems are not able to meet their foundational needs for safety and protection. A holistic understanding of the intersection of violence, disability, gender, and culture, among other factors, is necessary if we are to, as an ethical and moral society, keep providing young people with cognitive disability with safety, support, and access to all the opportunities people without disability enjoy.

4.7 Conclusion

This chapter has told part of Amethyst's story using a life map process. Using an intersectional ecological systems framework, Amethyst's story was then analysed to understand the different system-level failures. The failures explored in this chapter have contributed to Amethyst's life experiences being the antipathy of core human rights principles. At the core of disability human rights are general principles including dignity, equality, humanity, and full and effective participation and inclusion in society (CRPD Article 3(a), (c), (d), and (e)). These general principles are advanced and protected through the human right to live free from violence; to social security, housing, mental health support, education, and work; to support of transition within life stages and across domains; and to fully and effectively participate in decision-making processes. Across this book these rights are analysed primarily from a disability human rights perspective.

Disability human rights in the CRPD are transformational, but, as illustrated by Amethyst's story, the siloing of human rights by identity can contribute to systems failures. The need to respond to intersectionality was recognised in the drafting of the CRPD (Bantekas, 2018; Mykitiuk and Chadha, 2018). Accordingly, Article 6 addresses the particular vulnerabilities created by gender, whereas Article 7 addresses the particular vulnerabilities created by childhood. Amethyst's story, however, also includes the additional vulnerabilities created by her Aboriginality and South Pacific Islander heritage. Whereas the CRPD responds to childhood and gender, the additional vulnerabilities created by Indigenous and minority culture was not recognised in the CRPD with a stand-alone article (Harpur & Stein, 2018). The CRPD Committee has exacerbated this failure by inconsistently dealing with the heightened issues of Indigeneity and minority cultures. Illustratively, the CRPD Committee's first Concluding Observation on Australia addressed the heightened vulnerabilities caused by Aboriginal and/or Torres Strait Islander status in its analysis in Articles 1–4 and under Article 14 (United Nations Committee on the Rights of Persons with Disabilities, 2013, Paras. 12, 31, and 32(a)). In its next Concluding Observation on Australia, the CRPD Committee addressed the intersecting vulnerability of Aboriginal and/or Torres Strait Islander status when addressing Articles 1–8, 10, 13, 14, 16, 20, 24, 25, 27–29, and 31 (United Nations Committee on the Rights of Persons with Disabilities, 2019, Paras. 4(e), 5(e), 6(e), 8, 9, 11(a), 12(a) and (b), 13(d), 14(d), 15, 16, 19(a) and (b), 20(a) and (b), 25(d), 26(d), 27(a), 28(a), 29 (b), 30(b), 39, 40, 46(b), 47, 48(a), 49(c), 50(c), 51(c), 52(a), 53, 54, and 58). Thus the CRPD Committee has devoted considerably more attention to the heightened vulnerability of Aboriginal and/or Torres Strait Islander people with a disability.

CHAPTER 5

Experiences of Young People with Cognitive Disability

The Complex Road to Adulthood

Accessible Summary

- Becoming an adult involved lots of changes and challenges for young people with cognitive disability.
- Many services, and sometimes families, judged young people badly because they had a cognitive disability.
- Young people needed help to be independent, but this wasn't always given to them.
- Some young people were lonely, and found people who they thought were friends who later abused them.
- Aboriginal and/or Torres Strait Islander young people and young people from culturally and linguistically diverse backgrounds needed others to understand and respect their culture.
- LQBTIQA+ young people wanted love and acceptance to help them as they became adults.

5.1 Introduction

The world's 1.4 billion people worldwide who live with disability, when compared to the broader community, are less likely to attend school, secure renumerated work, own their own home, have and raise their children, enjoy a social life, or be permitted and supported to vote in elections (UN Chapter One: Overview – Realizing the Rights of Persons with Disabilities: The Compelling Reasons). These challenges and barriers impact every step of young people with cognitive disability's journey to adulthood. This chapter presents the experiences of young people with cognitive disability through what was often a turbulent journey transitioning into adulthood. For many young people the transition to adulthood is a time of multiple changes across many life domains.

In three sections, this chapter identifies the core themes that have arisen from the data that paint a picture of disadvantage, discrimination, and marginalisation at every level of the young person's experience. Section 5.2 addresses the overarching complexity impacting on young people with cognitive disability transitioning to adulthood. The young people in our study experienced emerging adulthood as especially complex, often facing additional barriers related to their experiences of disability and their reliance on both informal and formal systems of care and support. The interplay of developmental, cognitive, psychosocial, physical impairment, and health concerns alongside experiences of violence, abuse, and neglect highlights the vulnerability of this group of young people.

In addition to disability, young people also had other identities that create vulnerabilities. Section 5.3 analyses the impact of intersecting vulnerabilities related to Indigeneity, culture, sexuality, and gender that also sat outside traditional normative ideals of transitioning to adulthood. These identities were often unsupported by services and systems and presented additional challenges for young people. Many of the young people in this study showed resilience in the face of these challenges; however, their stories indicate that more could be done to support their transition to adulthood. An intersectional ecological approach highlights the complex layers and systems that young people with cognitive disability encounter and must learn to navigate, and the need to consider these in terms of their transition experiences. This was consistently highlighted by the young people, their parents, support network, and practitioners.

Finally, in Section 5.4 of this chapter there is discussion as to how the Convention on the Rights of Persons with Disabilities (CRPD) offers protection to young people with cognitive disability who are transitioning to adulthood.

5.2 Experiences in Transitioning to Adulthood

The experiences young people with cognitive disability had during their transition to adulthood often ran counter to what society expects from those without a disability. Social responses to young people with cognitive disability are discussed in relation to their impact on youth transition. Others' perceptions and expectations of what a disability 'looks like' could profoundly influence the experiences of young people with cognitive disability and their access to both formal and informal support. In addition, the supports provided to this group of young people may be inadequate and counter to their developmental needs. Young people with cognitive disability often experienced loneliness and disconnection as they transitioned to adulthood.

Ableist Understandings of Adulthood

Young people with cognitive disability in this study shared experiences of transition to adulthood that often ran counter to what society expected. Assumptions made by services and systems around emerging adulthood were often ill-informed and ableist and shaped transition as having a predetermined end. Australian laws provide that a person reaches the age of majority at the age of eighteen, and thus a person becomes a legal adult on their eighteenth birthday. But the normative notion of many services that, at the age of eighteen years, a young person is suddenly an adult, with all the associated responsibilities and knowledge, is unrealistic for most young people and especially problematic for young people with complex support needs. These assumptions around youth transition are compounded when many young people with cognitive disability may have not been supported to learn to make decisions by themselves and relied on parents and other adults to do so for most of their childhood. For others, there was an absence of support from family members and significant others, which left them without any information and guidance in making informed decisions about their lives.

Transition to adulthood for young people with cognitive disability does not always coincide with normative understandings of human development. For example, Becky, who described herself as having dyspraxia and dyslexia and had a biological age of twenty-five years, saw herself as just really starting her transition to becoming an adult woman. Becky explained that being an adult means taking responsibility for things for herself, which she liked. Her realisation of the importance of adult independence was only just emerging, later than what may have been socially expected:

> I feel more that I need to become more responsibility [*sic*] for myself since I'm twenty-five now. And Mum always kind of coddled me and everything like that, always helps me out and stuff like that. But I've come into the realisation, since I've moved into this place, I need to take care of myself. I can't rely on anybody. Yes, my Mum and Dad will give me money if

> I need it, but I don't want to rely on them because they're not going to be there all the time. I need to rely on myself.

Becky's account shows how important a sense of independence and responsibility can be for any young person, including young people with cognitive disability. Her transition to further independence may have been longer than other young people's but nevertheless was a source of pride, and the transition appeared to be supported by her family.

Not all young people in this study experienced appropriate supports for their stage of cognitive, social, and emotional development. This was very evident with regard to Amethyst, a twenty-nine-year-old First Nations Australian young woman with autism who became enmeshed in a horrifically abusive intimate relationship with a convicted paedophile (as described in Chapter 4). Her mother consistently pleaded with police to intervene, highlighting that her daughter's cognitive and developmental stage was not that of an adult. Despite having evidence from a psychiatrist, Amethyst's mother was not listened to. Police reportedly considered Amethyst an adult who was making her own choices about staying with an abusive perpetrator. In addition, there was a concerning lack of understanding from the various services involved. The Queensland Police and the Domestic, Family Violence and Vulnerable Persons Unit overlooked the impact of Amethyst's level of cognition and framed her experience as Amethyst's right to exercise 'choice' as a victim of domestic and family violence in remaining in an abusive relationship.

> Mother of Amethyst: I was at the police station three or four times a week. In desperation . . . Yeah, I even emailed the police commissioner in desperation because I got nowhere. Her psychiatrist actually . . . looked into it and I said, 'Should I go and confront him?' He said, 'Don't, he's dangerous.' Police were well aware of him. So, I emailed the police commissioner. On Boxing Day morning, I got a phone call from somebody from the Vulnerable Adult Unit, you'd think that's what their job is, a vulnerable adult. She rang me and she said, 'We went out. Covered in bruises from head to toe, but we asked her if she wanted to leave, and she said no.'

Amethyst later told her mother that the perpetrator was behind the door with a machete, and even though she wanted to leave she was afraid to say so, as he was there threatening her. The police had visited multiple times, but each time Amethyst was too frightened to leave. It was only when she eventually found an opportunity to run away that she was able to escape this situation. The lack of support received by Amethyst during this time was partly attributed to a failure of the system to understand Amethyst's stage of emotional, social, and cognitive development. It also was a refusal to act, and a failure of the system to appropriately respond to domestic and family violence.[1] For young women such as Amethyst, ableist attitudes intersect with broader social injustices related to violence against women.

Normative, ableist views on young people's development were most noticeable in the stories of young people with cognitive disability with complex communicative support needs. Angela is the stepmother of Danni, a twenty-two-year-old young woman with profound intellectual disability and severe cerebral palsy. When Danni turned eighteen, formal services and supports radically changed. Danni was no longer eligible for the medical and allied health services in the children's hospital she attended, and she was referred to adult hospital services. Angela described this transition as complex, confusing, and leading to a reduction in the support that was needed. Normative understandings of adulthood were an imposition on the family and bore no reality to Danni's experience. This was only one example of the failure of systems to accommodate the individual developmental needs of Danni. As Angela explained:

> You just get this complete unknown about what's out there, often there isn't anything, and then how to deal with all of the everyday things around the person. How do you operate their banking and how do you get her a passport and what do you do about voting, and how do you think about, I guess, all those little, everyday issues, as well as the big things about she's going to leave the school and what is she going to do? And then she's going to leave the children's system, which, in our experience, was amazing. And then you get launched into the adult health system, which is not amazing.

These accounts indicate that those who provide formal supports to young people with cognitive disability may have narrow, unhelpful understandings of young people's transition to adulthood. Services and systems can fail to acknowledge that the developmental trajectory of young people with cognitive disability may differ to other groups of young people. While both Becky's and Amethyst's mothers attempted to explain the differences in development in terms of cognitive age, a rather rudimentary explanation of development, this may have been the only communicative tool at hand to explain the need for appropriate accommodations. Even then, this did not guarantee that professionals responded appropriately. Amethyst's mother was unable to convince police of her daughter's needs related to her

[1] The systemic nature of this failing has been well recognised, as demonstrated most recently by the investigations into the police response to domestic and family violence in Queensland (Commission of Inquiry into Queensland Police Services Response to Domestic and Family Violence, 2022, www.qpsdfvinquiry.qld.gov.au/about/assets/commission-of-inquiry-dpsdfv-report.pdf).

disability, even after sharing a professional assessment from a psychiatrist. Where the young person's cognitive disability is visibly evident to others, as in the case of Danni, who had profound intellectual disability, there was still not enough priority given to the young person's stage of psychological, emotional, and social development.

These poor responses to transition are clear examples of systemic neglect of young people with cognitive disability. Services have a duty of care to afford young people the opportunity and necessary supports to learn to make their own decisions and allow them autonomy as young adults, but this must also be tempered with an understanding of the young person's developmental needs, and appropriate support to safeguard young people from violence. Neglect and other forms of violence can also occur in the way disability is socially constructed by others. The next few themes illustrate how certain constructions of cognitive disability have serious implications for young people.

Being Dehumanised: From Cute to Confronting and Frightening

There are many ways in which disability is interpreted. Some interpretations are inaccurate and potentially dehumanising. This study has uncovered examples of perceptions of cognitive disability that change in relation to the young person's age. Practitioners, young people, and family members pointed to stereotypes of children with cognitive disability as 'cute and vulnerable' and therefore safe to associate with – a perception that can extend into adulthood. However, adults with cognitive disability were often described by others as scary and dangerous, even as not human, in this way dehumanising the person. Thus, the 'cute' young person can suddenly be transformed by others as someone who is to be feared. These constructions can lead to further challenges around exclusion and discrimination.

A point made by a professional from a disability employment service is that for young people with cognitive disability there is the added challenge:

> that they're beginning to lose that cutesy feel of young kids, not cute. Everyone, 'Let's support them,' but then all of a sudden you see a grown adult who has an intellectual disability on a bus, and I don't like this at all, but we've heard it directly, that people are frightened of it. And it's not right and it's a perception that needs to be changed, but we've literally had people talk to us about how [frightening] these adults with intellectual disability can be to the general population.

When the construction of people with cognitive disability as 'cute' persists, it leads to infantilising adults with cognitive disability. The mother of Sophie, a young person with Down syndrome, discussed how the general public can regard Sophie as 'cute'. This is apparent when identifiable figures, such as police officers, talk down to Sophie using 'baby language'. These constructions of Sophie as child-like, when she is twenty years of age, have led others to underestimate her capacity. Sophie's mother described Sophie as a young woman with a lot of capacity who subsequently becomes discouraged by barriers and obstacles. Ongoing infantilisation and the associated lack of understanding about Sophie's abilities have created challenges for Sophie in relation to community access and participation and continue to impact her experiences as an adult.

In contrast, Hilde, a neurodiverse young person, explicitly identified being treated as if she was not human. She reported that her experience of disability led her to be dehumanised. She used the term 'monsterisation' in that she had been made to feel like she is a monster because of her disability. For Hilde this involved her own mother being scared of her and wanting to 'destroy the monster'. Hilde reported that her mother threatened to kill her, along with her father, who was also neurodiverse. Hilde also shared that this came from others in the community – 'I've lived my life with a high level of background radiation of "people like you should be dead".'

TBone's story is another example of being misunderstood and judged on the basis of his disability and behaviour. TBone is a First Nations Australian young person who was diagnosed with autism and pervasive developmental disorder not otherwise specified (PDD-NOS). At the age of ten, his parents found out he had been sexually abused and went to report this to the police. TBone was interviewed alone, which increased his anxiety. The combination of the trauma and the nature of his disability resulted in TBone having a 'meltdown', where he was kicking and screaming. His mother described that:

> a police officer then proceeded to drag him by the scruff of the neck from the back area where we were at the station, all the way through the station kicking and screaming and basically tossed him out the front door and said, 'Do you want to go to jail? Because if you keep up this shit you'll end up in jail.'

The response by police towards a ten-year-old traumatised child with a disability resulted in TBone's re-traumatisation. This example shows a complete disregard and dehumanisation of a child with cognitive disability, constructing TBone's behaviour as unsafe, rather than as a trauma response and genuine expression of distress. The punitive response further highlights the consequences of dehumanising persons with disability and the associated fear.

These examples of social responses speak to the pervasiveness of stereotypes surrounding the lives of young people with cognitive disability. The effect on emerging adulthood and identity development is likely to be detrimental and set the context for further episodes of discrimination and abuse.

The Invisibility of Disability

The disability of some of the young people in this study was not always visible to others. There may have been many reasons for this, including some young people appearing to have a high degree of independence and life skills, some young people having less severe forms of cognitive impairment, and young people masking their disability to others. Young people with cognitive disability and complex communicative support needs were also made to feel invisible by services and systems that deemed them 'too disabled' to provide adequate support.

A comment from Angel, a young person with intellectual disability, illustrates the problems associated with not having one's intellectual or cognitive disability recognised:

> From my experience, unless you're seen physically or physically known as having a disability, people tend to treat you really shitty. Yeah, because it's all mental they just either think you're really weird or they just don't treat you very kindly at all.... People with intellectual disabilities kind of slip under the radar because we don't necessarily look the part. So yeah, it'd be nice for that to be seen more as a priority, the same way as every other disability is.

In addition, practitioners reported that the invisibility of disability resulted in young people not being diagnosed, particularly in the out-of-home care and youth justice sectors, which created significant barriers to access to necessary supports. Without a formal diagnosis or functional assessment, many young people with cognitive disability in these systems missed out on appropriate help. This is supported by the research in this area (Baker Collins et al., 2018).

In contrast, parents of young people with cognitive disability and complex communicative support needs reported that their children's disability was so apparent to others that services, systems, and society rendered these young people invisible. Angela, the stepmother of Danni, aged twenty-two, explained:

> Well, it's that our society is just not set up to even think about people like Danni. We are the doubly invisible, right? So, I'm invisible because I'm doing that kind of work [carer]. My husband and my family, my thirteen-

> year-old who's grown up knowing that she's going to have to do that work when we're dead, provided Danni lives that long, and that Danni is invisible.... For example, she had a seizure once at [name withheld] Shopping Centre and it was that duality of you are so invisible, but also so visible. Everyone knows that something catastrophic is happening with this kid, but no one will look at you, let alone come up and go, 'Can I help you?'

Similarly, Peter, father of Kim, a young woman with profound intellectual disability, reported that Kim had become depressed at school, and he found out that she had been given a magazine and sat 'in the corner out of the way'. When Peter challenged the school principal, he was told that 'Their job is to look after the majority of people. They can't look after everyone.' This experience highlights the challenges for young people being able to participate in something as important as education fully and meaningfully. At the same time, these experiences suggest the deeply discrediting impact of an ableist discourse, resulting in an unspoken social devaluation of persons with cognitive disability and complex communicative support needs (Goffman, 1963).

Denial of Agency: Not Being Disabled Enough

Linked with this notion of invisibility are the challenges associated with others' expectations of what a disability 'looks like'. This was identified by a few of the young people, their family members, and practitioners; importantly, it resulted in restricted access to support.

Hilde stated that she was initially diagnosed with Asperger's syndrome and described herself as 'hyperlexic', appearing as more 'high functioning' than she is. This created contradictory challenges in that 'you're high functioning, that's used to deny aid. And if you're low functioning, that's used to deny agency.'

Similarly, Cody who has obsessive compulsive disorder (OCD) described the challenges associated with not coming across as sufficiently 'disabled' in that he presents as articulate and intelligent. Cody described his disability as 'really exhausting that people seem to think just because I am intelligent that I can't be ill or sick or need help . . . I try and get help, I think, but no one wants to help me because I'm supposed to know how to do it myself.' Cody experienced being blamed and judged as being lazy when he asked for help. For both Cody and Hilde, not fitting the stereotype about what is 'disabled enough' resulted in discrimination in terms of denial of support, unfair expectations of independence and agency, and feeling judged.

Too Costly

Both Angela and Peter, parents of young people with profound cognitive disability, referred to the emphasis on funding and fiscal considerations by services when it came to supporting their family member, who was often referred to as 'too costly' by these services. Services were often not appropriately targeted to the needs of the individual, but rather were driven by a philosophy of economies of scale. Peter provided the example of accessing a short-stay accommodation for young people with disability for his daughter Kim. Peter stated the respite centre would 'have the numbers at 100 per cent so they make lots of money. And if it's overcrowded, it's noisy.' Peter felt that the design of such centres did not provide an opportunity for people with disability to have sufficient privacy and quiet time, as the noise from the main living areas would carry into people's rooms. This proved to be an inappropriate option for his daughter Kim, yet there were few other alternatives for the family to access respite care.

For both Angela's and Peter's families, the frequent message from professionals and funding bodies was that much-needed support for their young person was not affordable. The solution by both families was often to create their own care arrangements and engage in concerted and sustained advocacy efforts to improve their young person's life. The toll of such efforts can be great for many families, as both Angela and Peter attested to, as they were constantly having to battle and advocate for basic support for their children. This is a common experience for parents and carers of people with disability, with the cost to their own well-being and health often overlooked.

Inaccurate and unhelpful assumptions about young people with cognitive disability are significant barriers for young people and their families as they seek to belong and to contribute to their communities and society. In the next subsection, the impacts of these deeply held biases are examined in relation to the part they play in stifling young people to achieve independence in their transition to adulthood.

Over-protection and Low Expectations

The journey to gaining independence for many young people with cognitive disability can be protracted and stifled by the supports around them. Our research identified challenges for young people with cognitive disability who lived in environments and accessed systems where everything was controlled and often 'over-controlled' for the young person. This infantilising over-protection from family members and disability workers often denied young people the right to make decisions for themselves and to develop important life skills. In essence, it demonstrated that others around a young person with cognitive disability could have limiting beliefs about a young person's capacity to learn new skills and grow into adulthood. Vivienne, a practitioner from a regional self-advocacy service, highlighted how this has a negative effect on young people with cognitive disability on multiple levels, not least in terms of empowering them to be independent as adults:

> I was contracted to go into a group home to do a survey with the people who had just moved in there and it was just horrendous. So, there was one person there, she was buttering peanut butter on her toast and the staff member was yelling, 'That's enough peanut butter for five bits of toast.' And this woman has a history of self-abusing, and as soon as that happened, she went over, turned on the gas hub and put her hand in it. And I'm sitting there thinking, 'Oh my God. There's no way. Just none of this should have happened this way. No way.'

The danger highlighted here is that over-surveillance and control not only deny agency but can actively distress some young people with cognitive disability and lead to further harm. Young people with cognitive disability may seek to reclaim their personal power within relationships through behaviours that challenge. These behaviours may be a means of communicating to others their need for personal agency.

The importance of having and/or promoting self-determination, dignity of risk, and informal support networks in the young person's ecology was identified by several practitioners in this research. Lorna, a practitioner working in an advocacy service in Victoria, Australia, emphasised how formal services can have an important role to play in recognising the potential of young people with cognitive disability:

> I think finding some way to create community independence, realising that everyone can grow within their capacity or when they have opportunity, then no matter what the person's disability is, that they can grow.

This practitioner, along with many others in this study, felt that there was a need for a holistic recognition of the individual as a person with their life ahead of them. This involves having a service system that supports the person's hopes and dreams and that is person-centred rather than process- and rules-driven. In subsequent chapters we will show how well different service systems fared in supporting young people to build independence and transition to a full and meaningful adulthood.

Seeking Connection

Social connection with supportive others is another factor that can greatly assist a young person's transition to adulthood. The body of research into the impacts of social isolation on the social determinants of health further highlights the importance of social connection (Holt-Lunstad, 2022; Holt-Lunstad & Steptoe, 2022). Unfortunately, the findings from this research indicated that the young people with cognitive disability often experienced loneliness and disconnection as they transitioned to adulthood. Social isolation can be detrimental to the development of life skills, to feelings of belonging within one's community, and to achieving taken-for-granted goals of adulthood, such as further education and employment. Social isolation may also set the context in which abuse and exploitation of young people can occur.

Many practitioners explicitly identified the challenges and risks associated with young people with cognitive disability whose only social networks were family or formal services. Jan, a specialist practitioner working with persons with intellectual disability, reported that her service ran therapeutic groups to assist young people to learn how to establish informal friendships:

> Jan: We also do therapeutic groups, which is a week group program which we've developed over the years. And then the one we're doing at the moment is called You and Me. So, it's basically about teaching people how to make friends, what different types of relationships look like, what's okay, what's not okay.... Because that hopefully not only tries to keep them a little safer but helps them build friendships. Because the biggest problem is, with most of our clients, that they're so lonely that they'll accept any offers of contact or friendship. And grooming is huge.
> Interviewer: So that makes them a lot more vulnerable.
> Jan: So vulnerable. Loneliness is probably the biggest problem.The need to understand and experience supportive friendship was a key aim for the therapeutic work in Jan's agency. By unpacking the elements of helpful relationships, it was hoped young people with cognitive disability would not be drawn into exploitative relationships with others, which could lead to emotional, sexual, and financial exploitation.

Friendship with peers not only was seen as a protective factor by practitioners and professionals but was also associated with the development of independence in young people. Monica, an advocate for persons with disability from culturally and linguistically diverse backgrounds, also discussed how relationships for this group were often confined to family members and paid support staff. She felt this could restrict young people from taking risks in the community, using public transport independently, and learning how to manage money. It was felt that the emphasis on allied health supports under the National Disability Insurance Scheme (NDIS) failed to adequately address the need for community connection and engagement.

Poor experiences in schooling can also lead to social isolation and reduced opportunity for connection. TBone had ongoing difficulties at school, due to his traumatic history of sexual abuse and lack of appropriate behavioural support. TBone ended up being home schooled and was not able to develop a friendship network around him. His mother reported that at the time of the interview, TBone's only friend was his father.

Young people with cognitive disability often develop strategies to overcome loneliness as they transition into adulthood. When there is a lack of supportive familial and friendship networks, the young person may seek to create their own family. Riley, a practitioner working with persons with intellectual disability who were survivors of sexual abuse, provided examples of young people making their own families:

> There's probably a few young people that I have in mind whose experiences of family rupture, of family dissolution, whether that's from statutory intervention or whether that's just from domestic and family violence or ... there's a number of different motivations that young people might have, but that sense of wanting to parent or wanting to start a family or wanting to be a part of a rich, meaningful, supportive, loving family. I think that there's very little validation of that drive for young people. And then, particularly for young people with intellectual disability, they're often pathologized for acting on that ... so [they may] not be engaging in safe sex, but also not being given information to make informed decisions around that. And so, their hopes or needs or motivations might be being exploited by the people around them or the people that they're having sex with, but also being blocked ... not being supported to make informed decisions by support staff.

Riley's example shows that if a young person with cognitive disability is not assisted to develop supportive, affirming relationships outside formal service provision, they are likely to end up in exploitative relationships as they strive to fulfil that need. Service providers can assist the young person with cognitive disability to be discerning around how to meet the need for relationship, but as identified by practitioners and professionals, they often fail to help the young person make informed decisions to prevent exploitation occurring. An inherent barrier is the lack of access to sex or relationship education in schools for children and young people with cognitive disability, which increases the risk of exploitation (Strnadová et al., 2022).

Some young people with cognitive disability in this research showed examples of reaching out for positive supports and connection through pets. For example, Goldie, a First Nations Australian young woman with autism, talked about alleviating the loneliness of making the transition to independent living through the support of her pet dog. The importance of pets has been recognised in providing a source of companionship and alleviating loneliness and emphasises the need to consider social support connections holistically (Lawn & Kaine, 2022).

Our research has shown that transition to adulthood for young people with cognitive disability may be stymied by ableist assumptions and contradictory responses from others around the young person. Young people with cognitive disability we spoke to often found a way to assert their agency despite the lack of social support to do so. The next two sections take into consideration the influence of cultural understandings on transition and discuss the issues and experiences facing Aboriginal and/or Torres Strait Islander young people with cognitive disability, young people with cognitive disability from culturally and linguistically diverse backgrounds, and LGBTIQA+ young people with cognitive disability.

5.3 Intersecting Vulnerabilities and Transitions to Adulthood

Young people with cognitive disability have other identity categories than those related to their disability. This research pays particular attention to those identities related to being a First Nations Australian young person, being a young person from a culturally and linguistically diverse background, and identifying as a LGBTIQA+ young person.

First Nations Australian young people with cognitive disability can face a myriad of challenges as they approach adulthood. These challenges can include intergenerational disadvantage. Colonised service responses can result in culturally unsafe service practices. Similarly, young people with cognitive disability from culturally and linguistically diverse backgrounds are likely to experience significant barriers as they transition into adulthood. Services can fail to respond appropriately to young people's cultural background and history of migration. There may be poor access to interpreters, and services may fail to accurately assess the young person's disability. Young people who identify as LGBTIQA+ may experience discrimination in relation to their sexuality. This can lead to poor treatment, abuse, and violence from others, including peers, family members, support workers, and professionals.

First Nations Australian Young People with Cognitive Disability and Transitions to Adulthood

As previously mentioned in Chapter 1 of this book, terms such as 'cognitive disability' are not always embraced by young people so-labelled. This may be especially true for Aboriginal and/or Torres Strait Islander young people, who belong to communities that regard disability as part of everyday life, and do not regard disability labels as culturally or socially appropriate (McCausland & Dowse, 2020). The researchers therefore refer to this term with some caution, to denote Aboriginal and/or Torres Strait Islander young people who require additional support with both intellectual learning and developing conceptual, social, and practical adaptive skills (Schalock et al., 2021).

First Nations Australian young people with cognitive disability can face a myriad of challenges as they approach adulthood. In this research, Aboriginal and/or Torres Strait Islander young people with cognitive disability and the practitioners who worked with this group identified intergenerational disadvantage and culturally unsafe service practices impacting on youth transition. First Nations peoples in Australia were colonised with the coming of European explorers and settlers. As with other countries, colonisation (1870s to mid 1920s) resulted in First Nations peoples being forced off their country. Many were placed in Christian missions and schools as part of a process of assimilation into Western culture. Key to this was the attempted decimation of their culture and customs (Gray & Hetherington, 2013). In the 1910s government policies resulted in the government-sanctioned removal of children from their families, referred to now as the 'Stolen Generation'. The impacts of ongoing policies underpinned by this discourse have resulted in cumulative and intergenerational trauma and affects all domains of life, with higher rates of unemployment; over-representation in the child protection, youth, and adult criminal justice systems; poor health and mental health outcomes; and economic, education, and housing disadvantage (Bennett, 2013; Department of Justice and Regulation, 2005; Gray & Hetherington, 2013). Within this context, First Nations children and young people living with cognitive disability experience a further degree of complexity in the challenges they encounter.

Intergenerational Experiences

This research includes findings that relate to intergenerational experiences of living with a cognitive disability within some Aboriginal and/or Torres Strait Islander families. Dan and John, two First Nations practitioners who worked for an Aboriginal and Torres Strait Islander Community Controlled Health Service, discussed how cognitive disability could be present in several generations of some families. In the holistic support they provided First Nations families they shared that they saw situations where they believed a young person and their family/kin all had a cognitive disability. In many of these situations, the young person and family had not received any formal diagnosis to confirm this, and thus had limited understanding of the nature of cognitive disability or associated disability supports. John provided the example of a mother who, he believed, may have her own learning disability, and was struggling to control her child's behaviour. The mother had difficulty understanding why her son could not do things as quickly as his sibling.

The intersection with past trauma was a common theme among First Nations young people with cognitive disability and their families, impacting on the young person's life. Annette, a lawyer who works with First Nations Australian people in the criminal justice system, talked about the impact of intergenerational trauma because of overarching practices of child removal:

> Often, it's a narrative of being removed. Especially with Aboriginal and Torres Strait Islander clients, it's a narrative of being removed from family and culture. And that even if there may have been neglect in the household because of their own parents' issues with drugs or alcohol or whatever, often, and not always, it's the removal which is worse, and being removed from family and not being connected with family is worse. So, then that's where the abuse and the neglect and trauma happened, ... in juvenile detention or in state care or in foster care.

The effects of intergenerational trauma permeated family relationships and the ability of family members to adequately care for young people with cognitive disability. Parents, grandparents, and other kin could have their own issues they were working through, which created challenges to attending to the needs of the young person. Dan and John, First Nations youth workers, highlighted situations where family members they worked with did not recognise that their actions in fact constituted abuse. This was attributed to a lack of education or understanding but also a result of 'repeating what they experienced when they were younger. It's just kind of had that snowball effect' (Dan).

Dan and John shared several examples of how trauma histories impacted Aboriginal and/or Torres Strait Islander young people with cognitive disability. John spoke about a young person he was helping:

> There's trauma ... father passed away, mum's involved in drugs.... There was ADHD [attention deficit hyperactivity disorder] in there.... Then it just leads onto violence in school and stuff and falling behind in classes, which is a reoccurring thing with the young people we work with, I guess.

Dan shared how he supported a young person with cognitive disability who experienced neglect:

> [He] was put in care at a very young age, I think maybe one year old, they've suffered trauma from the father's suicide, I know that it was pre-natal drug use. And I know there's been some diagnoses, but from what I understand there's like a big gap too from what certain doctors have, whether it be the psychologist from the DOCS [Department of Child Safety] versus ours in the clinic. I guess it's been my job at the moment to try to put that all together. Because I've seen three different pieces of paper with six different diagnoses.

Both examples depict experiences of grief and loss and disconnection from important relationships. The support from the systems involved in each young person's life appear to be less than ideal, with difficulties in communication across agencies, and gaps in expertise to diagnose. Youth workers such as Dan and John are required to integrate all this conflicting information about the young person and ameliorate the effects of an education system in Australia that does not always provide safe and positive educational experiences for First Nations young people. These factors can add significant barriers to young people with cognitive disability approaching adulthood.

Colonised Service Responses to Aboriginal and/or Torres Strait Islander Young People with Cognitive Disability

Both First Nations young people with cognitive disability and practitioners reported problems with the ways in which services and systems responded to cultural needs of young people. One example was the failure of formal systems to recognise a person's cultural heritage. When Amethyst, a First Nations neurodiverse young woman, was finally able to run away from her violent abuser, she was incarcerated:

> Because at school we got taught to ask ... for these three people if they apply to you. So, I asked for someone who I can call, to see a lawyer or officer, like the PLO [Police Liaison Officer], if you can get that across to a

> PLO that you are Indigenous. I just kept asking for the PLO and they're like, 'You're not indigenous,' and I'm like, 'Yes, I am' [crying].
>
> And then I never, not once, saw a PLO. And they turned all my lights off, and I'm scared of the dark. I'm terrified of the dark.... I was seeing things and hearing things and feeling things. Oh my God, it was crazy.

Failure of the criminal justice system to acknowledge Amethyst's culture impacted on her psychologically at a time when she was fleeing from a horrific experience of abuse, exploitation, and neglect. This experience has been corroborated by research in this area, identifying significant systemic gaps in the cultural responsiveness of mainstream services (Department of Justice and Regulation, 2005; Victorian Equal Opportunity and Human Rights Commission, 2013).

Cultural responsiveness calls for a flexible approach to service provision, which was not always present in the accounts of participants in this research. Dan, the First Nations Australian youth worker, provided an example of an Aboriginal and/or Torres Strait Islander young person with cognitive disability who had disengaged from school for the last twelve months and had not left his house for approximately six months. The education system appeared to create further barriers rather than supporting the young person and identifying solutions. Dan explained, 'I know my ... client's on a scholarship and then they're like, "Well, we will pull the scholarship if this person does not attend any further,"' showing inflexibility and lack of understanding.

Finally, service systems often failed to adequately respond to the complexities behind young people's lives. The First Nations young people with cognitive disability involved in these stories appeared to have complex presentations, indicating that they were likely to have more than one diagnosis. Many Aboriginal and/or Torres Strait Islander young people with cognitive disability have co-occurring mental health issues, as discussed by Dan:

> I guess mental health is a big thing with young Mob[2] with cognitive disabilities. Because some of them are falling behind in school and things like that. It all begins to snowball; their mental health will decline significantly. So, I guess that's been a big thing. It's just kind of trying to get them reengaged because they're disengaging.

[2] The term 'Mob' refers to a group of Aboriginal and/or Torres Strait Islander people associated with a particular place or country.

Dan intimates here that mental health issues were closely connected to young peoples' disengagement with education and experiences of social isolation, both of which impact transition. Service systems need to acknowledge both the strength and resilience of First Nations young people with cognitive disability, as well as the significant disadvantage facing this group. Without culturally safe, adequate, and timely responses, a young person can further disengage from support.

This section has outlined the importance of tailoring responses to First Nations Australian young people with cognitive disability so that they consider what is culturally safe to the young person, and what will assist the young person to connect to community and support transition. Without this, what was evident was systemic-level neglect. Similar priorities are necessary for young people with cognitive disability from culturally and linguistically diverse backgrounds.

Young People with Cognitive Disability from Culturally and Linguistically Diverse Backgrounds and Transition to Adulthood

Young people with cognitive disability from culturally and linguistically diverse backgrounds are likely to experience significant barriers as they transition into adulthood in Australia. This is because of the dual challenges of being from a culturally and linguistically diverse background and living with a cognitive disability (Kappelides et al., 2021; Lewis, 2021; Royal Commission into Violence, Abuse, Neglect and Exploitation of People with Disability 2021). The findings have shown that this group of young people may struggle with the English language and experience shame, stigma, and lack of understanding from those around them, including the ethnic communities to which they belong, as no community is entirely free of ableist bias. Young people who are from a refugee background have also experienced significant trauma, which can further undermine their well-being, adding further challenges. In this section we present the experiences of practitioners who worked with young people with cognitive disability, as the research team were not able to meet with the young people themselves.

It is important to recognise the breadth of diversity of experiences of people from culturally and linguistically diverse backgrounds. In Australia, the term 'culturally and linguistically diverse' refers to people who have been settled in Australia for decades, such as the Greeks and Italians who came out post war. The term also refers to more recent immigrants and those who have settled in Australia on humanitarian visas or who are seeking asylum. Consequently, there is no 'one size fits all' label when referring to people from culturally and linguistically diverse backgrounds and their experiences.

Failing to See the Young Person through a Holistic, Sociocultural Lens
Practitioners talked about the importance of taking a holistic sociocultural lens when considering the needs of young people with cognitive disability and their transition experiences. This includes recognising the intersection with their environment, community, and cultural values and beliefs. Additionally, understanding the sociocultural constructions of disability and support was highlighted, as these add another layer to the already challenging impact of systemic level discrimination and racism. However, practitioners identified the lack of thorough and culturally appropriate assessments in understanding the needs of the young person with cognitive disability, further exacerbated by limited culturally appropriate supports. Practitioners highlighted how the combination of these factors can impact the development of meaningful responses to a young person's experience of transition.

The following case study, conveyed by an academic, Barbara, whose research specialises in this area, emphasises the complexity and necessity of holistic assessments that consider the context and the sociocultural history of the young person:

> A young person aged eighteen came to Australia as a refugee. The young person had experienced an acquired brain injury due to a bomb landing on his house in the Middle East. His parents had left him in a refugee camp in another country while they tried to get refugee status. When they finally were able to bring him out to Australia, language and comprehension issues meant that the services who became involved were unable to manage his behaviour.. . . So, he was put under a restrictive practices regime,[3] which . . . the family described as like a domestic violence situation. They felt that they couldn't say much because . . . he was getting . . . better than what he was getting before he came to Australia.. . . And when we're talking about refugees [who] . . . come to Australia, we're talking about people [who] . . . may have been in refugee camps for twenty years, where medical services are really poor. I mean, the young man that I talked about, they took him to a European country, and . . . they just could not get a diagnosis to what was actually wrong. But the good story is, he's in a much better place now.

[3] Restrictive practices are any interventions that impact on the rights or freedom of movement of a person with the primary purpose of protecting the person or other people from harm. They include chemical, environmental, mechanical, and physical restraint, and seclusion.

This example shows how services, through their lack of understanding of a person's cultural background and history of migration, may struggle to support a young person with cognitive disability appropriately. Language barriers may alienate the family from having important input into the young person's care. In this story, the family also felt they should accept what was on offer, as in comparison to previous service experiences, there was some improvement for the young person.

Practitioners also highlighted the importance of engaging with extended family of young people with cognitive disability from culturally and linguistically diverse backgrounds. Due to the additional challenges regarding language and cultural constructions of disability, being able to support and educate the family to best support the young person becomes critical. Recognising the different cultural values regarding family is likewise important.

Monica, an individual advocate who works with persons with disability from culturally and linguistically diverse backgrounds, relayed an experience of supporting an eighteen-year-old young woman who had level two autism[4] and required substantial support. The young woman was living at home with her family but had informed the support coordinator[5] who was assisting her in the NDIS planning process that she did not want the family present at the planning interview. The planning assessment relied only on the young woman's self-reported accounts of her abilities, and the family, who did not speak English, were not aware of what was included in the young woman's plan. The support coordinator arranged for an urgent review of the young woman's plan, to arrange for the young woman to move out of home. The support coordinator made this recommendation because of a concern that the young woman was being financially exploited by family and that the young woman was being forced to pick up her sister from school. Monica identified that the support coordinator had never spoken to the family about any of these concerns:

> And so, we had this meeting, with an interpreter, and we found out that the reason she [the young woman] was picking up her little sister from school

[4] The reference to level two autism refers to the severity of autism in a young person. Someone with level one autism 'requires supports' in social communication and behaviours. A person with level two autism 'requires substantial supports' in these areas, and a person with level three autism 'requires very substantial supports' in these areas. Further information can be found in the American Psychiatric Association's fifth edition of its *Diagnostic and Statistical Manual of Mental Disorders: DSM-5* (2013).

[5] Support coordinators assist a person with disability to build their capacity by helping them to understand and use their NDIS plan and connect them with supports and services.

> was because she had nothing to do most days and it was just a way of getting her out of the house and giving her a role to do in life. So, she was asked.... And the finances, she was getting regular kind of pocket money and then the rest of the money was being put into savings for her.... She [the support coordinator] just heard one side of the story of someone with quite significant cognitive impairment and just took it as gospel, without doing any work with the family. And the family were at the stage of saying, 'Well, you just go,' because it had become so negative.... So basically, the big problem was that there was a ... support worker who really just completely undermined the long-term safety and security of that woman by isolating her from her family.

Monica was able to open the communication between the support coordinator and the family and assisted the young woman to access services and short-term accommodation outside the home with the support of her parents. This example highlights the added layer of understanding required by workers that considers social and cultural factors. While the agency of this young woman to make independent decisions as an adult is critical, this does not exclude the importance of considering cultural nuances and a culturally informed framework when supporting young people with cognitive disability to transition to adulthood.

Difficulties Understanding, Accessing and Accepting Support

A holistic approach to supporting young people with cognitive disability from culturally and linguistically diverse backgrounds involves addressing the challenges associated with accessing culturally appropriate supports. Many families from these backgrounds do not know what supports are available in Australia, and this can be further compounded when the parents do not speak or understand English. In addition, a family may come from a culture where it is expected that it is the parents who will solely take care of their children with disability.

Monica gave an example of a Vietnamese young person with cognitive disability who was in her mid-twenties and wanted to live independently:

> Her parents definitely saw it as their role to care permanently for their daughter.... It happens in all cultures, I guess.... But if you come from a community where there's no support for people with disability, and therefore there's been generational expectation that if you have someone in your family with disability that you will care for them all your life, then it's a huge change to think that you won't. And also, [there is] a loss of face amongst others in the community, that they might be seeing you're not doing the right thing by your children if you're allowing them to live independently.

Without appropriate cultural support, the needs of this young person to experience any type of independence and agency as she transitioned into adulthood were restricted, thus potentially denying her rights to freedom and choice.

As noted in the above example, accessing support may incite feelings of stigma and shame for young people with cognitive disability and their families. Darius, a social worker who also lives with a disability, discussed his experiences in supporting families from culturally and linguistically diverse backgrounds and their reluctance to apply for disability support:

> I got a client, she's from Lebanon, with her husband and they got the child with Asperger's.. . . I have to struggle with them basically to link them . . . to the support that we have in Australia, and they don't want it. The lady was keep telling me that, 'Oh Darius, look, I don't want anyone to know that my child has got Asperger's.' I said to her, 'Hey Adeline, look at me, as a person with a disability, I am a person with a disability, I am trying, and I have been a practitioner for eleven years. And look at me, I have [to] carry a cane and I go to work, and I study here.' It took me three years . . . to be able to help this child.

Other cultural barriers highlighted by practitioners included how the individual and their family and community understand the term 'disability'. Stigma and shame regarding terms like 'disability' can pose significant barriers to accessing support. As Darius shared, 'Look, when I do my needs assessment, . . . we get the section that we have to discuss about their disability. Okay, when we say "disability, mental health", [the person with disability says,] "Oh, no, no, no, no, no, no. I am not crazy. I'm not crazy." So, we have to break it somehow.' Darius highlighted how for some people he works with, disability is associated with mental health and with being 'crazy' and the stigma associated with this.

Shame regarding disability can be reinforced by country-of-origin communities, and families may thus be reluctant to seek help. For example, Barbara reported that families may hold very different sociocultural beliefs, 'particularly . . . for things like cognitive impairments, [beliefs] can revolve around witchcraft, possession by spirit, karma. And if you think like that, your health-seeking behaviour is quite different.'

Young people with cognitive disability from culturally and linguistically diverse backgrounds can thus become invisible unless they are linked into services that can work with the families to assist them in recognising and accepting the disability and supports available. Without targeted cultural support that recognises the nuances around beliefs and values, the implications for the child or young person are that they can miss out on much-needed support during critical stages of their development, having long-term negative consequences for their transition to adulthood.

Poor Access to Interpreters

A further challenge for young people with cognitive disability and their families from culturally and linguistically diverse backgrounds is access to interpreters. Darius shared the following example:

> I received the report from the psychologist. It's a huge report for one of my clients with autism. The mother [is] from Syria.... And I received the report from the psychologist, it's about thirty pages, and she said, 'I don't understand this report. I want to read it.' I spoke to some services. They said if we want to interpret that in Arabic it cost thousands and thousands [of] dollars. So fortunately, because I speak the language, . . . I went to her place, and I was able to basically skim that report and read it and translate [to] her in Arabic. Not in written, but explaining to her in Arabic. So, it took hours and hours [nine hours] to basically, as a practitioner, to support someone to understand the aspect of that cognitive disability.

This family was fortunate to access support from Darius, but this is the exception for many families where accessing appropriate interpreters is limited. Barbara (the academic) highlighted the added difficulties for young people with cognitive disability and their families who do not have access to technology, or where using a phone interpreter rather than face-to-face contact is the only option. Without access to appropriate interpreters and translation services or resources, many young people with cognitive and their families are ill-informed about what services and supports are available. This in turn creates additional barriers for the young person with cognitive disability as they transition into adulthood. It may also be an impediment to a young person to report any experiences of violence to appropriate authorities.

Culturally Inappropriate Assessments

Practitioners identified the barriers faced by young people with cognitive disability from culturally and linguistically diverse backgrounds in gaining accurate diagnostic assessments of their disability. Without a diagnosis, there is limited, if any, funding for support, including support for transition. Monica provided the following example, highlighting how services may fail to identify a young person's cognitive disability and the devastating outcomes that result:

> So, for instance, one of the young men I've been working with, he arrived in Australia when he was eighteen. He had an assessment through

> Centrelink[6] that said that he could work more than eight hours a week independently. He was connected with a disability employment service that found him a job and sent him off to work on his own, and the second day he was let go because he couldn't do the job that he was asked to do.

The young man subsequently spent seven years unemployed at home with no disability support and being cared for by his mother. The young man was referred to the advocacy agency where Monica works by his general practitioner, and Monica was able to arrange for an occupational therapist and psychologist assessment, which determined the young man had a significant intellectual disability. This new information led to a reassessment by the state social security service (Centrelink), access to NDIS school leaver employment support, and work skills training. Monica emphasised the need for wraparound supports for this group of young people:

> Now, his mum is a refugee, single mum with little English, so she didn't know what services were available, where to go to. So those are all barriers, like the lack of English, the lack of use of internet, the belief that they'd been offered an attempt at finding them employment, but it hadn't worked, so he was then on his own.

Providing an accurate assessment of a young person's needs involves understanding that the person may have difficulties answering questions due to language barriers, which may not be disability-related. Barbara explained:

> I think back to a young man whose family I interviewed, and because he couldn't speak English and the service providers couldn't understand him, they were just going to [think], 'This is all to do with his cognitive disability,' not considering that he might have language issues around just conversing in English, let alone anything else.

Poor assessment can also occur when professionals fail to account for the adverse life events young people with cognitive disability may have experienced. Barbara shared the opinion that doctors and specialists overlooked a myriad of issues facing culturally and linguistically diverse people. She stated, 'Particularly for people who've come as refugees, where some of their responses are natural responses to flight and trauma and deprivation and it's just lumped together and not looked at holistically. It's all pathologized.' Taking into account the impact of trauma requires careful attention and a focus on understanding the unique needs of the individual and their experiences holistically.

[6] Centrelink is the government agency that provides income support and other payments to Australians.

Barbara's example also highlights the insidiousness of ableism, where a person's disability is understood as the single reason for difficulties or challenges. This reductionist understanding has implications for what services are offered. Governments may subsequently fail to take responsibility for providing culturally appropriate supports and services, as 'disability' is seen as the only issue to be responded to.

The findings on young people with cognitive disability from First Nations Australian and culturally and linguistically diverse communities demonstrate how the experience of disability can often be context-dependent and have multiple cultural meanings. The experience of transition often involves young people navigating multiple social identities as they approach adulthood. To prevent and respond to abuse and violence within young people's lives, services and systems need to broaden their understanding of young people's lived experiences and look at the interplay of many factors. The following section examines the experiences of LGBTIQA+ young people with cognitive disability in this study.

LGBTIQA+ Young People with Cognitive Disability and Transitions to Adulthood

There were four young people who identified as LGBTIQA+ in this study. Each young person had different descriptors for their sexual identity, demonstrating the diversity of people who can belong to this group – Angel (aged twenty-four, LGBTIQA+, pronouns he/him), Becky (aged twenty-five, non-binary, pronouns she/her), Milly (aged twenty-one, pansexual, pronouns she/her), and Simon (aged thirty, intersex, pronouns he/him). At the time of being interviewed, three of these young people (Angel, Becky, and Milly) were living independently with formal support from disability services, and one young person, Simon, was living at home with his parents. The intersection of disability and their diversity in terms of sexual identities added a further layer of complexity for these young people as they transitioned to adulthood. Some of the key themes are now discussed.

The young people who identified as LGBTIQA+ shared a variety of experiences of poor treatment, abuse, and violence from others, including peers, family members, support workers, and professionals. Becky reported disturbing accounts of physical and sexual assault from family members and acquaintances, and Milly experienced emotional abuse and neglect from her birth family and domestic violence from her intimate partner. Simon, who was still living at home with his parents, experienced physical and emotional abuse from other persons with disability in school and in his current education program. He also experienced emotional and psychological abuse and neglect from disability support workers and a health professional. In telling their accounts, young people did not explicitly indicate whether these acts of violence were connected to heteronormative discrimination, but the researchers contend that sexual identity must be considered if young people's experiences of violence are to be understood from a holistic lens.

Learning to Love Oneself

As part of participating in this study, young people with cognitive disability were asked to share their thoughts about what it meant to become an adult. Angel, Becky, and Milly all conveyed that adulthood was a journey towards self-acceptance, a point of overcoming the legacy of earlier experiences of bullying, rejection, exploitation, and unfair expectations from peers, intimate partners, family members, and education authorities.

Part of self-acceptance involved learning to love oneself. As Milly shared, 'It's hard for me to see what love is and what love isn't, how to be treated, how to not be treated, because I never had that. I've never been loved before. I've never had that security of being loved . . . so I had to sort of learn to love myself.'

Angel was able to build his sense of self-worth by engaging in activities he loved, such as circus skills, where he discovered new talents and received recognition from others. Even in these positive environments, Angel disclosed that he still needed to consciously challenge old beliefs:

> Because going into those places where I can grow and do the thing that I'm good at, even though I know that I'm good at what I'm doing, there's still all that trauma of going, 'Well, you're not going to be good enough because you never were good enough when it mattered.' And that still kind of sits with you.

Becky spoke about helping others to be comfortable with who they were, and that self-acceptance and love became easier as one got older. She spoke of how her father used to be homophobic and that the only support she received while at school was from her mother. Becky acknowledged that she still felt fearful of others' judgements of her, recalling previous anxiety she had in attending a vocational educational training provider, also referred to as a Technical and Further Education (TAFE)[7] college in the clothes she wanted to wear:

[7] Technical and Further Education (TAFE) colleges are government-run tertiary providers of vocational training ("What Is TAFE (Technical and Further Education) and How Can It Benefit You?," tafecourses.com.au).

> I had anxiety. I had anxious. I had all these things going through my mind. How are people going to judge me? How are people going to look at me? How are people going to treat me differently? How are people going to do this? How are people going to do that? And that's why I never did it [chose the clothes she wanted to wear]. I'm still not doing it today. I do it in my room, but I don't do it when people are around.

Becky, Angel, and Simon spoke of experiencing anxiety and how this impacted their sense of well-being and ability to feel good about oneself and interact with others. Angel explained how he has learnt to manage his anxiety:

> Yeah, the overwhelming anxiety of having to go inside yourself and kind of like suck up all that fear in order to go outside the house, it takes a lot. So, it's just a lot mentally, of trying to suppress all that. Trying not to be as scared as I would be on the inside compared to what people would see if I was to show it.

The above section has been a small exploration into the transition experiences of LGBTIQA+ young people with cognitive disability. The young people highlighted the additional challenges associated with the intersection of heteronormative and ableist discourses generally, but also more particularly during their journey of transitioning to adulthood. While these findings are limited, they reflect the broader research about discriminatory attitudes towards people who identify as LGBTIQA+, while also adding the additional layer of living with a cognitive disability. Much can be learned from young people about the additional challenges they experience as they transition to adulthood. The young people in this research raise important questions about the importance of a holistic approach that considers the intersecting identities of each young person so we can best support them through their transition to adulthood journey.

5.4 Approaching Youth Transition through a Disability Human Rights Lens

The CRPD grants rights to young people with cognitive disability in their transition to adulthood journeys. Illustratively, the General Principles of the convention enshrine principles of equality, non-discrimination, and respect for the evolving capacities of children with disability (Article 3). These General Principles endorse all rights, including transition rights. The General Principles of equality are supported by other overarching articles in the convention, such as the right to equality and non-discrimination found in Article 5, and Article 6 on women with disability.

Article 6 includes obligations upon states to take all appropriate measures to ensure the full development, advancement, and empowerment of women with disability. The CRPD Committee's General Comment No. 3, on women with a disability, explains that states must ensure the advancement and empowerment of women with disability throughout their lifespan (United Nations Committee on the Rights of Persons with Disabilities, 2016, Para. 22). An illustrative example applicable to the transition between youth and adulthood is the General Comment No. 3 requirement to ensure that women with disability are provided comprehensive sexuality education to enable them to make informed choices (United Nations Committee on the Rights of Persons with Disabilities, 2016, Para. 40). Other examples of transition rights will be highlighted in subsequent chapters as relevant.

5.5 Conclusion

This chapter has focused on illustrating the challenges and context experienced by young people with cognitive disability transitioning to adulthood. Young people with cognitive disability are misunderstood by society. This misunderstanding of disability can include family members of the young person. Transitioning to adulthood is difficult for everyone, and the presence of disability creates additional challenges. Service systems and other supports were often not provided to young people with cognitive disability, creating greater vulnerabilities. This resulted in social isolation and reduced development opportunities, and led to abusive situations. Young people with cognitive disability often had intersecting attributes that led to heightened challenges. Social identities related to aspects such as culture and sexuality also need to be acknowledged, respected, and responded to if we are to truly support young people with cognitive disability in their transition to adulthood. The next chapter outlines the specific types of abuse, violence, and neglect experienced by young people in this study.

CHAPTER 6

The Many Faces of Violence

Accessible Summary

- Young people with cognitive disability, families, and practitioners reported many acts of violence against young people.
- The violence included:
  - physical abuse
  - sexual assault/abuse
  - neglect
  - exploitation
  - emotional and psychological abuse
  - domestic and family violence
- Young people were abused by other young people with disability, family members, partners, practitioners, and services.
- Young people in this book found the strength to speak up and tell their stories of violence.

6.1 Introduction

The previous chapter explored the barriers young people with cognitive disability experience in their transition to adulthood. In three sections, this chapter explores how violence is often present in the lives of young persons with cognitive disability from childhood to adulthood. Young people with cognitive disability, their families, and practitioners recount in this chapter assault, rape, and torture, as well as considerable systems failures that are causing these rights violations.

The voices of the young people with cognitive disability, their families, and practitioners have demonstrated the breadth and depth of violence and abuse being experienced. In Section 6.2, this chapter shares their experiences, which have been organised into different categories of violence. Section 6.3 then analyses the causes of increased vulnerability, before Section 6.4 positions the violence presented in this chapter from a disability rights perspective. However, it is important to note from the outset how difficult it is to separate acts of abuse, violence, neglect, and exploitation into different 'types' of abuse. By doing so it falsely implies that these violations of personhood are discrete, singular events. This fails to consider how disruptive and damaging these acts are across all domains of a young person's life, and that the abuse is only one of multiple facets of the prejudice, discrimination, and marginalisation a young person can experience. Therefore, the examples provided here overlap into the different categories, and it should be recognised that there is significant complexity surrounding these events.

While these acts of violence may be presented at the individual level, the complex intersections at the meso, macro, and exo levels are evident in the stories of the young people. Furthermore, at the chrono level, it is important to recognise the cumulative effects of violence, and that events earlier on in childhood can and have had enduring consequences for young people as they transition to adulthood.

6.2 Types of Abuse

The quantity of experiences of physical violence reported, from property damage to choking, illustrates how violence is impacting the lives of young people with cognitive disability. Sexual violence, from childhood sexual assaults to rape to children being born from rape, is explored in its own section. Neglect from those who should be providing support, from physical neglect to emotional neglect, traumatizes the lives of young people with cognitive disability. Related to this are the experiences of exploitation that are reported, where perpetrators have taken advantage of young people with cognitive disability to achieve their own physical, sexual, or financial gains. Young people with cognitive disability have a heightened vulnerability to emotional and psychological abuse, and this chapter presents a range of examples where this is manifesting. Related to emotional and psychological violence are the experiences of bullying, analysed next in this chapter. Domestic and family violence is explored separately due to the specific nature and harm caused when violence is perpetrated in settings that should be safe.

Physical Abuse

There were an overwhelming number of accounts of physical abuse experienced by the young people with cognitive disability in this research, confirmed by practitioners who uniformly highlighted how they supported young people who experienced this. The common theme identified for all participants was the overarching failure of communities to provide appropriate levels of prevention, early intervention, and targeted support to young people with cognitive disability who experienced violence. Jan, a practitioner, highlighted this when she talked about the need for a cultural shift in how community members need to respond and be responsible for the people around them, in terms of the well-being, safety, and protection of all young people, including young people with cognitive disability.

Practitioners identified a vast range of physical abuse examples with the young people they worked with, which included abuse by parents, siblings, partners, friends, strangers, and other young people in controlled environments such as residential care facilities and youth detention. Often incidents of physical abuse were accompanied by other forms of violence. The experiences of Lorna, a disability advocate from Victoria, highlighted the multifaceted nature of violence when she shared an experience of a young person with cognitive disability who had been placed in youth detention:

> I worked with a guy, he had some petty crimes when he was young and then he was accused of a more serious crime and put into juvie at the age of twelve and he was held on remand in juvie for twelve months while that crime was waiting, I guess, to go to court. And in that time, he was physically and sexually abused by all the other guys in the juvie and it really messed him up. He wasn't guilty of the crime. So, he spent twelve months in hell when he hadn't done anything. And again, it just made his trauma more that it just kept happening and the cycle kept going.

This example shows how abuse is seldom one isolated incident, which can result in cumulative harm and trauma, and that certain settings, such as correctional settings, which house together groups of disenfranchised and disadvantaged young people, can increase the risk of physical and other forms of abuse.

Further supporting this is the story of T, who has experienced a range of violence throughout his life, including most recently in his public housing where he has been attacked by neighbours. T described how traumatic this had been for him:

> One day I had [come] home and all my plants at my front door, my bonsai pots and what-not were all are smashed, and I was just like, 'What the fuck?' and he comes flying out of his unit. We had no quarrel before this, it's just he had been triggered by something, which I ended up finding out. And he came out and come up to me with a large butcher's knife and he attempted to stab me.... He's a very small stature gentlemen, so I was able to wrestle my way out of that. He tried to kill me, and it was pretty full-on crazy.... And that traumatised me. I dream a lot and it infiltrated my dreams.

Cody described experiences of abuse from a National Disability Insurance Scheme (NDIS) worker, who 'actually put me on a choke hold'. While Cody stated he complained, he was told initially by the NDIS Quality and Safeguards Commission[1] that because the worker had left the job, no action could be taken. The matter was later pursued with the Administrative Appeals Tribunal,[2] and an agreement was made to waive debt Cody owed to the service provider if Cody did not press charges against the worker.

These three examples of physical abuse show how this form of violence can be enacted in institutional settings by other young people, in the young person's home environment, and in the context of receiving disability support.

Sexual Assault and Abuse

Sexual assault or abuse can also have devastating impacts on the health and well-being of young people with cognitive disability. Of the twenty-seven practitioners who participated in the research, seventeen talked about working with and supporting young people with cognitive disability who had experienced sexual abuse. The issue of sexual abuse was present across multiple organisations, locations, and young people.

Vivienne, a disability advocate from Victoria, commented that in her experience approximately 70–75 per cent of women with intellectual disability whom she worked with had experienced sexual assault. Leanne

[1] The NDIS Quality and Safeguards Commission is an independent agency established to improve the quality and safety of NDIS supports and services. The NDIS Commission regulates the NDIS market and handles complaints about the quality and safety of NDIS supports and services (www.ndiscommission.gov.au/participants/how-ndis-commission-can-help-you).

[2] The Administrative Appeals Tribunal is an independent body that reviews, among other government decisions, decisions relating to supports under the NDIS (www.aat.gov.au/about-the-aat).

(a practitioner) confirmed this pattern, sharing her experiences of working in a service supporting people with cognitive disability:

> When I was at [service], we went on an outing one day with . . . five young women; all had intellectual cognitive disabilities. And we were sitting, talking just in the circle, and the five young people, they found it really hard to connect, but at just one stage, I don't even know how it got started, but they started talking and every single one of them had been sexually abused as a child.. . . Yeah, it really hit me that here we are, 100 per cent in this group of people had been sexually abused as children.

This anecdotal evidence of the prevalence of sexual abuse is quite alarming. What may be even more disturbing is the lack of specialised services to assist young people with cognitive disability who have experienced sexual assault. A degree of moral angst was evident in the accounts of practitioners in this study of the capacity and willingness of the service and criminal justice systems to adequately address these issues. Some practitioners, such as Jan, a sexual assault counsellor, expressed concerns that cases of young people with cognitive disability (particularly young men in this group) were not being referred to supports. Others, such as G, a disability professional, spoke of the futility of systems such as child protection systems in protecting young people from further harm and sexual assault in out-of-home care.

Experiences of sexual abuse were reported by eight of the nineteen young people in this study – Becky, Amy, April, Sophie, Amethyst, Rachel, T, and TBone. The young people's accounts vary in level of detail, and therefore not all are recounted here. Several accounts refer to the abuse occurring when the young person was a child, demonstrating the long-term effects on a young person. Other accounts indicate that the abuse was perpetrated when the person was a young adult. Two young people, Amethyst and Sophie, experienced sexual abuse in both childhood and early adulthood, an illustration of how sexual abuse can repeat in different forms over an extended period. Amethyst's story of sexual abuse is considered within the context of her whole life in Chapter 4 of this book.

April (aged twenty-four) reported being sexually assaulted by her mother's boyfriend on three occasions, the first in grade 7, again in grade 10, and the last in 2016. The first assault was reported to police, and her mother separated from her boyfriend; however, they appeared to have been reunited as he assaulted her again in grade 10, at which time he went to prison. After his release, her mother's boyfriend offended against her a third time in 2016. April noted that nothing happened to him after she told the police. April described being supported by her father and sister, with whom she has contact and support. April's mother continues to have contact with the perpetrator:

INTERVIEWER: Yeah. Does Mum have any contact with him still?
APRIL: Yeah.
INTERVIEWER: What's that like for you?
APRIL: At first, I was shocked, but I can sort of see he might be better. He might have changed.This shows a level of forgiveness by April; however, it also raises the risks that she continues to experience because of this ongoing relationship.

TBone, a First Nations Australian young man, was sexually abused by a friend of the family whom they used to visit each week. The gatherings would involve several children from different families. His mother reported that TBone had been socially excluded by the other children at the house, because he was 'different' due to his disability, which made him feel upset and angry. The fourteen-year-old son of a woman who came to live in the house they visited reportedly started to sexually abuse TBone over several years before his parents realised what had happened. It was only after the family stopped associating with the people in the house that TBone disclosed the abuse. He was aged ten at that stage. It is not clear how old he was when the abuse first occurred, but it appeared to be around the age of seven or eight. TBone's behaviour had become more and more aggressive, and this out-of-character aggression was more noticeable when they were visiting the house in question. TBone's mother reported that she did not understand the cause of the behaviour at the time.

The externalising behaviours that resulted from the abuse had long-term consequences for TBone and caused strain within his family. The abuse impacted on TBone's education, where he eventually had to change to home schooling. TBone's mother explained that school became 'too much' for him. In addition, TBone's parents had difficulty responding to his aggression, as his mother explained:

> So yeah, we've really struggled. Really struggled. I even had to call DOCS [Department of Child Safety] at one stage, because I wasn't coping, and I felt that I was doing wrong to TBone. Well, I was, I was abusive. So, I just couldn't cope with him. Could not cope. So yeah, he's had a period where he's been out of the home. It only ended up being six weeks. I think a month or six weeks.

TBone's story shows the far-reaching implications of such a traumatic experience on a young boy who held onto the secret of sexual abuse for so long. The sexual abuse led to challenging behaviour, which in turn resulted in reactions from his mother that she described as abusive. In the interview, TBone's mother talked about the abuse; TBone did not speak about his experience directly, only confirming what was said. It is recognised that recalling these experiences would have been very disturbing for him.

Practitioners also drew upon several examples of sexual abuse of young people with cognitive disability. Gabby, a social worker who manages a service supporting people with cognitive disability who have experienced sexual and domestic and family violence, shared the story of Rachel, an Aboriginal woman with intellectual disability. Rachel's story highlights the complex intersection of culture as an Aboriginal woman, having a cognitive disability, and living in a small rural community. Rachel experienced sexual and physical violence in her hometown and reported this to police. In doing this, she experienced 'blood blowback' from the community (retaliation from her community for reporting the incident to the police). She felt compelled to leave her community because she was not safe, even though she reportedly had a supportive kin network.

Rachel moved to Brisbane and lived in hostels and emergency accommodation where she experienced physical assault as well as domestic and family violence. Gabby described Rachel as 'being shipped from one place to another and nobody knew how to actually help her feel safe or give her somewhere to recover and feel supported'.

Rachel then moved into a public housing unit where she was sexually assaulted by an unknown intruder. This highlights some of the inherent challenges with public housing policy and delivery, which congregates people with complex support needs together. Rachel was then transferred to another public housing unit with increased security; however, she was sexually assaulted by someone she knew from her community, resulting in the birth of her child. This again highlights the gaps in supportive services and, in particular, a lack of culturally and disability-appropriate supports that could safely meet Rachel's needs. Rachel's separation from her support network and country, and poor agency responses by emergency accommodation services, contributed to the increased violence she experienced. The key messages Rachel wanted to share was the importance of being listened to despite having an intellectual disability and having safe housing and ongoing support.

T, a neurodiverse young man, demonstrated the potential connection between sexual abuse and precarious living situations. T spoke of a time when he felt unsafe with a housemate who appeared interested in him sexually. T had to fend for himself from a young age due to his mother's mental health issues. This meant finding places to live as a teenager, resulting in unstable and unsafe housing situations. He shared,

> And then me and my brother went our separate ways for a period, and I went to live with somebody who had a spare room, that was friends of my brother. And he turned out to be a very seedy gentleman. I did not like the way he would look at me or speak to me. It was very sexual, very unnerving.

T had the insight to move out of this situation because of the lack of safety. His account shows that not having a supportive home and family can increase the vulnerability of young people with cognitive disability to acts of sexual abuse.

Riley, a sexual assault worker, talked about a young woman with an intellectual disability who from about eleven years of age engaged in high-risk and increasingly criminalised behaviour. Riley and their service became involved with the young person when she was twenty, through a referral from her mother. The young woman constantly sought out relationships where she was regularly exploited by men. More recently, the young woman was in a 'relationship' with two men in their thirties and forties who allegedly coerced her into sex work. The young woman was being supplied with drugs (methamphetamine, it was believed) and was trapped in a cycle of debt to these men. One of the consequences was that the young woman presented to hospital on several occasions with drug-induced psychosis. Riley described the gaps in how the health and mental health systems responded:

> The hospital had, and continued to, refuse to initiate any treatment authority or emergency examination authority. And I think this young woman was potentially a frequent presenter at hospital, but, basically, the mental health and acute care team at hospital were not interested in any kind of safeguarding response. It was very much a kind of quick turnaround and then discharge her back into an unsafe setting in the community with this justification that she was choosing to engage in whatever behaviour that was happening in her life and her circumstances.

Riley explained that the mother had told hospital staff of the danger her daughter was in when she was discharged from hospital, but this did not change their response. Police were also aware of the young woman's circumstances but did not assist. Riley stated:

> I think the police saw this young woman as someone who was effectively a troublemaker, up to no good. She's making her own bed, she can lie in it, that sort of thing.

The young person interacted with numerous systems; however, no one took responsibility for her in terms of her safety. Riley encapsulated this as 'So, multiple systems saying, "No, it's mental health," or, "No, it's disability," or, "No, it's individual choice."'

Lorraine, a lawyer who supported people in prison, shared an example of sexual abuse of an incarcerated young person with cognitive disability. The example involved a young man with foetal alcohol spectrum disorder who was being 'stood over' by other prisoners who were seeking sexual favours. In this confined environment there were not many safety options available to the young person. Lorraine posed the question, 'How do you navigate that situation without, yourself, resorting to violence to attack that person?' This example shows how youth detention centres and adult prisons, which are intended to reform and correct those who enter them, can repeatedly expose young people with cognitive disability to sexual, psychological, and physical violence.

These experiences of sexual abuse and other co-occurring acts of violence have a destructive impact on the person as a child and as an adult. The effects of these events on the young person with cognitive disability, their families, and communities are likely to be under-reported here, because of the brief time interviewers had with each participant. A common theme to these accounts is the precariousness and inadequacy of formal support services, and how such supports can fail to respond to or assist the young person with cognitive disability in their recovery but also can serve to perpetuate and extend the cycle of violence in the young person's life.

Neglect

The presence of neglect was also a consistent theme and, as with the other forms of abuse, was not a discrete event. Neglect had many faces. At times it involved neglect of a physical nature, where tangible resources such as food and a safe place to live were denied. There were also examples of emotional neglect, where young people were not supported, encouraged, or provided appropriate opportunity to grow into adulthood. Systemic neglect also was discussed by practitioners, which involved passive, indifferent responses to young people's needs by systems.

Young people with cognitive disability shared many examples of neglect. Cody, a young man with autism and OCD, spoke of difficulties with support workers who would not teach him how to cook, saying he was 'happy to learn if the workers teach me, but some of them won't teach me how to cook things. I want to learn to cook things. I want to learn how to clean things. Some don't want to teach me anything at all. And you can't just get it right after one time. You need more than one time to get it right.'

In addition, Cody shared his frustration at not being listened to when he requested some personal space from the workers: 'And sometimes I've asked the workers to give me space and it will take them like ten times before one of them will even leave. I say, "Please leave the unit so I can have some space. Please leave. Please leave." By the tenth time or something I get angry because they're not leaving when I asked them nine times politely so far.' Both examples show the disregard workers had for Cody, depriving him of the privacy he needed in his own home, not meeting his needs, and failing to see him as a person who wanted to develop his independence. This treatment by workers likely had an enormous impact on his transition to adulthood.

Goldie, a First Nations Australian, disclosed the painful impact of experiencing emotional neglect from family members:

> My whole life has been sad, but mostly with my dad. And living with my mum, it's not like she abused me, but she severely neglected me.. . . She didn't really want me either, so there was a lot of rejection and abandonment there.. . . She didn't want to spend time with me, didn't want to sit next to me. If I came home crying, she didn't care, she didn't want to know. Anything I want to talk to her about, she just didn't want to know. She wanted as little time with me as possible.. . . I don't know, some families go camping, some families go to the beach for the day out. My mum never did anything like that with me.

Such experiences would be destabilising and traumatic for any young person. The impact was likely to be even more devastating for Goldie, who had been diagnosed with a number of complex mental health concerns, including borderline personality disorder, complex post-traumatic stress disorder, anxiety, and major depressive disorder.

T (aged twenty-nine) also reported experiences of neglect from his mother, who struggled with depression and periods of wanting to commit suicide. At the age of sixteen, his mother informed T that she was going to move out and that he had to find his own place. T explained, 'I begged her not for that to happen. But [she did it] for her mental health and whatever reason she wanted to. She was exhausted from being a parent.' T had a transient childhood, moving from place to place. He witnessed domestic and family violence between his mother and her partners, and, when his mother moved away, he survived living in caravans and campervans, until he sought public housing. T described this time of early adulthood as learning to make do on very little. 'I had to learn to survive. So pinch toilet paper from places and go find where [*sic*] can help with food vouchers.. . . So, a lot of accessing charities.' T had no choice but to develop a great deal of resilience and resourcefulness to survive.

TBone (aged nineteen) experienced neglect from workers who were paid to support him in assisted living. There was a lack of consistency of support from these workers, who did not follow through with what they promised or what was needed. This was detrimental to TBone's mental health: he engaged in acts of self-harm and withdrew from social contact. These difficulties put his life on hold. He had difficulties feeling well enough to find employment, and needed admission into hospital to manage his mental health on multiple occasions. Of concern was that in one instance, he was sent to hospital in an ambulance on his own without a support worker, and without the agency informing his family:

> MOTHER OF TBONE: No one was with him the whole time. And I stressed [about] . . . it, because I was that stressed out after the last one, I emailed and said to them, 'Look, he needs help. He needs to see a psychologist. He needs to be able to talk these problems through.'
>
> TBONE: It still hasn't happened.
>
> MOTHER OF TBONE: Yeah. And they were like, 'Okay, we'll get onto that. He really does. Sorry that you feel so stressed out about it.' Yeah, and things just aren't being done that he needs.. . . Apparently, it happens to most of the clients, because most of the clients don't have family to actually go back to them and say, 'Look, they need this.'. . . Yeah, so basically where he is at the moment, they're not abusing him in any way, as such, but yeah, they're not meeting his needs.This example demonstrates how neglect can also involve forms of emotional abuse and systems abuse. TBone's mother appears to have been told that this type of neglect is to be expected for young people with disability accessing this service.

Practitioners all highlighted neglect as a major experience for the young people with cognitive disability they worked with. Emma, a practitioner who supported young people and their families, talked about neglect being present for about 90 per cent of the young people with cognitive disability who used her service. She gave the example of a young person with cognitive disability who had returned home after leaving care:

> The young male who's moved back with his mother post-eighteen, they both have impairments.. . . He provides money, obviously, to keep the household going, but he is, I found out, not receiving any meals. He buys the groceries with his mother and then that's kept from him still, even as an adult. So, you're seeing the cycle of that neglect come back.

This example of physical neglect may have been a repeat of childhood experiences for the young person.

Exploitation

The term 'exploitation' can have different meanings to different people. In our research, it refers to acts of abuse where the perpetrator takes advantage of the young person with cognitive disability to achieve their own physical, sexual, or financial gain. It was not a term that was regularly used by the young people who participated in this research, and co-researchers with cognitive disability also needed assistance in understanding the meaning of the term. This is not to say that young people's accounts did not provide examples of what constituted exploitation, but rather that the construct was new to them. For the most part, it was practitioners who spoke of exploitation, at times as a broad descriptor that was applied to all types of abuse. Matthew, a practitioner who had over thirty years' experience of supporting young people with cognitive disability, discussed the pervasiveness of exploitation in young people's lives:

> Well, when I came to the organisation, I remember being here the first week.... I went around and talked to lots of people, and they were all young people with disabilities, they were all in their twenties, and I remember thinking by the end of the week that, 'If there's any shit that can happen to people in the world, it's happening to this group of people.'... So, my sense was that if there were any individual disadvantages, structural disadvantages, system disadvantages, exploitation that can happen to people, it was happening to this group of people.

As with the other types of violence mentioned in this book, exploitation, whatever its form, was seldom a discrete event. It could be perpetrated by family members, friends, and partners. There were also examples of exploitation by services, real estate agents, and commercial businesses. Exploitation could occur in face-to-face interactions, as well as via online platforms. This section discusses exploitation within the context of relationships, financial exploitation, and exploitation by services and systems.

Financial exploitation of people with cognitive disability was highlighted consistently; this was generally explained as due to the trusting nature of the individual being taken advantage of. Kristen, a support coordinator, explained how scam telemarketing could financially exploit young people, sharing, 'I know a few young people who've been scammed for money through particular phone calls.... [Without] really good informal support networks, they're not able to identify that it's a scam.... So, they'll follow the link, they'll lose all their money, they don't understand why they've lost it.'

Amethyst, a First Nations Australian young woman (aged twenty-nine), experienced financial exploitation from the host families where she was placed by the disability services. In each of the three families she was placed with, she was exploited financially. One host family made Amethyst work without pay by caring for their children. In two of these arrangements, she was not provided with adequate meals, and in her final placement with a host family, a man with whom she had previously become intimately involved regularly visited, and took a considerable amount of money from her. All the host families were paid by the state disability service to provide adequate care for Amethyst, yet neglected to keep her safe and contributed to the trauma Amethyst had experienced over her lifetime.

David, a young man with autism and complex communicative support needs (aged twenty-one), also experienced financial exploitation. David's mother recalled an incident with a support worker, whom she believed also had autism:

> When he took David out in the community, obviously we sent money for lunch for David, and so he would say that David shouted him Subway.... So, basically, he was stealing David's money to buy his own lunch. Like I said, I'm pretty sure he was on the spectrum, so he could rationalise that in his brain. I don't think it was a 'You owe me money.' I think it was just ... he wasn't managed very well or trained very well by someone.

David's mother ensured that the worker ceased working with David. Her story points to the need for better training and supervision of direct care staff. The role of service systems and their potential to exploit are explored in Chapter 7 onwards.

Emotional and Psychological Abuse

Emotional and psychological abuse is quite often invisible, yet it is as significant in its impact as other types of abuse. As commented earlier, it is difficult to neatly separate one form of abuse from another as emotional abuse is usually associated with physical and sexual abuse and neglect. The humiliation and loss of dignity resulting from emotional abuse can also have a devastating impact on a young person's self-esteem at a time when the young person is forging a new identity as a young adult.

Hilde, a neurodiverse young person (aged eighteen), described witnessing significant emotional abuse by her mother towards her father for 'his autistic traits and characteristics', which he reportedly saw as normal behaviour. Hilde started to notice this at the age of about twelve and spoke out about this to her mother:

> So then on, it was us [Hilde and her father] versus her apparently, since she decided it was like that. So basically, from then on, since I started noticing, she started just not caring and being horrible to him in front of me, which was very bad for me, not just to witness it, but also if you're emotionally abusing somebody due to their autistic traits and there's somebody else at

> the table who has the same autistic traits, I don't think that's just aimed at one person.

The psychological cruelty inflicted on Hilde's father was directed at his disability, which in turn caused mental anguish for Hilde, who had the same disability. She shared how she questioned her own worth as a result: 'Essentially, while I biologically, scientifically know that I'm human, sociologically and culturally, I'm not sure that I am . . . maybe I'm not a human being if, in the minds of a lot of humans, I'm not.' This profound insight goes to the very core of the harm caused by disability discrimination, and the significant impact it has on people questioning their own personhood.

Emotional and psychological abuse was not just confined to within the family for young people. Professionals could perpetuate feelings of anguish and shame through their interactions with a young person. Goldie, a First Nations Australian young woman with autism (aged twenty-two), had previous experiences of emotional abuse from her family; however, she also shared how workers, whose role it was to support her, made her feel rejected:

> There was this one worker, she was really aggressive in her tone, in the way that she was talking to me. And I asked her to just be respectful, and then she started yelling. And then she walked out of the unit and the manager came over, and the support worker was standing next to the manager, they were both standing on the driveway, and I said to the manager, 'Why can't you get someone else to fill this shift?' And the worker that was yelling at me jumped in and said, 'Ha, ha, because no one wants to work with you.' And that made me feel really upset when she said that.

Goldie, as with others who reported similar experiences, was in a vulnerable position because she relied on support workers. Psychological abuse from support workers can be particularly damaging because of the unequal power relationship between worker and young person. In this situation Goldie talked to the manager of the facility, but they said they could not replace that worker due to a public holiday, which left Goldie without support.

Goldie relayed another example of abusive treatment by a worker related to withholding medication and emotional abuse. She explained, 'There was another worker that said to me that it's not all about me, and she doesn't want to go get my medication, which I didn't understand, because it is all about me. That's what I'm paying them for.' While Goldie recognised the validity of her needs and rights being met, without a system there to support her by providing appropriately trained and qualified staff who can do the job with respect, dignity, and empathy, she remained at risk. The unequal power relationships with workers and the manager in this case create further levels of vulnerability that are systemically driven.

Cody, a neurodiverse young man with OCD, gave examples of emotional abuse from medical and mental health professionals:

> Even as a kid, doctors and stuff, even professionals, they blamed me for an illness that I never chose to have. Psychiatrists literally blamed me for obtaining OCD . . . [that] it was my fault to get OCD in the first place. They blamed me for an illness that I had no control over. And that, to me, is very disappointing from professionals. And they never asked me permission if I wanted the medication, the psychiatrist. They didn't ask my permission because I was a kid, and that's kind of messed me up a little bit.

He expressed concerns about the disempowering effects of medications making him 'numb'. Cody explained, 'Basically it doesn't allow you to stick up for yourself because you're so sedated.' The prescribing of psychotropic medication had become an indicator to Cody of the power health professionals exerted over him.

Bullying

A form of psychological and emotional abuse is the act of bullying or harassment. It involves an ongoing and deliberate misuse of power in relationships, through intimidation, threats, and coercion. Most of the young people with cognitive disability experienced bullying at school. There were also examples of experiencing bullying within families and by practitioners and other people who lived in the same house or complex as the young person.

Simon, a young man with Down syndrome (aged thirty), identified the sad times in his life as being bullied at school by other children. Simon described a time when three boys bullied him and recorded the interaction on video. He also talked about being yelled at by students at school, and an incident where a student drank his milk and threw the container at him. When asked how this made his body feel, Simon explained he felt 'cold and hot . . . shaking and shivering' and that these feelings could last for 'a long time'. Simon talked about feeling 'terrified' from the behaviour of other students. These experiences left him feeling upset and hurt.

Simon also identified other examples of bullying at school, including a teacher's aide pushing Simon too fast in the wheelchair, which scared him. Simon said he told the person to stop but they did not, highlighting the lack of control he felt. Simon was so scared that he did not tell his mother for a long time and was afraid to go back to school. What is striking about this is that although the bullying and abusive behaviour occurred several years ago, it was still uppermost in Simon's mind. Simon conveyed feelings that appeared quite visceral when he described the incidents and reported having nightmares about this. In addition, Simon also experienced bullying from a doctor when he went to hospital after drinking something that made him very unwell. The doctor reportedly was verbally abusing him, and the nurse had to inform the doctor that Simon had Down syndrome. This poor professional behaviour shows a lack of respect for the person and is indicative of discriminatory attitudes towards young people with cognitive disability.

Experiences of bullying can impact negatively on the transition to adulthood for young people with cognitive disability. It may be detrimental to a young person's development of self-worth, foster excessive compliance to authorities, and lead to high levels of anxiety.

Hilde also talked about her experiences of being bullied and abused at school:

> Went to kindergarten, it was horrible. I was bullied. Went to school, it was horrible. I was bullied by the teachers as well as the students, as well as emotionally and verbally, physically, quite systematically from the students and systematically emotionally from the teachers. The teachers also did physically abuse me.... I was physically abused by teachers in high school. But that wasn't their hands on me, that was them trying to physically block my path.... Look, I would say about 50 per cent of teachers have been outright abusive to me and I would say ... that 45 per cent have been entirely complicit in this abuse, and I would say that maybe 5 per cent have been good. At the same time, maybe 75 per cent of my teachers were well meaning. That doesn't excuse that they were harmful.... As somebody in the autistic community, I think ..., any neurodivergent group, we know especially well, even more than other disabled groups, that people who are well-meaning and think they are helping us are the ones who do the most harm, usually.... That in no way entitles or excuses their behaviour.

Hilde eloquently articulated some of the systemic-level issues in terms of attitudes and values where people being 'well meaning' can be an excuse for outright abuse, discrimination, and neglect. Her account points to a need for a cultural shift within the school system in order for young people on the spectrum to feel safe and welcome within that environment.

Similarly, Goldie, a First Nations young person, reported being bullied at school, including having teachers who did not care. Goldie described her feelings: 'I felt like real shameful about it and I hated myself for it.... Life was actually pretty depressing in my childhood.... It was just shit the whole way through. There wasn't really many good moments. It was pretty rare to have a good moment.' This highlights the impact of cumulative experiences of emotional and psychological abuse for young people, and how young people can internalise the harmful messages from others.

G, a practitioner who worked with young people with cognitive disability exiting Child Safety[3] and youth justice systems, highlighted a number of the common themes practitioners identified about bullying:

> There was one school that many of the young people had all been to and all spoke very negatively about that experience, and it was a special school.... Yeah, humiliation and harassment, like bullying, just negative experiences with their families, really connecting with their self-worth. I'd say probably all of the young people that I work with have depression or anxiety on some scale, which is definitely not helped by that.

G also talked about bullying behaviour extending to the workplace for this group of young people: 'Some of the young people . . . haven't had to work because of the discrimination, but also have gotten to that point and then been discriminated against and left . . . essentially.' This highlights that even when a young person obtains employment, bullying and discrimination can continue, which then further limits opportunities to fully participate in society and achieve one's goals and hopes.

Domestic and Family Violence

Domestic and family violence featured prominently in the accounts of several young people, which was also supported by the experiences of the practitioners. This is consistent with the research that identifies one in six women experience physical and sexual violence in Australia and that two in five women with disability (40%) have experienced physical violence after the age of fifteen compared with women without disability (26%) (AIHW, 2023, 2022). Some of the domestic and family violence experienced by young people in this research included young people witnessing violence in the family of origin and being involved in violent relationships that included coercion and control.[4] Of the twelve young women involved in

[3] 'Child Safety' refers to the state government department that investigates reports of alleged harm or risk of alleged harm to any child or young person under eighteen years.

[4] Coercive control involves manipulation and intimidation to make the person/victim scared, isolated, and dependent on the person who perpetrates the violence. It can include isolating the person from friends and family, monitoring activity, restricting autonomy, and controlling the body.

the research, all but four experienced domestic and family violence by partners or family members. This was further reinforced by practitioners who shared their experiences.

Leanne, a social work practitioner who worked with parents with intellectual disability, shared that everyone she worked with experienced domestic and family violence:

> One [young woman] in particular that I'm working with, she's had her ribs broken, her teeth are all knocked out, she's had facial surgery, she's had [her] nose broken, she's been strangled until point of unconsciousness. She says that each of the children were conceived by sexual abuse. She's been restrained by him in a house, held hostage. That's one person. And then the others [service users] are all varying degrees of that. There's a lot of coercion and control. Because people are so vulnerable and so needing to have a relationship, they put up with … a lot of manipulation, and they don't always recognise it for what it is.… And then when they've had a baby by that person, they find it really hard, I think, possibly harder than people without intellectual disability and who don't have such significantly limited support networks, to let these relationships go.

Leanne's discussion highlights how social isolation and poor support of young women with cognitive disability can perpetuate domestic and family violence, as it becomes exceedingly difficult for young women to leave the perpetrator.

Emma, a practitioner who worked with youth and families, talked about how a young person's need for an intimate relationship could override their priority to stay safe. She gave the example of a young person with cognitive disability who also had significant medical concerns. The young woman was involved in 'a very significant DV [domestic violence] relationship, still is, no safe adults in her circle'. This young person experienced a ruptured oesophagus from the domestic violence relationship. Emma explained the intersection of physical and emotional abuse, neglect, and exploitation in the life of this young person:

> There was drug use, and this relationship had gone on for eight years, since she was a teenager. So, there was a lot of coercion, a lot of control, financial abuse, emotional, physical. So, you [as a practitioner] have to pick your battles obviously, and what is the most significant thing that needs attention. So, it was getting her to hospital, but because of the abuse in the domestic violence relationship, in her intimate relationship, she was fearful that he would leave. She would rely on him a lot and feel that that was the only way she was going to keep him around. So, sometimes she would purposely not take insulin, because she was diabetic as well; she would purposely not look after herself, not understanding the real consequences of

> that or understanding the conversations that we have about DV and that power and control cycle, or who else is out there that you could talk to, to get support.

Young people's experience of domestic and family violence could be of long duration. Goldie, a First Nations Australian young woman with autism, experienced abuse and neglect throughout her life. She described her mother taking out a domestic and family violence order on her father when she was aged four. At the age of fifteen she was placed in out-of-home care; however, from the age of sixteen she lived in homeless shelters for about two years. At the age of eighteen she moved in with her father. It is important to note that there was an order (likely a child protection order) that said Goldie could not live with her father until she was eighteen. When Goldie moved in with him, she experienced further abuse:

> But with my dad, it was definitely abuse. He wanted me, to use me to clean up for him and do things for him, but he was very abusive, verbally, physically, was violent, aggressive. He was horrible. He was horrible. It was much worse living with him than it was with my mum because he was literally abusive. My mum was just neglectful. So, yeah.

Goldie described her father as being violent and exploitative towards her. Goldie reported eventually 'escaping' him and getting her own unit around the age of twenty-one with the support of a domestic and family violence organization. However, even after she left, Goldie talked about her father visiting her once a week and being violent towards her. It was not clear at what stage in her life these visits occurred, but nonetheless it resulted in ongoing fear. Goldie explained, 'Well, he was always violent.... So, every time it came to Sunday, his visit day, I was always scared as it was. And there were times that he bashed me, which made my fear come true.' What becomes evident with Goldie's story is the multiple types of abuse she has experienced – namely, domestic and family violence, neglect through her mother, and, it appears, systemic-level neglect when in out-of-home care. Each of these experiences highlights the pervasive effect of violence in different manifestations across significant periods of a young person's life.

The experiences of domestic and family violence for Amethyst (a neurodiverse First Nations young person) were endured over a long period. Amethyst reported being physically attacked, drugged, isolated, choked, and having her head shaved by an abusive partner. The perpetrator was successful in filing a domestic violence order (DVO) against Amethyst, despite this abuse. Amethyst also experienced violence by other male perpetrators throughout her life, commencing at the age of eleven. More details of her story of experiencing horrific violence are shared in Chapter 4 of this book.

Findings also highlighted how family members and significant others can become abusive towards children and young people with cognitive disability. Young people with cognitive disability may need considerable physical, emotional, and financial supports that may result in caregiver stress (Lightfoot, 2014). Family members may require unique knowledge competencies and skills to adequately attend to these needs (Flynn, 2021). A lack of recognition and understanding of the disability of the child or young person can lead to them be misperceived as being, for example, 'lazy' or 'wilful' and can lead to acts of domestic and family violence.

Angel, an LGBTIQA+ young person (aged twenty-four), only recently realised that he had an intellectual impairment, even though he stated that his parents knew from an early age. Angel stated that his parents did not want to label and treat him as 'special'. Angel reported that this did more damage in the long run because he would always be thinking, 'Well, they [his siblings] can do it, I can't . . . I don't understand.' Angel talked about different family members, particularly an aunt, grandparents, and his father, using emotional and physical aggression to force Angel to complete certain tasks:

> Yeah, it was always the same thing, 'If you're not going to try, then I'm going to force you. Then if you're not going to get it in your own time, then I'm going to beat it into you' kind of thing. So, kind of that old school mentality is like, 'I'm going to harden you up and pretty much scare you into getting you to do what you can't do.'. . . So, I was being made out to be the dramatic person and then they were doing normal type of discipline. It was like, 'Oh, your kid was acting up, so I flogged him.' Instead of actually saying, 'Your kid was annoying me, so I pushed him down the stairs' type of thing.

Angel felt his parents never protected him, yet he relied on his family as his 'safety net', which meant following their rules. Part of his transition into adulthood involved achieving independence from his family, and because of his experiences this included changing his name and distancing himself from them.

A theme that emerged was the lack of knowledge about supports and services for survivors with cognitive disability of domestic and family violence, along with gaps in what services there were or could provide. Survivors of domestic and family violence need to know there are others outside the abusive relationship who can provide assistance, and be confident that when they reach out for support, they will receive it. This became evident for Amy, who described herself as having a behavioural disability and who had been in a domestically violent relationship with the father of her three children. At the time of the interview, the father was in prison. Amy identified the lack of support she received from the statutory child protection system, and the difficulties of reporting abuse from her partner, for fear the perpetrator may find out and punish her. As Amy explained about reporting any kind of abuse, 'I learnt not to because no one really helps me. That's the problem.'

6.3 Causes of Increased Vulnerability

Relationships are always connected with violence, and young persons with cognitive disability are often at heightened risk due to their desires to belong, to be accepted by others, and to have connections and relationships in their lives. Addressing and responding to violence is more complicated where the violence occurs from other young people with cognitive disability in institutional/organisational settings such as schools and supported employment.

Social media misunderstandings about consent and exposure to predatory support workers are factors that increase young persons' vulnerability to sexual violence. Abuse is not always caused by rogue agents, but instead is sometimes permitted by law in the form of restrictive practices. Systems that should protect are reported in this chapter to often fail young persons with cognitive disability when it comes to them reporting violence or having others report on their behalf.

The Relational Context of Exploitation

> G [practitioner]: But yeah, I'd say exploitation is always relational. That's, I think, because of the isolation that these young people experience, it's the easy drive, easy motivator. And I think a lot of them aren't aware of it. It's just like, 'That's what you do for your friends.'

Many of the practitioner participants discussed how exploitation of young people with cognitive disability arose out of the desires of young people to belong, to be accepted by others, and to have connections and relationships in their lives. When young people felt lonely and isolated, they could welcome the presence of others into their world without question.

For example, Amy reported helping 'the wrong sort of people' after leaving school, whom she called 'fake friends', who financially abused her, by asking for money, coming to stay at her house, and asking for food.

These 'fake friends' were known by either the Department of Child Safety, police, or parole officers. Amy moved away from the area she was living in to break off contact with these people, but said they followed her, often sighting her at the train station.

Lyn, a support coordinator from a disability service, spoke of the difficulties some young people with cognitive disability had in setting healthy and appropriate boundaries with others. The yearning for friendship could result in boundary violation and exploitation:

Lyn: One of the other team members have one as well where she's just got a [Department of] Housing house, has been couch surfing for months, and now she has all these other people couch surfing on her couch, using her to do that, and she's possibly going to lose her housing because she's helping these other people.The example given here of the young person allowing others to stay with her resulted in this young woman losing her unit. Another support coordinator, Sonia, explained that not all young people had a supportive parent to ask advice from: 'So there's no protective factor for them, for them to be able to say, "Hey Mum, do you think I should give them $50 because they don't have bus money?"' Without support and education to discern who may be exploitative, young people with cognitive disability could potentially lose their homes, be blacklisted by public housing, and experience further poverty and isolation.

Examples of exploitation were prevalent in the experiences of young people with cognitive disability who had previous involvement in the child protection system. A young person could experience exploitation from those who were closest to them and then later return to their birth families after being in care and re-enter an abusive and exploitative environment. Mary, a practitioner who supported young people with cognitive disability exiting care, explained that young people's decision to return to their family of origin was often because they 'desperately want secure, loving relationships'. Goldie, a First Nations young person, returned to her father after leaving care and endured domestic and family violence within this relationship. She also reported that other members of her immediate family had exploited her:

> My sister and my brothers, like you said about just stealing the credit cards, they used me for everything. Take my smokes, take my money, my sister stole my car. My brother told me that he's happy to give me a rope to help me kill myself because I had an argument with this girl that he liked. And they're in their thirties, my sister's nearly forty, they're a bit old to be doing that. But, of course, they abuse the youngest, who can't fight back. And yeah, they just used me and bullied me.

Emma, a practitioner who supported children, young people, and families, also referred to the complexity involved when a young person returned to their birth family. She gave the example of a young man with cognitive disability who returned to his mother's home at the age of eighteen:

> [He] has been living with her and doing everything for her, even though he has quite a significant disability, taking her shopping, taking her to her appointments, but then on the flip side, he can't have a routine, he can't always consistently go to TAFE or consistently go see his peer groups when he goes for community access through his NDIS plan.... So he's really at a disadvantage.

In this example, it appeared the young person had been placed into the main carer role in the family, which impacted on his own disability support needs.

Many times, when the young person returned to the birth family home, there were multiple acts of abuse and exploitation, often by more than one family member, as described by Mary (practitioner):

> So, lots of degradation, putting people down, making them feel awful. Those family of origins not understanding their disability, 'So lazy, you're this, you're that, you're whatever.'... Lots of financial exploitations, because it's great to get kids back when they're sixteen and they've got their DSP [Disability Support Pension] and you've got, at that point, it was $600 a fortnight coming into the household ... lots of threats of violence, I would say as well.

Mary explained that other members of the young person's family could threaten the young person to hand over money, and that the perpetrator often had complex issues of their own that were influencing this behaviour. She added that many in this group had experienced fractured and unsafe relationships, and it became more difficult for this group to understand what a safe and respectful relationship looked like.

G, a practitioner who supported a similar group of young people, shared that exploitation also often occurred outside the birth family. Young people could be exploited through payday loans; young people who used drugs were exploited by drug dealers where they ended up owing money. Another practitioner, Matthew, said young people with cognitive disability could also be criminalised because they end up becoming the 'fall guy', where other 'friends' convince them to do something that was illegal. A strong link was made between young people wanting friendship and connection, and them not knowing what constituted healthy, safe relationships. This could lead to harmful personal relationships and experiences of exploitation.

Responding to Abuse by Other Young People with Cognitive Disability

Practitioners and family members identified violence that can occur from other young people with cognitive disability in institutional/organisational settings such as schools and supported employment.[5] When the instigator of physical and other forms of abuse is a person with cognitive disability, it can raise ethical concerns for professionals as to how to respond.

For example, Kim (sixteen years) was bitten eleven times by another student in a special school setting. Her father pursued the matter with teaching staff, pointing out that the problem lay with poor supervision, rather than locating the issue with the young person with disability who committed the act.

Practitioners from an employment service identified the difference in their view of 'behaviour' and deliberate violence that occurred within supported employment settings, where a person with cognitive disability could act out against a support worker or another employee:

> Look, I mean, when you're dealing with autism, I mean, there's some really challenging behaviours, clearly, at times. So, clearly, we've logged incidences over the years of participants acting out . . ., sometimes in an environment; it might be even with another participant or acting out against a support worker, lashing out quickly. I wouldn't consider that often violence. That's a behaviour or an uncontrollable behaviour, not intentional.

While these types of incidents may be routinely recorded by organisations, the question remains if it constitutes actual abuse as the practitioners did not regard these acts as 'intentional'. This creates a moral and ethical dilemma, as the 'perpetrator' of the harm may be someone who also has significant vulnerabilities that need to be acknowledged.

The same employment service provided further examples of their employees with cognitive disability being involved in potential harm of other employees:

[5] The term 'supported employment' often refers to work undertaken in Australian Disability Enterprises. These provide support to people with disability who are regarded as having high support needs to engage in work, often in a sheltered workshop environment at below minimum standard wage (www.dss.gov.au/disability-and-carers-programs-services-for-people-with-disability/supported-employment).

> And then on top of that, I mean, we've had incidents of inappropriate touching between supported employees when they're in a lunchroom or something along those lines. We report them straight away, we investigate them, we make sure that people are aware of their obligations to report to police, and all these different sorts of things. So, we go through those, but often it'll be two employees just doing things they shouldn't be doing.

This highlights the complexity involved when young people with cognitive disability are grouped together, but it also raises questions about how individuals are supported to understand consent and the difference between appropriate and inappropriate touch. In this case, the manager, who initially investigated and escalated the matter, connected employees to appropriate relationship education and supported their families with additional resources.

Contributing Factors Leading to Sexual Abuse

Unsupported Use of Social Media

Practitioners generally talked about the risks of sexual abuse of young people with cognitive disability, particularly young women, when engaging with social media platforms. Jan, a highly experienced practitioner who works in a disability-specific sexual violence service, described some of the challenges for this group in negotiating and navigating their understanding of sex and sexuality and the associated risks. Jan provided the example of a young woman she was working with who taught her about 'anime porn':

> She's in year 10 and she and her friends all watch this shit. Not a lot shocks me, but she was telling me about the conversation between her and some of her friends in the school playground about [sex] with four guys at the same time.

Jan explained that many of the young people she supported became fixated on these messages from social media: 'They know and think and talk about this stuff all the time.' Jan raised concerns that this ended up normalising abusive behaviour. Similarly, Chantal, a disability advocate, expressed concerns about the young women she supported accessing Tinder and other dating platforms without appropriate support.

Understanding Consent

The unique needs of young people with cognitive disability were highlighted time and again, including young people's vulnerabilities around understanding consent. Jan continued her story about the young woman who had taught her about 'anime porn'. The young woman had been sexually assaulted when she was about fourteen by her older brother, who has autism. The abuse was not reported to authorities. At school, a seventeen-year-old boy asked the young woman to be his girlfriend and Jan reported that young woman agreed because she wanted to be 'the same as her peers'; however, the issue related to her understanding of her rights around consent and her body:

> He [the boyfriend] told her if they were boyfriend and girlfriend, that sex was normal. And he did ask her if she consented. And she said, 'Yes.'... Okay, so yes, she consented. So, when he wanted to do something she didn't really like or didn't feel comfortable with, he would say to her, 'But you consented.'

Jan identified the challenge of how to provide appropriate education, noting that most of the young people her service worked with had no sex or relationship education or even information about menstruation. Other practitioners also talked about the need for education programs that assisted young people to understand how to make decisions that can act as preventative measures.

Disability Support Workers as Perpetrators

Jan also discussed the vulnerability of young people with cognitive disability to being groomed, particularly in cases where the perpetrator is a support worker and who has regular, unsupervised access to young people. Jan shared that nearly a quarter of cases of abuse of people with cognitive disability in their Victims of Crime data were committed by support workers. She told the story of a young man with autism who had just turned eighteen and had a passion for trains. After leaving school he did not have much to do and would go to the local train station to watch the trains. People started to get to know him, and the train station staff kept an eye on him. However, a man who was a support worker, wearing his agency shirt, started to talk with him and groomed him so that the young person ended up going back to his place to supposedly look at the perpetrator's train set. The young person ended up being sexually assaulted multiple times, and the perpetrator reportedly had told him that that was what male friends did. It was only when he told his mother because his bottom was getting sore that anyone found out. A further disturbing point about this story was that the case went to court and the perpetrator was convicted and sentenced, but when the judge asked him if had anything to say, the person said 'I am not a perpetrator. I am not a pervert. I waited until he was eighteen.'

Other examples provided by Jan relate to male support workers doing night shifts in share houses with young women with cognitive disability. Jan shared stories of support workers taking advantage of the young women, who in turn started to think of them as boyfriends. In one case, the violence and power escalated:

> I listened to the stories from this guy and from the client, and it's almost like the sex wasn't enough, then there has to be some sort of physical violence that's involved in the sexuality, like the restraints and not feeding, 'If you don't do what I want . . .' [The case went to court and] I supported her [the young woman who had been assaulted] because they needed an interpreter because she's basically non-verbal.. . . They [the perpetrators] were sitting there laughing and making fun of her in the courtroom.

Both examples demonstrate the power imbalance inherent in the relationships between support workers and young people. Young people with cognitive disability may be taught by services to trust their support workers unconditionally. The workers in these examples violated this trust, engaging not only in sexual assault, but also in emotional and psychological abuse, wilful deprivation, and physical violence.

Reporting the Sexual Abuse

Most of the young people with cognitive disability who survived sexual abuse in this study had negative and unsupportive experiences of reporting the abuse. They were often not believed and/or subjected to practices by the criminal justice system that failed to accommodate their disability. Examples included not having the case progressed and or police failing to intervene at the time when the abuse was occurring, as was the situation with Amethyst, whose story is shared in Chapter 4. The reliance on verbal statements made reporting difficult for TBone and Sophie, who struggled to describe what happened in words.

Being believed is important for any survivor of sexual abuse, and the stories of the young people reflect how distressing this was to them when they were not. Not being believed was likely to leave young people vulnerable to further abuses. Becky (aged twenty-five), who was raped, described her negative experiences when reporting this to the police:

> I told them [police] and they still wanted me to keep on describing the details and keep on describing the details and keep on describing the details. I did it three times. After that, why do you want to keep on reliving that memory? I told him three times. I told them when I was there, I told them when I was in the hospital. He [police officer] came whilst [I was] in hospital. I had to tell them again in the hospital. And he came and saw

> me at [housing service] and asked me to describe it again. I just said, 'No. I don't want to keep on going through this. Stop asking me.'

These interactions were retraumatising for Becky, who did not receive any counselling at the time. She also shared that only one person believed her and that other people she confided in called her 'a fucking liar'.

Sophie, a young woman with Down syndrome and autism (aged twenty), first reported an incident of sexual assault to police when she was at school. Sophie's mother described police as unsupportive. She was not allowed to be present with Sophie during the police interview. The police officer who interviewed Sophie was described as intimidating: 'he was six feet tall and was wearing a visible gun and taser'. Sophie was asked closed questions, which elicited single-word responses, and she reportedly answered 'no' to many of the police officer's questions. Sophie and her mother were later advised the police were unable to proceed with the complaint. Sophie's mother expressed how she was very disappointed by this, considering Sophie had confirmed the assault to the teacher and her general practitioner. Sophie herself referred to police in negative terms, while not able to explicitly talk about what happened, saying, 'I want to kill the police.' Her overall language at times in the interview suggested she experienced significant trauma from this experience.

Sophie was later sexually assaulted by her sister's ex-boyfriend. This was reported to the police, and Sophie's mother stated that the police encouraged Sophie to accept a lesser charge than sexual assault, which was offered by the prosecution, but they refused to do so. At the time of the interview, the ex-boyfriend had pleaded not guilty, and Sophie was therefore required to testify in court. Sophie's mother said she paid for a lawyer to fight this and to ensure Sophie was sufficiently advocated for. These experiences demonstrated a lack of understanding and appropriate practices that are focused on supporting the victim of the crime, and in fact illustrate the lack of fundamental attention to the rights of the person to have access to appropriate support during reporting. Ultimately, the right for Sophie and her family to prosecute a crime against her was being denied or hindered.

Professionals who witness sexual abuse within the agencies they work for can also have a difficult time in having their concerns attended to. A support coordinator from a disability service talked about reporting sexual abuse of a client by a co-worker 'that was not taken as credible at first disclosure and was taken to the police and then not able to be prosecuted due to lack of cognitive capacity in the victim'. The support coordinator also raised human resources grievances about the work colleague, which were not responded to appropriately. While the work colleague was found to be a perpetrator of significant abuse in the long run, what was morally distressing for the complainant was that she could not prevent ongoing abuse while her organisation did not act. She said,

> If we can't listen to me, as a person with an ability to be articulate and very assertive, then how can we listen to a person who has a cognitive impairment and who can't speak in a basic sense and might use keyword sign as well to communicate their needs?

Some settings can also make it very difficult to report sexual abuse because of the potential repercussions to the victims. Lorraine, the legal practitioner working with prisoners, highlighted the ramifications of disclosing abuse for the victim within the prison system, stating that 'if word gets out that that's what you've done, it doesn't matter where you go in the prison situation, it's going to be bad'.

Two young people with cognitive disability received support by services after being sexually assaulted. Amy (aged thirty) reported experiencing multiple acts of sexual and physical abuse by others in the community and had an ongoing fear of retaliation if she reported the incidents. Her most recent experience occurred within the week prior to her interview. The research team were ethically required to follow up with participants on any disclosures of current, unreported abuse, and ensure that the young person had appropriate supports around them. In Amy's situation, she was supported by a specialist agency for persons with cognitive disability who had experienced sexual abuse. Her worker was actively supporting Amy to talk through the issues and discuss her fears about reporting. Amy was weighing up her options from these discussions:

> They said, because this person's not known to me, it's just a random person, so they said it makes it hard. They said the only thing they could possibly help me with is if I report it, it would come under criminal court.

April (aged twenty-four) also received support by services after being sexually assaulted by her mother's boyfriend. She reported the abuse to her teacher at school, who then contacted the statutory child protection service, and the police became involved. April described feeling supported by her teacher, father, and sister. It appears that each time the abuse happened, she had the courage to tell the police, and on the second occasion the perpetrator was incarcerated. However, the perpetrator was not convicted the first or third time he committed the abuse.

Receiving emotional and psychological support after the abuse was the exception rather than the norm for most of the young people who had experienced sexual abuse in this research. Most of the young people did not receive appropriate counselling support at the time of the abuse but were connected to formal services at the time of the research interview. The process of recruitment for this research through gatekeeping agencies meant that the young people with cognitive disability who participated were accessing supports in the process of their recovery. Despite the resilience young people demonstrated, the aftermath of the sexual violence and other forms of violence was still evident in their lives.

Restrictive Practices

There were numerous examples of restrictive practices within this study's findings. Many of the stories relayed by participants were examples of overt restrictive practices, involving physical or chemical restraint. Participants raised concerns about the necessity of such actions and the long-term effects on the young person with cognitive disability.

A few practitioner participants shared examples of restrictive practices that occurred within the family setting. John, an Aboriginal and/or Torres Strait Islander youth worker, identified this in the context of a First Nations family not recognising and understanding that the young person had a cognitive disability:

> I've worked with a young person and the family is really struggling to understand his cognitive disability. They don't understand why he can't do certain things as quick as ... his youngest sister. And so, he struggles with telling the truth and kind of identifying what truths are, so they've put cameras around the house everywhere and they're kind of always watching his every move, like whether he takes things from the fridge and there's like alarms being set off. I could see that like it's definitely across that line, ... where now he's kind of declining mentally from it and he's always on edge. And I feel as though when I go in there, I have to ... take him out of that environment because it's just not healthy for him.

Rod, an occupational therapist who had experiences working with young people with autism, identified restrictive practices in terms of chemical restraints as:

> quite a common thing, particularly with autistic clients, and usually it's to reduce unwanted behaviours. Usually there's a behaviour of concern. Some can be really, really bad, like headbanging or self-harm, but usually they'll try and dull that by giving the child antidepressants or stimulants. But the parents don't really know that that's actually a violation. It's just given to kids just willy nilly ... so when you discuss that with them it's kind of like, 'Oh, you mean I don't have to actually medicate my child? You mean there are actual other ways?'

Rod explained that there were many behaviours of concern that arose in younger children with autism, which could include high-risk activities such as running on the street, self-harming, or repetitive head-banging. His concern was that medications, such as Concerta (prescribed for attention deficit hyperactivity disorder), were often seen as the solution to supporting young people:

> What happens is usually children are linked in with antidepressants or stimulants quite young. So, they've been dulled to that point, and it just becomes second nature. [The parents are] just like, 'Oh yeah, he's got Concerta, and he's got this blah, blah, blah medication.' But then you question the parent and be like, 'Why is he on Concerta? What do you think he's on Concerta for?' 'Oh, it's to control his behaviours of concern.' 'What's his behaviours of concern?' 'He talks a bit. He likes to talk in front of the teacher.'... And I'm like, 'That's not really a behaviour of concern that you need chemical restraint for.'

Both examples of family involvement in restrictive practices highlighted the importance of providing accurate information and resources to family members so they are better able to support the unmet needs of young people with cognitive disability who present behaviours of concern. The medication of young people with autism also indicates poor practice among medical professionals and school systems in responding to complex behaviours, which can suggest lack of understanding and or resources to support them to best meet the needs of the young person.

There were many examples of service providers engaging in restrictive practices with young people with cognitive disability, and it was not always clear from accounts whether these were acts of last resort, and whether agencies had the legal authority to engage in such practices. Nevertheless, Chantal, a disability advocate, described restrictive practices as denying 'the right to treatment to address the actual underlying issue, which is often ... trauma and that experience of abuse or bullying or violence'.

There can be devastating after-effects from restrictive practices. David, a young man with autism and complex communication support needs, exhibited physical behaviour at school that resulted in him being physically restrained by teaching staff. His story was shared by his mother, who reported that 'there were a few times when they'd have to pile on him, restrain him', instigated by the vice principal, which was described as a trigger for David. His mother attributed his behaviour in part to his hormonal changes during puberty as well as environmental factors. She described the physical restraint as 'a bit of a catalyst to some yucky times' and discussed how her son suffered from trauma for a long period afterwards. What becomes evident is the lack of more supportive and preventative measures to best deal with a child or young person's behaviours. Acts such as having teachers 'pile' on top of a young person would not be sanctioned with children without a disability.

A support coordinator in a parent-led organisation identified restrictive practices in terms of a hostel manager restricting tenants' access to water. This type of restrictive practice could be described as an act of wilful deprivation. The hostel manager allegedly removed the taps in the hostel so residents could not drink when they wanted to. It appears this was the manager's way of preventing bed-wetting by women with a cognitive disability, thereby limiting the staff's workload. While the support coordinator reported the matter to the NDIS Quality and Safeguards Commission and advocacy organisations, they said no one took the inquiry seriously.

Cody (aged twenty-two) experienced restrictive practices within a private hospital setting. He recalled that at the age of eighteen, the nurses threatened him to take his medication. According to Cody, they told him if he did not take the medication, they would send him to a public hospital adult ward where he was afraid of being abused. Cody shared that he was prescribed medication that was numbing, which distressed him. Cody identified the harm he experienced in relation to being threatened, having his freedom of movement restricted, and being denied a choice about his treatment. While Cody was there as a voluntary patient, he said he was not able to leave the hospital when he asked to.

In a similar vein, G, a practitioner who supported young people with cognitive disability exiting child safety and youth justice systems, identified working with young people who experienced forced treatments and interventions from mental health services and schools. G provided the following example of restriction on freedom of movement:

> I work with a young woman who shared with me that she went to a special school, and they locked her in a classroom because they didn't want her to leave. Part of her disability and her coping was to escape situations where she felt trapped or felt unsafe, so she would just leave school and go for a walk. I mean, she was quite young at this point, so I understand why there were safety concerns around that, but I feel that locking her in a classroom is probably not the most useful.

This act of mechanical restraint added to the negative experiences the young woman had in the school environment, and the worker was now seeking to reconnect the young person to school after twelve months' absence.

While many of these examples point to harmful practices, the complexity involved is recognised. The practitioners from an employment service talked about this complexity in terms of making decisions to ensure that the young person and others are not harmed. They shared a situation with a young person who had no behaviour support plan in place. This young person would 'lash out with scissors and things like that' within their employment setting, and this behaviour posed a significant risk to others. In this case the parents were against the implementation of any kind of restrictive practices; however, the service needed to comply with workplace health and safety obligations to keep staff, employees, and the young person safe. In addition, the young person shared a home with other persons with disability, who had to move out due to safety issues. The service applied for guardianship to engage in restrictive practices with this person. This presents a complex ethical issue about whose safety is prioritised, how risks are managed, whether restrictive practices should be used, and how these practices are monitored and minimised.

Annette, a solicitor who worked with incarcerated young people, defined solitary confinement as a form of restrictive practice. She explained that the policy of her service was that solitary confinement should not be used for more than fourteen days and not used for more than a very short period with anyone with a disability or mental health condition. Annette explained that the new Queensland Human Rights Act 2019 specifies that the least restrictive methods must be used; however, how this is monitored is problematic. The lack of therapeutic support for young people with cognitive disability within prison settings makes these practices especially harmful to a group of young people who often have co-occurring mental illness and extensive experiences of trauma (Ellem, Denton, & Davidson, 2020).

This section of the chapter has identified several factors that can increase the risk of violence against young people with cognitive disability. Many of these factors occurred within the context of relationships. Many of these risk factors are also a result of a lack of information shared with young people with cognitive disability and the failure to support young people to adopt protective behaviours. Other concerns are raised regarding the skill set and practices of service providers and authorities, which can lead to dehumanising responses to young people with cognitive disability, who deserve care and respect.

6.4 Understanding Violence from a Disability Human Rights Perspective

The violence experienced by young persons reported in this chapter is especially addressed by Articles 16 and 6 of the CRPD. The drafters of the

CRPD recognised the widespread violence against persons with disability and thus adopted Article 16 (Fennell & Keeling, 2018). Article 16 grants persons with disability a right to live free from exploitation, violence, and abuse. To realize this right, the CRPD requires states to take all appropriate legislative, administrative, social, educational, and other measures to protect persons with disability, both within and outside the home, from all forms of exploitation, violence, and abuse (Article 16(1)). Relatedly, states must provide persons with disability appropriate assistance and support, including on how to avoid, recognize, and report instances of exploitation, violence, and abuse (Article 16(2)). States must also ensure all services are monitored both to reduce the risk of violence occurring and to enable intervention where it has occurred (Article 16(3)). This requires states to put in place effective legislation and policies, including women- and child-focused legislation and policies, to ensure that instances of exploitation, violence, and abuse against persons with disability are identified, investigated, and, where appropriate, prosecuted (Article 16(5)).

Whereas all persons with disability have a heightened vulnerability to violence, women with a disability are especially vulnerable. Recognising this heightened vulnerability to rights violations, the drafters of the CRPD included Article 6 (Mykitiuk & Chadna, 2018). Article 6 requires states to take a range of measures to address the intersecting vulnerabilities caused by disability and gender. The CRPD Committee has provided further guidance on Article 6 in its third General Comment (UNCRPD, 2016). General Comment No. 3 specifically recognises women with disability heightened vulnerability to gender-based violence, domestic violence, sexual violence, exploitation, and other forms of violence (at Paras. 8–10). In addressing Article 16, General Comment No. 3 provides a comprehensive list of types of violence, many of which appear above in this chapter, including physical force, rape, neglect, economic coercion, the absence of free and informed consent, psychological manipulation, and bullying (Paras. 31 and 33). General Comment No. 6 emphasises that states need to take additional measures, when responding to Article 16, to support women with a disability to live a life free from violence (Para. 62).

6.5 Conclusion

In this chapter, young people with cognitive disability, their families, and practitioners have provided a snapshot into how those young people are often living with violence and its aftermath. This chapter has reported on exploitation, violence, and sexual assaults, which have occurred from childhood into the adult lives of persons with cognitive disability. The outcomes from this violence have ranged from psychological trauma, children being born as a result of rape, and property harm through to struggles in effectively transitioning into adult life. The violence experienced by young people with cognitive disability profoundly impacts their efforts to grow into adulthood.

The CRPD grants persons with cognitive disability rights to live free from violence and requires Australia to enable this right to be exercised. This chapter has shown that, instead of protecting young people with cognitive disability, some laws permitted restrictive practices and other forms of abuse. Even where laws prohibited the violence, complaints of violence were often not acted on; young people did not receive support; and screening measures were either absent or flawed, so that perpetrators were able to gain access to those they could then exploit. The human cost of the failure to protect young people with cognitive disability are profound and call for a profound response.

CHAPTER 7

Young People and the National Disability Insurance Scheme

'The Standard Cookie Cutter Approach'

Accessible Summary

- This chapter looks at services. It focuses on the National Disability Insurance Scheme (NDIS).
- Services don't always recognise what young people with cognitive disability can do.
- They can neglect young people with cognitive disability. This can lead to violence and abuse of the young person.
- This chapter looks at how young people with cognitive disability found supports from NDIS agencies.
- Young people with cognitive disability had trouble getting onto the NDIS.
- Professionals, families, and young people needed to fight to make sure supports were helpful.
- The NDIS must get better for all people with disability.

7.1 Introduction

The book now turns to how violence against young people with cognitive disability can occur at a service and systems level. Previous chapters illustrated how policies and practices of supporting young people with cognitive disability transitioning into adulthood were not adequate in ensuring the well-being of young people and their families. This chapter focuses on Australia's first national scheme to support eligible people with a disability, the National Disability Insurance Scheme (NDIS). The analysis in this chapter begins with a focus on overall concerns with service systems for young people with cognitive disability, and then discusses findings in relation to the NDIS. Subsequent chapters will focus on other service systems, showing how systemic-level discrimination and discourse can construct young people with cognitive disability in unhelpful, debilitating ways. While each service system is examined separately in the coming chapters, it is important to note that difficulties also arise when service systems need to work together to support young people with cognitive disability.

In three sections this chapter will present accounts from young people, family members, and practitioners on how the complexity of the NDIS is limiting the support and outcomes for young people with cognitive disability. Section 7.2 explores how service systems overall can struggle to provide a coherent, supportive narrative around cognitive disability. It can be concluded that this systemic- and service-level treatment is a contributing factor to unfair treatment of this group of young people. We analyse how this unfairness operates across six subsections in Section 7.3.

Section 7.3 introduces the NDIS, providing a brief explanation on how this scheme operates and supports eligible people with disability, including most of the young people with cognitive disability featured in this book. The section then analyses a raft of system failures. This includes the challenges in navigating the evidential and administrative rules to access the scheme, and how the system defines what supports are available. In particular, the NDIS fails to respond to the long-term nature of cognitive disability, often reducing supports into adulthood. It also fails to appropriately respond to the individual needs of young people with cognitive disability, adopting a transactional approach that limits positive outcomes. Overall, participation in the NDIS requires constant advocacy by young people with cognitive disability and their support network, which can have a high impact on emotions and resources for all involved. Finally, in Section 7.4, this chapter analyses how the CRPD creates a right to access supports and analyses how the NDIS is currently not meeting Australia's international human rights obligations.

7.2 Systemic-Level Discrimination against Young People with Cognitive Disability

Service systems can struggle to provide a coherent, supportive narrative around cognitive disability, and this can be a contributing factor to the unfair treatment of this group of young people. Young people with cognitive disability may be an afterthought in many service systems. In systems that specifically cater for people with disability, the needs of young people with cognitive disability may be problematised as being too complex or costly. Decisions regarding who is in and who is out become a dilemma for many systems, and need is often determined through a deficit lens, according to fiscal and managerial considerations, rather than authentic need.

A deficit understanding of cognitive disability can infiltrate all aspects of a young person's life. When systems frame disability in this way, they can create significant barriers to young people with cognitive disability achieving their potential. Chantal, a social worker, raised this when she talked about having to advocate strongly for a young woman with cognitive disability to access the same school as her brothers, to be treated with the same consideration from doctors, and to ensure she attained a job after leaving school, which started out as a small business:

> And so they knocked on pretty much every door in their hometown, which is a regional community of Queensland, and started off with one business, and now she's grown that to where she has staff and she's got her work van that she's purchased. Then [the young person] wanted to have her own home and buy her own house. And [the young person] has got this great comment that [the worker] always talks about that, *nothing says inclusion more than having a mortgage* [emphasis added].

The young woman reached these achievements despite the barriers created in systems such as the health and education systems. Yet the issue is that these barriers create inherent inequity for young people with cognitive disability, and subsequent denial of the person's rights to health, education, employment, and financial and economic independence.

Systems-level abuse can result in a young person with cognitive disability's marginalisation and removal of their self-worth. The effects of this are not as readily apparent as other forms of abuse, but are nevertheless insidious, creating a situation where it is acceptable to not provide best practice – it becomes acceptable to have second-rate services for young people with cognitive disability, as evidenced in this book. This in turn leads to poor resourcing and high staff turnover, as practitioners who support young people with cognitive disability are equally devalued in such a system.

TBone's experience (aged nineteen, First Nations Australian) exemplifies this pattern of neglect. TBone required targeted support to address his self-harming behaviour and stabilise his mental health. There appeared to be a lack of support for his paid carers and frequent changes in staffing.

Workers left because they were not appropriately resourced, adding further instability into TBone's life.

Systems-level disregard for young people with cognitive disability is also evident in the siloed and fragmented ways in which services operate. The young people with cognitive disability featured in this book have made transitions across multiple support systems, and the failure of these systems to collaborate around a young person's needs adds confusion and chaos to young people's lives. Amy, a young parent with cognitive disability who has three children in care, illustrates this point as she sought support for her mental health issues as mandated by the child protection system. When asked if child protection professionals provide support, Amy responded:

> Well, they try. They tried last time, when I had to go [to the hospital] ... and they said, 'We can't help you because you're a Child Safety parent.' And because there's nowhere else for us to go, we make mental health backlogged because of all the Child Safety parents. So yeah, it's hard.

For Amy to meet the expectations of child protection authorities, she needed to access mental health services. She described the experience of being turned away from the hospital as one in which 'Child Safety parents' such as herself make the system 'backlogged'. She had internalised the problem of poor interagency processes and inadequate resourcing.

Matthew, a practitioner who managed a support agency for people with cognitive disability, considered inadequate resourcing as a form of systemic neglect. The impact of this neglect can create moral distress for some practitioners when they are unable to provide the needed support for a young person with cognitive disability. As Matthew noted:

> It's just when people's lives are really disadvantaged, and you, as a worker, feel that there are things you have to let go because you can't address everything, and are you being neglectful, that's an issue – I think that's a constant issue in your head all the time.... Is the frigging NDIS neglectful in that it doesn't recognise these systemic issues that are impacting on people with a disability? Is Child Safety neglectful in that this young woman has had two children and they've both been taken away at birth? And will her children go on to have children ... [who] will be taken away at birth?

The blatant disregard from government funding bodies to ensure holistic support for young people with cognitive disability can be disheartening for professionals who support this group.

Riley, a sexual assault worker, also identified the systemic nature of neglect for young people with cognitive disability. Riley talked about assumptions being made that the young person with cognitive disability lacks capacity and that there are low expectations that can then set the 'person up for poor well-being outcomes.' Riley added, 'So, I think . . . that in itself is a kind of . . . neglect . . . in the sense of just giving up and being really indifferent in terms of the long-term outcomes for people.'

Many of the above examples point to the need to go beyond individual acts of abuse and neglect and consider the driving influences of services, systems, and policies that set the context for such violations. The messages that systems give to young people with cognitive disability can be disempowering and soul-destroying. This chapter and subsequent chapters on different service systems take a closer look at how policy failure, the ways in which systems function, and the values they espouse play a large part in setting the background for violence against young people with cognitive disability.

7.3 Young People with Cognitive Disability and the NDIS

This section introduces the NDIS, a scheme that provides funding for supports and services to Australians with disability, including most of the young people with cognitive disability in this book. As illustrated in this chapter, the access to support under the NDIS for young people with cognitive disability is not always easy. This section of the chapter shows how NDIS system failures impact on young people with cognitive disability in their transition to adulthood.

Introducing the NDIS

The NDIS is the central mechanism through which most young people with cognitive disability in this study received daily support. The NDIS is part of an international trend in disability services to provide individualised funding to people with disability (Cortese et al., 2021). It is a system that, according to the National Disability Insurance Agency, is premised on the concept of providing 'choice and control' to people with disability who utilise the scheme (NDIS website). The scheme, which marked a historical shift in disability policy, uses insurance principles to provide support to people with disability over a lifetime, with the view to increase the level of independence of an individual with disability and to further their ability to participate. Each person with disability who is eligible for the scheme has an individual support plan that encompasses three categories of supports: (1) core supports to provide help with daily living, consumables, transport, and social and community participation; (2) capital supports such as assistive technology, home modifications, and specialist disability accommodation; and (3) capacity-building supports, including coordination of supports, increased social and community participation, improved living arrangements, enhanced health and well-being, finding and keeping a job, improved relationships, improved life choices, and improved daily living skills (National Disability Insurance Agency, 2022).

There was an overwhelming recognition of the benefits and value of the NDIS by young people, family members, and practitioners. One young person, Hilde (aged eighteen) explained that persons with disability 'fought and died for the NDIS'. Goldie (aged twenty-two) expressed gratitude for the help she was receiving through the NDIS:

> They pay for therapies and sanitary products and for support workers to do household stuff with me, like cleaning and laundry and the list goes on, and also to go out with me, go to the movies, go play putt-putt, and go shopping, take Bob [Goldie's dog] to different dog parks, and take me to my appointments, and join me at the groups. So yeah, I think I've got a lot of help. I think I'm pretty good with the help.

While the positives of the system were acknowledged by participants, there were several gaps identified within the NDIS that resulted in ongoing disadvantage and marginalisation for young people with cognitive disability.

Accessing the Scheme

Access to the NDIS requires that people with disability can adequately articulate their goals and aspirations (Collings et al., 2019). The onus rests with applicants and their families to prove their eligibility for the scheme and to understand the administrative rules associated with support (Soldatic et al., 2014).

Several concerns were raised in this study about difficulties for young people with cognitive disability in accessing the NDIS. Angel (aged twenty-four) spoke of his frustration with assessment processes:

> Everything at the NDIS you have to prove. It's great getting the supports that come from that, but, at the same time, I'm always having to be tested and I'm always having to prove to somebody else why I need the supports that I need. So I'm never not getting away from that like, 'Well, why do you need it?' I'm getting accepted for being the way that I am, but, at the same time, I always have to prove why I need the services that I need. It's like, 'Isn't the whole point is you understand why I'm on the service in the first place?'

The supports received through the NDIS were valued by Angel, but he reported feeling uncomfortable asking for and continuously having to justify his need for assistance.

Monica, a disability advocate for young people with cognitive disability from culturally and linguistically diverse backgrounds, shared the challenges this group face in getting onto the scheme. She was surprised that there was not sufficient outreach to young people with cognitive disability in special schools and by the number of clients she still encountered in these settings who were not connected to the NDIS. She had less confidence that this group of young people in mainstream schooling would be registered under the NDIS.

Chantal, another disability advocate, was concerned about young people with cognitive disability who had a co-occurring mental illness. She explained,

> It's the challenges to get into the scheme and to get through the processes, to get the functional supports that they need around their disability that would actually help all of these other things happening in their life is another particular challenge.

A Need for a Long-Term Focus

A key purpose behind the NDIS is to provide supports to participants that increase their capacity and develop their independence. Several authors have noted the neoliberal underpinnings of the scheme and have questioned the focus on producing 'self-actualised' individuals, who can actively select appropriate supports in the disability marketplace, and eventually achieve social and economic independence (Cortese et al., 2021). Such a focus may fail to account for the many social and economic barriers facing young people with cognitive disability, and lead to placing too much responsibility on the service user (Wiesel et al., 2019).

Several practitioners in this study felt that the scheme at times had unrealistic expectations that the need for funding for individuals would diminish over time. Rod, an occupational therapist who had experience working with young people with autism, noted how funding decreased for young people when they reached the end of high school. He felt this pattern almost assumed that the young person's disability would be 'fixed'. It failed to consider the crucial point of transitioning into adulthood and the supports needed to navigate this significant transition.

Mary, another practitioner, found that the NDIS did not account for the amount of time needed in developing rapport with young people with cognitive disability who had experienced violence and abuse. Time was required to build trust and to help young people to understand some of the dangers they may be facing in exploitative relationships with others.

Failing to Understand the Nuances of Support

It has been reported by several authors that young people with cognitive disability who have complex support needs are at high risk of not gaining adequate support from the NDIS (Bigby, 2021; Soldatic et al., 2014). Services under the NDIS may fail to account for the specific communication needs and decision-making challenges of young people with cognitive disability (Bigby, 2021).

Mary, a practitioner, regarded the skills in supporting young people with cognitive disability as nuanced and specialised. She emphasised the need to be available for young people when they are in crisis. It was felt that the system did not understand cognitive disability, and there was less flexibility in adapting the amount of support hours. Mary argued that the transition to a self-directed model of service delivery resulted in supports for young people with cognitive disability becoming more itemised. The need to measure the cost and time of providing help limited the responsiveness of the support.

Angela, the stepparent of Danni, a young woman with profound cognitive disability, also referred to a limited understanding of profound impairment. She confided,

> Honestly, I've never met a support coordinator who knew diddly squat about profound impairments or who could find me the unicorn of a decent program that wasn't, 'Park her in the corner and put her brakes on,' or, 'Take her out to the Coffee Club [a café chain] once a week.'

This lack of understanding of support needs raised fears about the security of long-term funding. As Mary shared, 'My real concern, which we know is happening, but they're not telling us, [is] that intellectual disability will be streamed as low needs.' Angela faced this fear every time Danni attended her planning review. The processes of having to go through reassessments, the need to justify funding of staff, and the amount of work caused significant stress for Angela.

The Prescriptive, Transactional Nature of the NDIS

Supports under the NDIS were often transactional in nature, involving a prescriptive set of resources and services, which did not always serve young people with cognitive disability and indeed created additional barriers. Chantal, a disability advocate, shared some of the unintended consequences:

> I think some of the structures, particularly around NDIS that have been put in place around supports coordinators and those different models, have

> some unintended consequences for this group in their gatekeeping and seeing themselves in this role of controlling what the person's plan and supports are.... Which they've only got a limited amount of hours and it acts as another barrier sometimes to thinking about innovative responses and doing things differently because we become stuck back in the transactional relationship stuff.

Cody (aged twenty-two) noted how support workers in his Supported Independent Living (SIL)[1] arrangement had come to itemise the cost of providing him transport to community places such as the local library:

> Their [SIL] workers just don't want to do it ... they used to say they have to spend money on it and so it's not worth it for how much they get back on fuel.... Apparently, ten, fifteen, twenty cents per – they get apparently, I think it's forty cents back per litre spent on fuel and they say it's not worth it. It might not be worth it for one trip, but it would add up.

In his discussion around NDIS supports, Cody spoke repeatedly of the business-like nature of paid work, the 'red tape' around getting assistance, and the financial costs of attending appointments with professionals. It appeared the transactional nature of service delivery was at the forefront of his experience with service providers. Cody argued that the scheme could be simplified by providing direct payments to scheme participants to allow them to decide what support they needed.

Matthew, a manager of a small service for people with cognitive disability, provided a stark example of how the NDIS may seek to mould its participants into a certain service user image, which was far from the reality of the young person's experience. He provided the background about a young woman with cognitive disability they were working with:

> She was in Child Safety, she was self-placing in Child Safety, two children while still under the age of eighteen in Child Safety, both children taken away at birth.... Appalling sort of histories of violence, abuse, trauma.... We were able to organise that she did get a NDIS package, big package. 180,000 [AUD] or something like that. We were doing some work with her, sort of outreach work going and connecting with her, dealing with a multitude of issues, and she's constantly in violent sets of relationships, lots of exploitation going on, poverty, homelessness, the whole lot, which has been going on all of her life

[1] Supported Independent Living is one type of home and living support for NDIS participants with higher support needs, who need some level of help at home all the time. "Supported Living," National Disability Insurance Agency, 28 June 2022, https://ourguidelines.ndis.gov.au/supports-you-can-access-menu/home-and-living-supports/supported-independent-living.

Guardianship was arranged for the young woman, and the guardian appointed a support coordinator from another service. Matthew's service provided the core supports for the young woman, identifying some of the challenges:

> The core support is paid much lower [than support coordination]; you're under a lot more financial pressures as an organisation to do that. Can you sort of attract the right sort of staff to do that sort of very complex work? We decided to go that route. So, we've got workers reaching out to her, connecting with her around a multitude of issues, including going and getting food parcels with her.

When the support coordinator found out what the workers were doing, she told the service that they should not be taking the woman to get food parcels, and recommended another agency. When questioned on this, the support coordinator was of the opinion that the young woman with cognitive disability needed to attend a disability day centre where she could learn about budgeting and not need food parcels. Matthew described the lack of understanding by the support coordinator of their work and frustration about this:

> So, working with this young woman who's been from this incredibly deprived, traumatised background, essentially homeless since she was about ten years of age, and when we were working with her about getting a food parcel, it's clearly not just getting a food parcel. We're in the car with her, there's a whole lot of counselling support going on around, just all around safety processes and stuff that's happening in a whole lot of relationships. There's all this work that's going on, safety planning, et cetera.

Matthew saw this as an example of the system's narrow perception of young people with cognitive disability that assumes the young person is middle-class, independent, and self-organised. There was no understanding of the extreme trauma the young woman had experienced throughout her life, only 'a scripted idea of what supports you offer through that system'. Similarly, Cody, a young person with cognitive disability, highlighted these concerns, saying, 'that's the thing, not everyone needs the same care, and they think everyone does. They're treating it as a standard cookie cutter approach.'

Amy, a parent with cognitive disability who had three children in the child safety system, felt she received little help from her NDIS support coordinator:

> She's got a very lack of understanding with parents in Child Safety. She's got no idea. And I think what I struggle with, that I have support workers

> and I like all my support workers and I'm happy, but the thing with NDIS and support workers is that there's no understanding, there's no knowledge in parents fighting this system, parents dealing with the system, parents that live in the system.

The Need to Constantly Advocate

Both Peter and Angela, parents of young people with severe and profound cognitive disability, spoke of the need to continually advocate for their family member under the scheme. The need for someone such as a family member to 'prosecute' the interests of young people with cognitive disability under the scheme has been noted elsewhere (Bigby, 2014, p. 94). Peter shared his perception of the difficulties in doing so and said, 'There is no formal way to hold NDIS to account.... You have to go through the AAT [Administrative Appeals Tribunal]. In reality, to do it well, it costs you thirty to fifty grand.'

Peter referred to the challenges that could arise when a NDIS participant and/or family member disagrees with the decision of the National Disability Insurance Agency. NDIS participants can ask for an internal review related to their eligibility for the scheme or the contents of their individual support plans. If the participant/family member is not satisfied with the outcome of this internal review, they can apply for an external review through the AAT, a tribunal that provides independent merits review of administrative decisions by the Australian government. Affordable legal representation is difficult to access for many people with disability and their families. Where the participant with disability has complex and high-care needs, appeals often require sophisticated expert evidence, which can be costly (Brookes & Ballantyne, 2019). Peter estimated to challenge the decision of the NDIS would take him approximately forty to sixty hours of work to be successful, involving gathering multiple assessments and reports from professionals who worked with his daughter.

The bureaucracy surrounding the system could potentially be very confusing to young people. Cody conveyed his understanding of the chain of responsibility in the system and the inherent gaps in achieving its goal to support persons with disability:

> I don't care who's designed it. I just say, 'Fix it.' That's all the same with the NDIS' LACs [local area coordinators].[2] Currently the LACs are the ones

[2] Local Area Coordinators support people with disability to find information about supports and services and assist in accessing the NDIS and creating and implementing a NDIS plan. "Local Area Coordination Partners," National Disability Insurance Agency, 17 July 2023, www.ndis.gov.au/

> who write the policies we follow, but they can't change the policies. The policies are restricted by the legislation.[3] Apparently, NDIS ministers do not have the ability to change the legislation.... So they're basically just buck passing.

Both Peter and Angela spoke of the long time it took to access assistive technology under the scheme and the work involved in applying – requiring skills in advocacy. Angela shared how she applied for a specialised wheelchair: 'I think it took me about twelve months to get the application together. And then it took the NDIS twelve months to review it.'

Sonia, Lyn, and Brianna, transition planning facilitators, also reported difficulties advocating for a young person with cognitive disability who was living in an 'unsafe house'. Comprehensive reports from an occupational therapist for modifications had been submitted to the NDIS but had been declined. The facilitators identified that there was no one they could talk to about this, that clinical reports were being ignored, and that despite one year of advocacy, the person's living situation had not changed.

7.4 Viewing Young People's NDIS Experiences as Disability Human Rights under the CRPD

The systems failures experienced by young people with cognitive disability in this chapter are more than just distressing; they are a violation of their human rights. The rights of persons with disability to an adequate standard of living and to social protection cut across many rights but are primarily protected by CRPD Article 28 (Cremin, 2018). Article 28 recognises that persons with disability have a right to social protections and requires states to take measures to realize this right, including access to social protection programmes and poverty reduction programmes, assistance from the state with disability-related expenses (including adequate training, counselling, financial assistance, and respite care), as well as a right to access to public housing programs (CRPD Article 28[2]).

The CRPD Committee has called upon states to target interventions for the needs of people with cognitive disability in a range of Concluding Observations, including those from Australia, Niger, Singapore, and Slovenia (United Nations Committee on the Rights of Persons with

understanding/what-ndis/whos-delivering-ndis/lac-partners-community#:~:text=Local%20area%20coordinators%20support%20people,live%20the%20life%20they%20choose

[3] The National Disability Insurance Scheme Act 2013 (NDIS Act) is the legislation that establishes the NDIS and the agency that governs the NDIS.

Disabilities, 2018B, 48; 2019, Paras. 4(a) and 5(e) and (f), 11(a), 37[a], and 51(a); 2019C, Para. 46; 2022K, Para. 54). Most relevantly for this chapter, the cross-cutting nature of rights to social protections, as well as persons with disability's rights in relation to the NDIS, was specifically addressed by the CRPD Committee in its last Concluding Observation on Australia (United Nations Committee on the Rights of Persons with Disabilities, 2019). In this Concluding Observation, the CRPD raised concerns about the significant proportion of persons with disability living either near or below the poverty line and the nature of eligibility restrictions limiting access to supports (United Nations Committee on the Rights of Persons with Disabilities, 2019, Paras. 51(a) and (b)). The CRPD specifically addressed NDIS failures under the principal areas of concern (United Nations Committee on the Rights of Persons with Disabilities, 2019, Paras. 4(a) and 5(e) and (f)). In particular, the CRPD Committee raised concerns about the disability assessment that individuals must undergo in order to be eligible to receive services through the NDIS, which, the CRPD Committee noted, still relies heavily on the medical model of disability and does not provide equal opportunities to older persons with disability, persons with disability from culturally and linguistically diverse backgrounds, Aboriginal and/or Torres Strait Islander persons with disability, and persons with intellectual or psychosocial disability (United Nations Committee on the Rights of Persons with Disabilities, 2019, Para. 5(e)). Relatedly, the CRPD Committee, when addressing women with disability under Article 6, was concerned with the low percentage of women and girls with disability, particularly of Aboriginal and/or Torres Strait Islander backgrounds, who have access to services under the NDIS (United Nations Committee on the Rights of Persons with Disabilities, 2019, Para. 11[a] CRPD). Finally, when addressing the right to adequate standard of living and to live independently in the community under Article 19, the CRPD Committee raised concerns that the NDIS requires persons with disability to live in particular living arrangements in order to access support (United Nations Committee on the Rights of Persons with Disabilities, 2019, Para. 37[a] CRPD).

7.5 Conclusion

The accounts from young people with cognitive disability, family members, and practitioners indicated that NDIS was considered a complex system to access, to negotiate in terms of support, and to influence in terms of improving outcomes for young people with cognitive disability. This complexity arose from the number of bureaucratic layers of accountability within the scheme, as well as the reductionist focus on what constituted support. Warr et al. (2017) reported similar findings with other groups of people with disability. These groups relayed that they received inconsistent information from the NDIS, and that the administrative requirements of the scheme were difficult to understand. Similarly, in this study, the energy required by stakeholders to navigate this system could shift the focus from the well-being of young people with cognitive disability to fiduciary matters. Like any other individualised funding model, the NDIS is dependent upon the existence of positive relationships and a supportive community in the life of a young person with cognitive disability. Without such supports, the system is likely to neglect or overlook young people with cognitive disability rather than ensure a meaningful transition to adulthood.

This chapter has identified that young people with cognitive disability are being required to surmount considerable evidential hurdles to access NDIS supports, and that this is creating a profound barrier that is delaying access to services for years or preventing access to any services. Services are short-term, often inadequate, and there is a constant need to gather evidence to justify the need. The experiences of the NDIS by young people with cognitive disability in this study are not consistent with their CRPD rights. To enable them to access services requires, at a minimum, that Australia improve its strategic responses to combatting the poverty experienced by persons with disability (United Nations Committee on the Rights of Persons with Disabilities, 2019, Article 52[a]). The complexity of disability assessment criteria and exclusion of persons with cognitive disability from NDIS must be reviewed and aligned with the human rights model of disability (6(e)). This must include simplifying, clarifying, and making NDIS procedures more transparent, including by making information publicly available and accessible (6(f)). This review must also ensure that the NDIS meets the diverse and intersecting requirements of persons with disability in all areas (6(f)).

CHAPTER 8

Don't Give Up on Us

Young People's Experiences of Education and Employment

Accessible Summary

- Young people with cognitive disability found school to be both good and bad.
- Things were good when young people had friends and teachers who listened and tried to help.
- Things were bad when the school wanted young people with cognitive disability to be like everyone else. Young people could be punished or neglected if they didn't fit in with everyone else.
- Leaving school could be hard. Young people with cognitive disability often didn't have a job or university to go to.
- The United Nations Convention on the Rights of Persons with Disabilities says that all people with disability have a right to a good education, and that people can be supported to get a job or to learn more after school.

8.1 Introduction

There has been a paradigm shift in how persons with disability operate as economic actors (Stein & Challenor, in press). Historically, public policies largely excluded persons with disability from the open labour market, expecting them to rely upon charity and to work in sheltered workshops

(Brennan-Krohn, 2016; Hoffman, 2013). While disability support services and other welfare agencies can help limit the impact of poverty, work is the primary means of rising out of poverty to economic citizenship. Bantekas, Pennilas, and Trömel (2018) argue that the right to work and employment is considered a fundamental human right, 'chiefly because it ensures the individual's sustenance, dignity (including self-worth) and wellbeing'. Education is one of the most essential resources that can lead to employment and empower people to succeed in life and to become economic actors (Harpur & Stein, 2019).

This chapter starts with an analysis of young people with cognitive disability's experiences of the transition through education to work. Section 8.2 emphasises that education is a key system that all young people interact with, and it plays an important part in a young person's transition into adulthood. For many of the young people, family members, and practitioners, their experiences highlighted challenges, barriers, discrimination, abuse, and neglect within this system. Section 8.3 considers the right to education for persons with disability within the CRPD framework, and how this requires appropriate support for young people to transition from school to university and/or into work.

8.2 Discounted Educational Opportunities Leading to Discounted Work Opportunities

Young people with cognitive disability in this book largely reported not being understood at school. They often did not obtain the supports they required to enjoy an equal educational experience as their peers without a disability. Friendships were considered important where they developed. Without friendship groups, education was isolating. Students were expected to fit into systems even when the system failed to acknowledge or make accommodations for the young person's disability. Leaving school created significant stress for the young person and their families, as there were often few opportunities for the young person to engage in meaningful activity. The young people desired educational and work settings to better support their transitions.

Not Being Understood

Education was and is important for Hilde, an eighteen-year-old neurodiverse young woman, who moved from one school to another in pursuit of an education. Hilde identified some positive and supportive teachers;

however, overwhelmingly she discussed her experiences of being in an oppressive system that failed to understand her neurodiversity. Hilde reported experiencing abuse from an early age:

> I used to get in so much trouble. When I was in Prep [preparatory school] I'd be sent to timeout, which was abusive actually.... And I'd sort of be out there for five minutes. The teacher would come and say, 'Are you sorry?' I'd say, 'No.' [The teacher would] come back in five minutes, 'Are you sorry?' 'No.' 'Are you sorry?' 'No.' It was like, 'When are you going to say you're sorry?' So I ended up spending big chunks of time out there, because why would I lie?

Hilde acknowledged that she did do some wrong things; however, this did not justify the punishment, highlighting that she was behaving in a way consistent with her autism.

According to Hilde she experienced abuse from approximately half of her teachers, but also highlighted that it was not always intentional. Hilde emphasised that 'well meaning' people who 'think they are helping us are the ones who do the most harm usually'.

Hilde discussed the importance of the system changing to support the young person with a cognitive disability. For the education system to truly understand the young person, it needed:

> to break down the harmful power structures and make everything, absolutely everything, not about people having things decided for them, but about people being supported to make their own decisions.

Hilde identified resisting authority and abusive practices in school from the age of six, where she supported other students, speaking out for them when she felt teachers were teaching incorrectly, and challenging teachers when they exercised their authority in discriminatory and harmful ways. Hilde recalled one teacher who was neurodiverse who she deemed 'incredible', stating that 'it was just astounding the difference it makes to have a teacher who actually says, "I want you to challenge me. If you think I'm wrong . . ."'. This teacher welcomed input from young people, and seemingly had greater understanding of what it was like to be neurodiverse.

Other young people also desired to have their disability understood and to be listened to by school authorities. Amy (aged thirty) described getting into trouble at high school and never having anyone listen to her side of things. Cody (aged twenty-two) identified that his obsessive-compulsive disorder was not understood at school, which meant not receiving appropriate support to help with his assessments. Cody identified experiencing panic attacks and reported being blamed, laughed at, and punished, and spending copious time in detention. Cody described school as being:

> designed for the person who's spotlight average. If you're above average in some areas and below in others, pfft. Completely below average, pfft. They might have some people who are completely disabled. They don't really have anything when people who are in between.

Getting the Right Support

There were mixed accounts as to whether the school system made appropriate adjustments and accommodations for young people's learning styles. Becky (aged twenty-five) identified struggling at school because of her dyslexia and dyspraxia. She reported not being able to be in a big class because she thought people were talking about her. Becky identified the importance of schools helping people who are struggling with their learning but said this support was not readily available to her. She explained her desire for teaching staff to reach out to proactively offer support:

> 'Can you please stay after class today? I need to talk to you.' Doesn't mean you're getting in trouble. You've got to ask them, 'Do you need . . . because I will help you. After all school hours are done, I will come in and I will help you with what you need help with.'

Becky's discussion suggested that teachers needed to adopt a less authoritative approach, and instead one that focused on genuine inquiry and concern for the young person. Unfortunately, Becky's memories of school involved limited support, which, in turn, restricted her opportunities:

> If I'd got that extra help, I probably could've passed with flying colours. But I couldn't because nobody offered it to me. I even asked for it, and they said no.

Similarly, Rod, an occupational therapist, reported systemic neglect of young people with autism by educational bodies, where they failed to provide appropriate educational adjustments to facilitate young people's learning. Thus, young people would leave school in year nine or ten. He spoke of the detrimental effects on the young person's self-esteem: when 'your school has given up on you, everyone else is probably going to give up on you'. The message this sends to people is 'I don't want to talk to someone who could help me because school's given up on me.'

In contrast, Cooper (aged twenty-three) highlighted positive experiences at primary school because he had supportive teachers who advocated for him. Cooper used a wheelchair, and while initially there were physical barriers, the school was able to get funding to build ramps. Being in a supportive school involved not feeling discriminated against and the presence of experienced and understanding teachers, who were trained in working with young people with cognitive disability. Having had a positive experience at primary school helped prepare Cooper to navigate high school.

Flexibility in support is crucial for some young people with cognitive disability. David, a young person with complex communicative support needs and autism, attended a special school for all his formal education. As David matured into young adulthood, the changes associated with puberty affected him and he experienced a turbulent time emotionally. David's mother reported that the school was able to be flexible with David's reduced hours of attendance, which assisted David to have a great final year. David's mother also commented on the connection that David had with teaching staff – some of the teacher's aides at school would provide support to David over the school holidays.

This highlights how it is possible for young people with cognitive disability to have positive experiences with the right supports at a systemic level. Where this was not present, as we have reported, young people had negative and harmful experiences, which could undermine their self-esteem and their agency as young adults.

Friendships

A key task of attending school is socialisation as children and young people develop friendships and connections with others. This can result in long-term friendships and a sense of belonging, factors that may also support a student's motivational, behavioural, social-emotional, and academic functioning (Korpershoek et al., 2020). Friendships can enhance the young person's capacity to undertake changes associated with transitioning to adulthood.

April (aged twenty-four) identified school as a positive time, talking about being engaged in sport as being fun and having 'good teachers' and 'friends'. It appears that April's experiences of school were inclusive and supportive, including being supported by her teacher after she reported her sexual assault. T (aged twenty-nine) described his experiences at school as being 'quite brutal' but also as 'fun' as he developed a network of friends. While this was also the time he started to experiment with drugs and 'wag [absent himself from] school' with his peers, the relationships were nevertheless important to T's self-esteem and sense of belonging.

Feeling Like You Don't Belong

Not all young people achieved a sense of belonging at school. This book has previously provided examples of bullying of young people with cognitive disability by their peers. This could reach a crisis point for them, which could lead to school disengagement. For example, Goldie, a First Nations young person who attended eight different schools, experienced bullying as well as the teachers not caring for or protecting her. Goldie left school at the end of year 10 and then attended a flexible learning centre.[1] Her experiences at school resulted in feeling shame, and Goldie described 'hating herself' because of these experiences.

This sense of not belonging could penetrate deeply, affecting the young person's sense of self. Becky, who identified as LGBTIQA+, talked about the impact of experiencing bullying and physical and emotional abuse at school from other students, which made her feel miserable. These included experiences such as:

> Nudging me on the shoulder, calling me a loser, that I was worthless ... getting their shoulder up and hitting me on the chin. Just pushing me around pretty much and just calling me names. Names that make you feel like you're actually worth nothing.

It was problematic for Becky when she was told by her mother to 'just ignore it', which she could not do and so reached a 'breaking point' where she could no longer handle things. She pleaded that school authorities should do something to address the issue:

> If someone's bullying someone, trying to set them on fire or whatever, because it's happened to me, suspend them, tell what happened to the parents, do something. Because it is not right. What's happening in these schools right now is not right. But we do need to get these counsellors trained in at least the basic form of people who are trying to transition or the people who are gay or the people who are straight and they don't know who they are. We need counsellors who are actually trained in that.

Bullying in schools is a system-wide issue, with research highlighting the detrimental impact it has on a child and young person (Rivara & Le Menestrel, 2016). When the basis for bullying is related to a young person's disability, gender, and other identities, it can perpetuate deeply held discriminatory attitudes and further exclude young people from a supportive educational experience (Armitage, 2021).

[1] Flexible learning centres are schools that cater for young people who may have one or more significant and complex support needs and who have difficulty accessing mainstream school (www.ereafsn.edu.au/what-is-a-flexible-learning-centre-4-2-2/).

Responses to Complex Behaviours in Schools

A key theme that has emerged from this study is the requirement for the child or young person with cognitive disability to 'fit' the school model or assimilate. Behaviours that sat outside what the system expected were often responded to poorly. For example, Rod, an occupational therapist, described his experiences with children with autism in a specialist school where the parents were encouraged to medicate the child due to their 'behaviours' that were considered disruptive to others or created 'risks'. This was identified as also occurring in mainstream schools for neurodiverse young people, highlighting the pressure on this group of young people to conform to a system designed by, and for, neurotypical people.

TBone, a First Nations young person, experienced significant difficulties at school. Although he attended a special education unit with specialist teaching staff, the school was unable to cope with his behaviour, which was aggressive and violent at times. The school's responses included going into 'lockdowns' and sending him home, and TBone ended up being home-schooled. TBone's mother described what happened:

> They were having to have ... lockdowns to keep the whole rest of the school in their classrooms while he was rampaging. Because he would actually go to classroom doors and shake them and windows and all sorts of stuff, yelling, screaming. Yeah, real guttural. It was quite frightening to the younger kids, apparently, as well because they had to – you're a shocker. They had to send notes home to the parents explaining. So it was really disruptive to the whole school.

This raises the important issue of how schools are equipped to support a young person who has a combination of behavioural issues associated with their disability, and who also may have significant trauma. Failure to respond well to such issues can be detrimental to the young person and to others in the school environment. Without adequate training and support, the end result is that the young person becomes excluded. This undermines their educational opportunities, leads to social isolation, and creates additional stressors for the young person's family, who may be left to deal with this alone.

Education Systems That Prepare Better for Transitions

Participants recommended that the educational requirements of young people with cognitive disability needed to be accepted as an entitlement and not as a something that could be ignored. The significant inequalities experienced in education led to various suggestions. Illustratively, for Cooper, having more awareness within schools of children and young people with cognitive disability was important to promote more inclusiveness. Relatedly, Becky drew from her personal experiences and recommended more consideration on how to better include and support young people in the education system who struggle because of their disability. Addressing transitions specifically, Monica, a practitioner, suggested

> really making sure that when people leave school, the next stage in life is set up and organised as much as people want it. We don't have to say, 'People don't have to do things,' but the range of options for people on leaving school should be very clear to them and their family.

Leaving Secondary School: Opportunities and Challenges

Many young people discussed leaving school as a significant event in their lives as they transitioned to adulthood and developed further independence. This transition was often discussed as an important milestone for the young person, symbolised by attending the end of school formal celebration.[2] Those who reported attending this event shared both positive and negative experiences. For TBone (aged nineteen), the school formal was a positive experience, involving all the formal rituals of hiring a suit, staying overnight in Brisbane, and celebrating. Similarly, Simon, a young man with Down Syndrome (aged thirty), still recalled the importance of this milestone as a marker of becoming an adult:

INTERVIEWER: What does that mean for you now that you're an adult and you don't have to go to school?
SIMON: I leave school. I've got a formal.
MUM: He had a formal.
INTERVIEWER: Yeah. And so, when you finished, your formal, how did that feel, going to your formal?
SIMON: It was good.
INTERVIEWER: Yeah?
SIMON: Yep.
INTERVIEWER: Did it make you feel like you were growing up?
SIMON: I am growing up so far.

Participation in school formals was seen by many young people as a major step in this transition, but also, if handled insensitively by school

[2] The school formal is a tradition in Australian schools of celebrating the end of high school.

officials, a reinforcement that the young person with cognitive disability was somehow different from other young people and did not belong. Cody (aged twenty-two) reported a negative experience of the school formal, one that further reinforced the discrimination because of his disability:

> And basically, that you've got disability, you're automatically just put into other people's groups of disability. For the school formal and everything, the only kid that didn't have dates, like boys sit here, girls sit there. They're like, 'Okay, we're giving you ten minutes to go and see if you want to work up the courage to get one. Get a date yourself or whatever.' And before they were even finished, I was about to get up to walk across to ask Helen to be into dance or whatever, just to have someone to be a dance partner or whatever.... But at the end they went, 'Nope.' Just before I went, they went, 'Okay, nope. You know what? Boys line up here. Girls line up here.' And the boys got pushed back to the end of it who were disabled, and so did the girls, and then let the girls all choose first.

While there were accounts from young people of experiencing bullying and discrimination in school, nevertheless, leaving this environment was seen as a significant challenge. School provided a sense of security and purpose through its daily routine and structure. Transitioning out from school for young people with a cognitive disability was often frightening due to the lack of alternative options in terms of education, employment, and sense of purpose.

After finishing secondary school, Angel (aged twenty-four) described his attempts to enter higher education and the barriers he experienced. Angel described receiving mixed messages about 'you can do it' from the education provider, which was followed up with messages about 'you're not going to last long'. Angel talked about no one wanting to help him because his IQ was too low, and teaching staff were not slowing things down to suit his learning needs. Having more robust support during his secondary education to help prepare Angel to undertake further study would have better equipped him. The lack of support closed opportunities for Angel to fulfil his goal.

Leaving school was often considered by many young people with cognitive disability as highly anxiety provoking, as they left the structured daily routine and regular social contact of school to transition to a place of uncertainty, where attending further education or gaining employment were not guaranteed. The destabilising nature of this transition is stressful for most young people, for those with cognitive disability the stress can be, and is, exacerbated by the significant barriers to other opportunities.

Finding Paid Employment

Practitioners and young people described the profound challenges confronting young people with cognitive disability seeking to transition from education to work. Practitioners explained that the education system failed to appropriately prepare young people with cognitive disability for work. They further noted that society and the labour market were often reluctant to see young people with cognitive disability as workers. One practitioner, Dean, who worked in a mental health service, explained that 'a lot of people I've supported in the past have finished school and not known what's next: "What do I do now? I haven't been highly employable or employed in terms of other people's perceptions."'

Failure to accommodate young people with cognitive disability in work environments could result in them being excluded from work or having very short-term contracts. Becky (aged twenty-five) explained that the longest time she had held a job was one month. In part this had been caused by employers being unwilling to comply with their legal duties and make simple adjustments to accommodate the young people. T (aged twenty-nine) explained that his disability (autism and fibromyalgia) required him to be able to adjust the room temperature and have more bathroom breaks. He was initially refused these adjustments until he provided copious medical records, which highlights some systemic discrimination.

For many young people with cognitive disability, the only options for employment are in more structured work environments provided by disability services, or 'precarious work'[3] with poorly paid and insecure conditions. Angel, for example, found traditional employment very difficult, and found working in the more precarious work sector more liberating as he could control his work schedule. Similarly, April described involvement in precarious work as 'it was just something that I could do at my own pace.' Cooper (aged twenty-three) also attempted to work as an independent contractor in a precarious work arrangement, by purchasing camera equipment, after he was excluded from standard work options.

When young people with cognitive disability do get work, then they are more vulnerable than other workers to abuse. Darius, a social worker and advocate for persons with disability from culturally and linguistically diverse backgrounds, gave the example of an African young person with a cognitive disability whom they could not find work for. Later, the young

[3] Precarious work sector includes the part time, self-employed, seasonal, temporary, agency, and casual work where regular employment conditions and benefits are inferior to more 'regular' type work.

person came to them proudly explaining they were working in fruit picking. They were being paid less than half the minimum wage but were happy as they had work. This placed Darius in a very uncomfortable situation: if he ensured the young person had their rights protected, then that young person would not receive any more casual work, thus highlighting the ethical issue of self-determination and exploitation.

Even when young people get work, their experiences of violence can negatively impact upon their ability to work. Amethyst (aged twenty-four) was living with her partner, a perpetrator of domestic violence. Her partner did not like Amethyst working three hours per week, as that was giving her confidence and independence; she had to quit her work and became more isolated as a result. Recognising the intersection of disability and experiences of violence is critical to best support people.

Despite system failures and inequalities in society, the young people with cognitive disability were actively seeking to secure work. Four participants said they were actively seeking work, and one said they were working, indicating this was of profound importance to them. When they were denied their right to work, it had a damaging impact on the young people. Angel (aged twenty-four) noted that he

> struggled to see how I'm supposed to get my independence. I want to physically be able to work. When you meet people, the thing that always gets brought up is, 'What do you do for a living?' I can't say anything, then I get really uncomfortable because I just have to say, 'I'm retarded. I can't do anything.' Because especially on the disability support pension, you either need to be studying or you need to be working. They need to see you do something, and I can't do either. And it's like, 'What do you want me to do?' I go out of my way to do either one. And every time I have done either one, I've had a mental breakdown because people have not been kind to me in those situations. I just want to be treated better anyways. Don't say you support people with disabilities, and then I walk in there and then tell me that I'm not suitable for the job because of my disability. It just doesn't make sense, does it?

When young people were able to exercise their right to work, they felt empowered and regarded the experience as a 'happy' event. The interview with Simon (aged thirty) illustrates the importance of work. When asked about when he was 'really happy', Simon responded 'my first job'.

To enable young people with cognitive disability to transition into work requires increased funding and improving the focus of systems. The young people explained how the system should change. T's lived experience has enabled him to develop a powerful vision for the role of disability employment supports:

> I suppose, in my head, I imagine the dream model being having the systems set up to eventually have to not need itself. A true employment service should be set up to not propel itself to trying to get more business. It should be doing everything it can to have as little businesses as it can. And that's the exploitation there. They're signing people up into their contracts, which are just to keep money coming in for the system.

T's comments provide a critique of disability employment services, which he saw as being more focused on gaining revenue than finding work for young people with cognitive disability.

Long-term employment is possible and should be the focus. Ben (aged twenty-five), a young person with autism, accessed a social enterprise for persons with intellectual disability. The provider focused on providing Ben the support he needed for work. This support was present throughout Ben's work experience and continues in Ben's work today. Ben had the same job for six years at the time of this report.

Service models also need to empower families. Angel, for example, turned to his father to help him find more interesting work and not to disability service providers. Similarly, TBone, a First Nations young person (aged nineteen) turned to his mother and Indigenous service providers rather than disability service providers. Some young people trusted their families more than external supports, while others trusted external supports. Critically, the system should not make young people with disability fit within the system to get help; it is the role of the system to meet the individual needs of young people with cognitive disability to enable them to transition to remunerated work.

8.3 The CRPD on the Importance of Transitions in the Right to Education

The right to education in the CRPD entitles persons with disability to demand support transition through their education journey from kindergarten/preschool to finishing secondary school, through to university and/or into work. The right to work continues the requirement to support transitions and requires states to enable persons with disability to transition through levels of work.

Education Preparing for Work

The CRPD includes state obligations to promote the rights of persons with disability to education (McCallum & Martin, 2013) Article 24 is 'one of the more strongly worded State duties contained in the treaty' (Stein, Barnett, Harpur, Porter & O'Cinneide, in press) and includes eleven paragraphs that provide further detail on what states must do to enable persons with disability to exercise their right to education on an equal basis with others. These obligations are extensive and aimed at providing inclusive education (de Beco, Lord & Quinlivan, 2018). Among the mandated duties are to facilitate 'full and equal participation in education and as members of the community', which requires providing comprehensive accessibility supports (United Nations Committee on the Rights of Persons with Disabilities, 2018, p. 15).

The transformational purpose of the right to education is stated in CRPD Article 24(1), which directs state parties to provide an educational system directed at developing a person's full potential and preparing them to operate effectively in a free society (see, e.g., Article 24(1) (a) and (c). Considering the CRPD provides that persons with disability have equal access to education (Article 24), employment (Article 27), and political activity (Article 28), the education system must prepare students with disability to engage in more advanced studies, participate in the open labour market, and enable them to become leaders of industry, the community, and the state.

The capacity of education to empower persons with disability to become economic actors is increased by the fact that the CRPD does not limit education rights to children, extending access beyond that of the Convention of the Rights of the Child, which limits itself to persons under the age of eighteen and the right to primary school education only. The CRPD has created 'an inclusive education system at all levels and lifelong learning' (United Nations Committee on the Rights of Persons with Disabilities, 2018, p. 14), thereby encompassing vocational, university, and graduate education. This right to lifelong education represents a substantial change in how persons with disability have enjoyed rights protection in this space (Chowdhury, 2011). By expanding the right to education from basic primary schooling to lifelong learning, the CRPD enables students with disability to demand disability-inclusive vocational, university, and graduate school education, under international human rights law for the first time (Harpur & Stein, 2019).

Transitional Rights and Work

Education plays a transformative role in supporting persons with disability to enter the employment market, informing and equipping them to identify and challenge oppressive work relationships. This can include being trained to identify and avoid exploitation, as well as being supported to transition to work arrangements that are compliant with the CRPD. Education plays a pivotal role in supporting persons with cognitive disability to aspire to all work options, not just targeting training to low-level work options, which has typically been the case.

The CRPD entitles persons with disability to demand equality in the labour market and work environment. This includes a work environment that is open, inclusive, and accessible to persons with disability (see Article 27(1)). The CRPD requires states to strive for genuine work equality, which includes the requirement to remove structural inequalities in the regulation of work. This includes not restricting access to employment opportunities and types of jobs, and promoting suitable arrangements such as 'sheltered work' and ensuring equal pay for equal work.

8.4 Conclusion

Safe, secure, inclusive, and appropriately responsive education can create a strong protective support system to scaffold any young person, and particularly young people with cognitive disability. Where this is lacking, it can create additional risk factors for abuse and discrimination. The findings of this research detail both supportive and harmful practices within schools. Young people with cognitive disability felt supported when they were recognised as students who deserved the opportunity to learn, make and maintain friendships, and be listened to. A sense of belonging in school, something that is fundamental to learning, was not always present for young people. If the young person had a history of trauma, this could manifest in complex behaviours and subsequent exclusion from educational environments. Responses from the educational system could lead to cumulative disadvantage, disconnection from peers, social isolation, and poor educational trajectories. The school system could become another source of abuse and neglect for young people, which can severely impact their transition to adulthood. Furthermore, the education system should equip young people to enter the employment market, either through higher education or skills development. Our research identified gaps in the ability to fulfil this responsibility to meet the needs of the young people. As evidenced in this research, Australia still has a long way to go to achieve its obligations under the CRPD. It is apparent that more must be done to ensure quality education for all young people.

CHAPTER 9

Housing, Home, and Mental Well-Being
The Need for Self-Determination and Safety

Accessible Summary

- Young people with cognitive disability deserve to live in a home of their choice.
- They also deserve to get help when they feel mentally unwell.
- This chapter looks at where young people with cognitive disability people live. Many young people felt unsafe where they lived.
- Some young people needed mental health services. It could be hard to trust mental health staff.
- Mental health services were good when staff really wanted to help and listened to the young person.
- Young people with cognitive disability should be helped to make their own decisions.

9.1 Introduction

Like any other young person, young people with cognitive disability can and should be supported to live in a safe home environment and access mental health support if needed as they transition to adulthood. In 2023 the World Health Organisation (WHO) recognised that housing and access to affordable health services of decent quality (including mental health services) are among the social determinant of health (www.who.int/health-topics/social-determinants-of-health#tab=tab_1). Unfortunately, mental health and housing services can also be sites of violence and abuse for young people with cognitive disability. In two sections, this chapter continues discussion on service systems and the experience of young people with cognitive disability of violence and abuse, with a particular focus on housing and mental health supports.

Section 9.2 of this chapter examines young people with cognitive disability's experiences of 'home'. Other research has found that many young people with cognitive disability experience a lack of choice in where they live and whom they live with (Fisher et al., 2021). This section highlights this lack of choice and the subsequent consequences. Housing insecurity, such as what was experienced by some of the young people with cognitive disability in this research, can lead to poor mental health outcomes, such as anxiety and depression (Park & Seo, 2020). Examples of housing insecurity, as well as experiences of financial exploitation and sexual and physical violence by young people with cognitive disability in the context of their living environments are discussed. This section concludes with a summary of what the CRPD asserts are the rights of persons with disability with regard to home. While the CRPD grants persons with disability a right to live independently in the community and to receive the supports they require to do so, our research identified gaps and challenges.

Section 9.3 of this chapter covers young people with cognitive disability's experiences of mental health services. The CRPD grants rights for persons with disability, which involves the right to disability-specific mental health services. Young people with cognitive disability typically experience poorer health outcomes in relation to mental health than the general population and are at heightened risk of mental distress in the transition to adulthood (Whitehead et al., 2021). During this life stage, young people with cognitive disability may experience increased anxiety and loneliness as they navigate changes in living environments, leave school, and seek employment (Young-Southward et al., 2017). In addition, young people with cognitive disability age out of eligibility for many services and are forced to access adult services that may not always cater to their needs (Kramer et al., 2019). This section highlights how many of the young people with cognitive disability in this study experienced abuse and mistreatment at the hands of mental health professionals. In other situations, young people were unable to access mental health treatment when it was needed. When mental health support was appropriately provided, this could act as a protective factor for young people against violence and abuse. This section concludes with commentary on mental health protections for persons with disability as outlined by the CRPD.

9.2 Young People with Cognitive Disability and Housing

The majority of young people who participated in this study lived independently from family in settings that were subsidised by the state or federal government. This included arrangements that were not specific to people with disability, such as community housing settings or public housing. Others, particularly those young people who required considerable assistance in daily living supports, accessed supported accommodation for people with disability. These supports could be provided to the person on their own by a disability service, or the young person could share supports with other people with disability in a group home arrangement. Some young people sought temporary accommodation, often as a result of escaping violence or due to experiencing poverty and/or other hardships. Temporary accommodation included boarding houses and hostels, domestic and family violence shelters, caravans, youth shelters, and homeless shelters. Whatever the housing arrangement, many young people reported less than ideal living environments to support their transition to adulthood.

Putting Up with What Is on Offer

> T (aged twenty-nine): I'm very thankful to have subsidised living, but really, at what cost? I simply just can't afford to live anywhere else.

Access to adequate housing that is safe and secure is recognised as a basic human right and is foundational to other aspects of an individual's well-being. Safe and secure housing is easier to obtain if a young person has a relatively stable life, a supportive educational experience, and adequate remuneration through paid employment. This was often not the case for the young people with cognitive disability in this study. Some young people, particularly those who had been in out-of-home care under child protection orders, had experienced periods of homelessness. Others relied on subsidised living, either through family, community housing arrangements, or public housing. It was likely that most young people with cognitive disability were receiving a disability support pension as their primary means of income, thereby also restricting their financial independence and subsequently their housing options.

Practitioners identified part of their role as supporting young people with cognitive disability to access housing, and for the lawyer practitioners, this included assisting young people with cognitive disability on parole or leaving prison to access accommodation. Significant challenges were identified in these transitions. Annette, a lawyer, highlighted experiences of young people being placed in boarding houses because of the lack of adequate housing for young people with cognitive disability and subsequently experiencing exploitation, including financial abuse:

> Being put in that situation where there's so many people in the one spot.. . . Exploitation is going to happen in those environments.. . . If, for example, . . . all the people on parole who had a disability could go into private rentals or supported housing with only a couple of other people who also had disabilities and had a support worker there, that would be the gold standard. But that's going to be too expensive.

Annette's comments demonstrate how housing support for ex-prisoners is driven by economic considerations, where it is more financially viable to house vulnerable people together, rather than provide safer options that could cater for individual needs, such as those arising from cognitive disability.

Practitioners from a disability employment service also highlighted the lack of appropriate housing for young people with cognitive disability. A young person with cognitive disability, even if they were in supported employment and could live independently, had limited choice. Dylan, the director of an employment service, also had serious reservations about hostel living:

> Because they [young person] can live in a normal environment, . . . they still don't have a large access to housing options. So, I know some of our guys, it's not as bad as it used to be, but [they are] living in hostels in the Valley and places like that, because they've got nowhere else to be.

Dylan referred to 'the Valley', an inner-city suburb that has many nightclubs and venues for entertainment and higher crime rates than other areas in Brisbane (Queensland Police Service Online Crime Map, https://qps-ocm.s3-ap-southeast-2.amazonaws.com/index.html).

Young people with severe and profound cognitive disability may also have difficulties accessing appropriate housing. Two parent participants, Peter (father of Kim) and Angela (stepparent of Danni), had been actively advocating to secure funding for their young people in the long term. Government assistance was not available, so the parents were required to self-fund housing renovations and invest in property to ensure the long-term safety of their young people.

The Precariousness of Housing

While living independently can provide a sense of dignity and achievement for young people with cognitive disability, housing arrangements may not always afford sufficient safety and security. Mary, a social worker, highlighted the risks for young people with cognitive disability in boarding houses and caravan parks, identifying that caravan parks have become more common sources of accommodation, replacing the traditional boarding houses. Mary described these accommodation options as locations where people are 'ripe for exploitation':

> And it comes back to some of that then fundamental stuff around young people with cognitive disability have the right to choose with whom they live, where they live . . . but how do we put those things in place so that that is somewhere that is safe and appropriate for them that doesn't escalate their trauma?

Mary explained that limited options meant that professionals place young people with cognitive disability 'in an environment that's just going to set them up to fail often'. She also referred to unscrupulous and unprofessional practices in boarding houses, citing examples where managers did not record rent being paid, and then asked for it to be paid again, thereby taking advantage of the residents living there.

Public or community housing, which in theory is meant to provide secure and affordable accommodation options, could also be sites of violence for young people with cognitive disability. There were several examples in our research of young people with cognitive disability experiencing abuse from other residents in the same housing complex. Rachel, a First Nations Australian young woman with cognitive disability, was sexually attacked twice in two different public housing units, resulting in her having to move each time, further destabilising her life.

T (aged twenty-nine) experienced considerable instability in public housing. T's childhood had been transient prior to accessing public housing. He had lived in a caravan, unaffordable private rental accommodation, and transitional housing until he could obtain a public housing unit. T described some of the challenges of living in the public housing unit block, including having a neighbour who threatened to kill him with a knife and having his plants smashed. T described being traumatised by this and subsequent experiences of violence living there:

> But I stayed at that unit block and new residents came in. And [the Department of] Housing's not really good at placing people. They placed somebody, a really chronic alcoholic, who caused so many issues. I've been attacked violently by him several times. I got punched, but nothing damaging other than to my mental health. I'd always be taunted and

> verbally abused from him just because he'd drunken a whole goon sack[1] that day type thing.

New tenants also created an unsafe environment. T described two people who would drink,

> to the point there was always broken glass everywhere and the police were constantly called on. Everybody had made complaints, but Housing did nothing about that. They really didn't. So, it got to the point where I had to get so many support letters from doctors saying, 'This is compromising my mental health.' Housing didn't do anything at first, but then I kept getting more people involved, more people involved to pull Housing up for their neglect.

The advocacy undertaken by T to find a safer and more supportive choice in public housing demonstrates an unresponsive system to young people's fundamental needs for security. After much effort, T was able to be moved urgently and was 'assured' it was a safe place. At the time of the interview, he had lived there for three years but described it as being 'horrific' where he has been 'a victim of crime here twice, violent attacks from guests from other units'. T said the impact on his mental and physical health was significant and that he was 'sitting on the edge of getting a diagnosis of PTSD [post-traumatic stress disorder]'. T was currently waiting to be moved to a stand-alone unit due to ongoing issues with other tenants. He had been waiting for about one year.

Amethyst, a First Nations Australian young person with cognitive disability, was targeted by another resident when she first moved into her public housing unit and then subjected to three years of abuse and torture from this man. Amethyst had previously been living in shared accommodation, and her mother pleaded with the service not to move Amethyst:

> So, it was about three months. They weren't able to find anybody suitable for Amethyst to ... So, they came to me and said, 'She can't stay here anymore. The funding's not here.... She's going to have to go into a unit.' And I said, 'No. That is totally against anything that I think is reasonable. Especially in a Housing Commission [Department of Housing] unit, she's going to be vulnerable, she's going to be a target.'

Becky (aged twenty-five) was supported by a community housing provider to live in her own home. While she was very proud of this

[1] 'Goon sack' is Australian slang for wine in a foil sack that has been removed from the box it was sold in.

arrangement, Becky also reported being sexually assaulted by someone who lived on the same floor. The housing service evicted the perpetrator because of this incident.

The practices of placing people with a history of trauma, abuse, and disadvantage in close proximity to others with similar experiences can create additional complexities for all involved. Young people with cognitive disability who may need assistance in building safe relationships can find their safety violated in such settings, as evidenced in this research. While it may be economically expedient for housing providers to offer congregate housing arrangements, it presents an unacceptable to risk to many young people with cognitive disability to further violence and abuse.

Forced Co-tenancy

Several young people with cognitive disability in this study had experiences of living in group homes with other young people with disability, where paid support was shared between residents. Common concerns for young people included incompatibility between residents, housing decisions being predicated on financial imperatives (rather than the young person's safety), and young people feeling powerless to change their circumstances.

Cody (aged twenty-two), who was living in Supported Independent Living (SIL) accommodation with support worker assistance, experienced abuse and neglect from his support workers as discussed elsewhere, but he also commented on his lack of independence and choice. Cody described his living arrangements as being designed for people with high needs who need twenty-four-hour support, which he does not. Cody described trying to move out of the accommodation for some time as it was 'terrible', and the workers did not interact or support him. The main barrier Cody identified was that National Disability Insurance Scheme (NDIS) funding was provided not to him as the service user but to the SIL program, so this restricted his choice to be able to live with support in a more appropriate setting:

> I just basically want an environment that I can truly call my own, because even when I was on a different provider, it still wasn't really my environment because I didn't really have a key or anything at all. And basically, it just feels like I'm being treated like a jailer, basically criminal, but basically a jail.

In this quote, Cody's experience of lack of choice to make his own decisions as to where and with whom he lived is equated with being punished by the disability service system.

The experiences of TBone (aged nineteen, First Nations Australian) further highlight some of the complexities for a young person with cognitive disability in living in supported accommodation when there is a lack of appropriate support. As with Cody, TBone had limited choice and was dependent on the priorities of the service provider. TBone was in an assisted living arrangement with twenty-four-hour support from the age of eighteen years. TBone described the first house as 'terrible' and talked about having other young people living there who were clients of the statutory child protection service. His mother identified how stressful this was for the family and how TBone had been taken advantage of by having money stolen and his property broken. TBone's mother explained:

> They used to pick on TBone, belt him up. Yeah, we were really concerned, because we were really stressed out because we thought that he would be going to a home where other disability people were. Not Child Safety. And that's a completely different kettle of fish.

TBone's parents were living in a caravan at the time and could not have him move in with them, so he remained in this unsafe environment. Subsequent experiences in group homes involved restrictions on TBone's freedom to associate with other young people, failure to provide social stimulation, and passive neglect of TBone's well-being. The impact on TBone was significant, and his housing situation led to his depression and self-harming behaviour.

Not all comments on group homes were negative. Two practitioners, Dylan and Greg, from an employment service, stressed the importance of a 'whole of life' approach by service providers who run group homes. This involved a focus on the quality of care, wraparound 24/7 support, and robust policies and processes to ensure the safety and well-being of the young person. The organisation had met several barriers from the broader community in establishing supported group accommodation, including complaints from neighbours about these homes and villas in their suburb. These neighbours did not want people with disability living in their street. It is important to note here that neighbourhoods also need to be welcoming to young people with cognitive disability, as this can also be an important protective mechanism against abuse.

Housing Options during Times of Crisis

Access to safe accommodation is vital for young people with cognitive disability at times of crisis, for example, escaping domestic and family violence. Rachel, a First Nations Australian young woman with cognitive disability, fled to Brisbane to escape domestic and family violence. Her practitioner, Gabby, said that Rachel was 'being shipped from one place to another and nobody knew how to actually help her feel safe or give her somewhere to recover and feel supported'. It was only when Rachel was engaged with a specialist women's housing support service that the important work of building trust and facilitating her recovery was able to occur.

For young people with cognitive disability who have experienced domestic and family violence, the additional vulnerability created by a system that places them in inappropriate accommodation was highlighted by two practitioners, Chantal and G. Chantal talked about placing a young person with cognitive disability in a motel as creating harm, saying, 'We often see that then, in those places, people experience a secondary trauma and exploitation because they're not given the right supports in that system around their vulnerabilities.'

G, a social work practitioner, also identified challenges to accessing appropriate homeless and domestic and family violence shelters for young people with cognitive disability needing support. Many of these shelters lacked an understanding about cognitive disability and could turn young people away, as G commented:

> The risk of accessing DV [domestic violence] shelters is that, well, they have – I don't know if they overtly say, 'There's a high risk that that young person could share that address,' but I feel like it's a fear, so it's a risk … essentially turning people away because their risk of violence is too high that it could put other people at risk, is the answer.

G's example illustrates the complex decisions emergency housing providers may be forced to make when considering the safety of all residents in a housing shelter. Domestic violence shelters need to maintain the confidential location of their residences and may be concerned that a young person with cognitive disability may mistakenly disclose that information to others.

A group of support coordinators also reported experiences of young people with cognitive disability in homeless or youth supported shelters being evicted from these settings. One young person with physical and intellectual impairment had kicked down the front door of the accommodation because it was jammed, and she could not open it from the outside. At the time, the young person felt that this was the only way they could get back inside to safety. The young person was dismissed from the accommodation and charged with property damage. Another young person, aged fifteen with severe intellectual impairment, was advised that if she did not clean her room she would be dismissed by the accommodation. She was required to sign an agreement that she would do so; however, she could not understand the purpose of the agreement and did not sign it. She was forced into homelessness. Lyn, one of the support coordinators, explained the challenges, 'So that's through mainstream services and a lack of education and understanding around how to best support people with cognitive and intellectual impairments in those settings.' These examples underscore how important it is that services have staff who have the knowledge, understanding, and skills to meet the needs of young people with cognitive disability.

G, a social worker, identified a systemic-level gap in providing crisis housing to young people with cognitive disability. She commented, 'If you need respite housing, NDIS will fund that. But if you're homeless and you want a respite from your homelessness, not funded.' The prescriptive set of supports under the NDIS could create further barriers and challenges for some young people with cognitive disability, perpetuating the cycle of abuse and harm by failing to address crucial issues. G provided the example of a young woman with cognitive disability at risk of homelessness:

> So, there's a young person who I'm thinking of specifically, who experiences homelessness a lot. And in the past, we have accessed her NDIS plan to find short-term accommodation or fund a hotel room. So, there was a long weekend where we were in [COVID-19] lockdown and all the shelters were shut. And basically, it was like she's on the street, we've got X amount of money in her NDIS plan, how can we get the support coordinator on board so that this woman's not homeless for the weekend? Because the other option is violence. Violence or on the street, were the options basically.

A Right to Live Independently in the Community

The inability of young people with cognitive disability to live safely in the community, as reported in this chapter, requires attention from the state. The CRPD frames the right to live independently and in the community as a human right and explains what states must do to realize this right. Article 19 entitles persons with disability to live independently in the community, as autonomous agents who possess the right to decide where to live and with whom. To enable this right to be exercised, Article 19(b) requires states to ensure that persons with disability have access to a range of 'in-home, residential and other community support services, including personal assistance necessary to support living and inclusion in the community, and to prevent isolation or segregation from the community'. Despite this, our research has demonstrated that young people with cognitive disability are having these rights denied or restricted due to government policies and funding. The consequence is that they have experienced further violence, exploitation, and lack of safety.

The CRPD provides guidance on how states must provide supports to enable Article 19 to be realized in its General Comment No. 5 on Living Independently and in the Community (United Nations Committee on the Rights of Persons with Disabilities, 2017). Powerfully, the CRPD Committee explains in General Comment No. 5 that Article 19 requires that states provide 'services that facilitate the transition of young people to adulthood, including support with moving out of the family home, starting employment and continuing into higher education' (Para. 46). The CRPD Committee explains that these supports are 'crucial in supporting independent living' (Para. 76). The CRPD Committee explores these obligations more in the Concluding Observations on States Parties, where the committee explains that these supports are disability-specific. Illustratively, young people with cognitive disability have particular needs that the CRPD Committee requires states to address to enable them to exercise the right to live independently in the community (United Nations Committee on the Rights of Persons with Disabilities, 2019, Para. 38). These supports must also target the broad range of needs that persons have when they are transitioning between living arrangements. These supports must extend to covering the physical and psychological needs of persons with disability (United Nations Committee on the Rights of Persons with Disabilities, 2019, Para. 38; 2022D, Para. 42(c); 2023A, Para. 40(a)). Reflecting this obligation, the CRPD has been critical of some states for failing to provide persons with disability mental health supports related to their right to live independently in the community (United Nations Committee on the Rights of Persons with Disabilities, 2022D, Para. 42(b)).

9.3 Young People with Cognitive Disability and the Mental Health System

This section of the chapter now turns to the mental health system and its part in the lives of young people with cognitive disability. Participants' accounts of the mental health system reflect the complexity involved in supporting young people with cognitive disability who have co-occurring mental illness. While young people with cognitive disability have a comparatively higher need for mental health support than other groups of young people, their access and utilisation of mental health services has been found to be poor (Sinclair et al., 2023; Whittle et al., 2018). The following stories underscore the complexity involved, the lack of trust some young people with cognitive disability had in mental health services, and ultimately the harm that can be inflicted when services fail to take time to build positive relationships with young people. At the same time, other experiences reflect some of the good work with young people with cognitive disability that is occurring through individual practitioners and services.

A Heightened Need for Mental Health Support

A vast majority of the young people with cognitive disability who participated in the research mentioned living with mental health issues. This is consistent with the comments of Matthew, a practitioner, who highlighted the higher incidence of mental health issues for young people with cognitive disability compared with their peers. Matthew noted, 'Adolescents with intellectual disability have a higher incidence than adolescents usually. And that's already a danger point, a risk point for any adolescents, or it's an even high[er] risk point for people with an intellectual disability.'

Chantal, a disability advocate, also stressed that the mental health issues of young people with cognitive disability needed to be addressed, and that often these issues were a result of abuse and violence in the young person's life:

> And the context of how people arrive at this point in their lives and the trauma and the violence and abuse that they have experienced that hasn't been responded to and dealt with and appropriate care provided to help them work through that, that then leads to this place of usually the exacerbation of mental health issues and experiences and then that escalation of behaviours.

Mental health support was vital for young people with cognitive disability who had been in out-of-home care, youth detention, or prison. Annette and Lorraine, both legal practitioners, highlighted the importance of having mental health support available to incarcerated young people with cognitive disability while in prison to be able to meet their needs. Furthermore, establishing these relationships prior to being released could provide an additional safety net for the young person. Lorraine stated:

> Sometimes that's the start of it, is just getting them to acknowledge that, 'Oh no, there's people who do care and can help,' and linking them in with those people and them being able to realise that. So, if that started in prison, maybe that would help when they do reintegrate back into the community as well.

The offer of mental health support was seen by Lorraine as a source of hope for young people with cognitive disability leaving incarceration, potentially assisting the young person to develop trust in helping professionals.

A Lack of Trust and Confidence in Mental Health Services

There were several accounts from young people that suggested a lack of trust in mental health authorities and their ability to support the young person through times of crisis. The story of T, a neurodiverse young person, includes accounts of physical and emotional abuse, restrictive practices, and systemic-level abuse. T has significant mental health issues and was frequently hospitalised and placed under involuntary treatment orders. T reported being given a sedative against his will, being given high doses of sedatives, and having his human rights ignored. T shared a recent hospitalisation for mental health issues:

> Just recently I had to be admitted to the hospital. They put me in under an EEA [Emergency Examination Authority] order,[2] due to they thought I was going to commit suicide, but that wasn't the case at all. I had called up the hospital and I was going to meet somebody from the mental health team there. And they said, 'Yeah, we'll meet you on arrival and talk through some things.' This was after that robbery had occurred and I'd just been shaken up and getting no sleep. I was sleep deprived and every single noise – I was hyper-vigilant with my surroundings. I still am. I'm over-aware of my surroundings to the point it's such a burden.
>
> And the way I was handled in the hospital was ridiculous. Security guards, they wanted to inject me with a sedative, and I said, 'No, you're not going to. You don't know what therapy I've done to not have to have anything of that nature in my body.' So, they had no one there to try to diffuse the situation. They took me to the wrong hospital, to [Hospital 1], when I was meant to go to [Hospital 2]. Security guards absolutely brutally handled me. It was terrible.
>
> They had to overdose me, well, give me a ridiculously high dose, sorry, of the sedative, because it wasn't working. I seemingly just faltered off. During the night, when there was no one there, I just got up and I walked and left the hospital because I'm just like, you know. I don't know how it properly

[2] When needed, ambulance and police officers can issue an Emergency Examination Authority order under the Mental Health Act 2000 (Qld). This authorises a doctor or mental health practitioner to enter premises to detain and examine a person without their consent, to determine whether further assessment of the person's mental state is needed (Treatment and Assessment Orders, MHLaw, mhlawqld.com.au.

> works, but seemingly you give up a lot of your freedom and your rights. Or you don't give it up, they're taken from you.

> And then I was manhandled back into the hospital by the security, and it was just disgraceful. And as soon as the mental health workers came, which was in the morning, they were just like, 'Why are you even here?' They're like, 'You don't seem like someone who needs to be here.' And I'm just like, 'They just mistook my words.'

> I was waiting hours for the ambulance to come, which I've done that by the request of the mental health worker I spoke to on the phone, who I spoke to through Queensland Health. I didn't even call the ambulance or anybody originally, but it took so long that I rung them back and I said, 'What does somebody have to do? Hurt themselves to get attention?'... But it was so barbaric. It truly was. Yeah, that was traumatising.... I'm never going to contact health advisors for my mental health ever again, because they've stripped your rights when it comes to things of that nature.

T's recollection of what happened during this hospital admission included sedation and physical restraint by mental health professionals that he did not consent to and regarded as a violation of his rights. These actions came further under question when he was told the next day by the mental health worker that he did not need to be there. At a systemic level, there was a lack of understanding and responsive service provision to a young person who is neurodiverse. T said this very clearly when he said, 'They stripped your rights.' Whether T presented a danger to himself at the time of admission is difficult to determine, but his account suggests that there was very little discussion with T after the event to help him process what happened. The experience left him wary and untrusting of mental health authorities, and he resolved not to contact them again for help.

Goldie (aged twenty-two), a First Nations Australian young person with cognitive disability who was additionally diagnosed with PTSD, anxiety, and major depressive disorder, had been involved with the mental health system from around the age of fifteen. She was placed in out-of-home care due to what appeared to be significant neglect and emotional abuse from her family. Goldie alluded to a 'shit' experience when attending a particular hospital in relation to her mental health, saying she was 'never going back'. Goldie did not expand on what happened, but her lack of faith in the system to support her was evident.

Cody, a neurodiverse young man, talked about his experiences of first seeing a psychiatrist at the age of thirteen when he was diagnosed with

OCD and how he felt the psychiatrist blamed him for developing this. Cody recalled his experiences with the public and private mental health systems when he was seventeen about to turn eighteen and being taken to a public hospital for mental health support by his father. While Cody was about to age out of youth mental health services, the hospital did not want to place him in an adult mental health ward, as Cody recalled:

> 'Because I don't want you to get abused.'... All the youth services had available ... for someone like me to stay was a tent, which is not the best situation for someone who needs a stable place to stay and learn how to be an adult and deal with new social norms and different rules.

Cody ended up in a private hospital facility where he described experiencing a range of abuses:

> Unfortunately, the hospital was awful. They basically left me in my own filth, they threatened me into taking medication, they gave me a room and a bathroom and a table and a bed. The bed was nice, the bathroom was nice, the TV was nice in my room, but what they did was very awful.
>
> They threatened me into taking medication.... And they came in and said to me, 'If you don't take this pill right now, we'll put you in a public hospital. If you don't take this right now, we'll get security on you.' That's what they said to me, these nurses.

Cody's example indicates that there is a lack of confidence, even amongst mental health professionals, in the ability of adult mental health services to provide a safe environment for young adults with cognitive disability. The safest option for Cody appeared to be a private hospital facility, yet this was an experience where Cody felt disrespected, neglected, and threatened into taking medication.

Dean, a social worker in a community mental health service, discussed how delayed response time by the system could also inadvertently undermine the confidence of young people with cognitive disability to seek help:

> I think one of the other challenges was, for example, you support someone to go to the emergency room, they're experiencing suicidal ideation, they've shared a plan and you'll go to the emergency room, and you'll sit there and you wait and then you wait a bit longer and you wait a bit longer and eventually the young person just gets the shits with it and says, 'Let's just go.' And then you're like, 'Righto, that's all I can do. I'm not going to try and force you to stay here. What am I supposed to do?' So, I guess supporting people to access services, and then for those services to not deliver or not be able to deliver was quite disheartening at times. That obviously hits close to home.

Long waiting lists in mental health services have been identified as problematic for young service users generally, as they fail to address the need for immediate mental health care. Without such care, there is the potential to aggravate mental health symptoms and ultimately lead to service user disengagement (Punton et al., 2022).

Failing to Provide Support

Supporting a young person with a dual diagnosis of cognitive disability and mental illness is a specialised area, which is often under-resourced as there are not enough professionals with appropriate skills and knowledge to work with young people (Kramer et al., 2019). The interplay between the two conditions requires an informed and considered response, which some mental health professionals may find too challenging. Misdiagnosis and a lack of appropriate knowledge and training are significant barriers to young people with cognitive disability finding appropriate mental health support (Whittle et al., 2018). This was the case for David, a twenty-one-year-old man with autism, complex communication needs, OCD, and other mental health issues. David lived with his family, who provided valuable support, but David's access to an appropriate psychiatrist was identified as a significant challenge.

The intersection of cognitive disability, mental health, and a culturally and linguistically diverse background creates even more barriers and challenges to accessing appropriate support. Monica, a disability advocate, shared the story of a young man with intellectual disability who left school at year 10 to attend literacy and numeracy courses at a Technical and Further Education (TAFE) college. The funding for the courses was cancelled, and the young man was expected to take the general course. He had no disability support services when he left school and none while undertaking TAFE. Monica described the impact of the lack of appropriate support:

> Eventually it led to extreme agoraphobia, and he didn't leave the house for five years. He didn't wash, he didn't shower, he didn't cut his nails, he didn't cut his hair, eventually, he wouldn't leave his room. And it got to the stage where people from the other townhouses were complaining because of the smell coming from the home. It was just atrocious.

The young person had supportive parents who were struggling, and while acute mental health services were called in, the young man only communicated with them lying in bed under his doona (duvet or quilt). The assessment was that he was not a danger to himself and therefore not 'an issue they had to deal with . . . it was behavioural, it was to do with his intellectual disability'. His brother called a helpline where they had a psychologist on call who specialised in dual disability and was able to involve the multicultural advocacy service where Monica worked. The young person was subsequently supported by Monica and the manager of the allied health team under Disability Services Queensland,[3] who spent months trying to convince him to leave the home and seek help. Eventually, an application was made for an involuntary treatment order, and he was admitted to hospital. After five years the young person had spent in isolation, he was able to access appropriate psychiatric intervention, and eventually moved out of the family home into supported accommodation. Monica explained the impact of these experiences:

> But the really sad thing was, when he was unwell, he developed ankylosing spondylitis and his neck all fused, all the bones in his neck, his spine fused. So, then he had a physical disability as well. And then a month ago he fell in the bathroom and now he's a paraplegic. So, that was two years after he got out from home, or two or three years, I guess. So, it's very sad. That whole thing is that if the mental health team had helped, or if his GP [general practitioner] could have done something to insist that – and the family saw the GP all the time . . . they knew them well, so I don't know how no one took responsibility for helping that young man or that family with anything. With just Disability Services, 'Oh no, it's Mental Health,' Mental Health, 'Oh no, it's Disability.'. . . And how two teams of Mental Health people could have been in their home and left without doing anything is – I just don't know how they could do that.

This is a stark example of how failure to appropriately assess a young person with cognitive disability can lead to devastating consequences. Monica highlighted the gaps in the systems when there is limited training, and accountability and responsibility: 'They must have seen so much, I guess, that it's no longer their responsibility . . . a normal human being with no medical background would think, "Surely there has to be something I can do to help this family," if you were in there.'

Helpful and Supportive Experiences with Mental Health Services

Where services have been helpful and positive, this has mainly been through individual practitioners and services who have a focus on

[3] Prior to the establishment of the National Disability Insurance Scheme, disability services were funded and operated at the state level in Australia. In Queensland, state-funded disability services was called Disability Services Queensland.

supporting young people with cognitive disability. Effective mental health support also involves having appropriate social and emotional supports that contribute to the overall well-being of the person.

Rachel, a First Nations Australian young person who has an intellectual disability and post-traumatic stress disorder (PTSD), was engaged with community mental health supports when she moved to Brisbane. A key source of support that complemented this has been a group run by a service for domestic and family violence and sexual assault for persons with intellectual disability, which was described by the service's coordinator, Gabby, as

> kind of multifaceted. It's quite a social … group, having a safe place to practice and build relationships for women with intellectual disability who've experienced trauma. And there'd be cooking, art and craft, pampering, self-care, and then a discussion group once a month. So, it'd be a topic that people were interested [in]. So, it's a bit of psychoeducation, but really building safety and recovery through reducing social isolation, a way to have some ongoing contact with the organisation too, because we know people come in and out of dangerous situations or might need feedback on a regular basis without giving up that individual casework all the time. It kind of complements that.

Core to this service was attention to creating a safe and non-confrontational environment for young people who are given the time to develop connections and build trust with others. It is also an environment where practitioners, who understand cognitive disability, can check in on young people's ongoing well-being, provide help as issues arise, and support the young person's access to mental health professionals if needed.

Amethyst, another First Nations Australian young person with cognitive disability, and her mother were also supported by the same service. They were engaged with a 'fantastic psychiatrist and an amazing psychologist', and these were facilitated through the above-mentioned service. Indeed, this service appears to have provided opportunities to empower Amethyst to participate in education and advocacy, demonstrating the power of specialised services that are able to cater to the complex needs of young people with cognitive disability and mental health issues.

Placing the Person with Cognitive Disability Front and Centre: Supported Decision Making

Addressing the challenges in accessing the right health services to meet the needs of young people with cognitive disability was a key message in the research for this book. This involves the need for access to the right services, an integrated approach, and a holistic approach. Participants explained that this this required the voices of young people with cognitive disability to be empowered through supported decision making. This was highlighted by Mary, a practitioner, who talked about the current 'low investment in well-being for people who have disability, particularly cognitive disabilities'. Addressing this requires increasing the investment; Mary explained the current system's

> low expectations of people with disability and lack of appropriately targeted and resourced systems and services to be able to really understand and help them understand what the issues are. For example, mental health issues rely on self-reporting, but the person with a cognitive disability and mental health issues can be dismissed when they self-report, but reports from other professionals are also dismissed

Relatedly, Dean, a social work practitioner, said that

> opportunities like this, for service users to have their voices heard, [are] probably much more important and so much more valuable than something I could share. Yeah. So, more opportunities for people to really express how they're feeling, what they're going through, what kind of supports that they need and what they think would be helpful, I think, is really important.

Echoing this theme, support coordinator Brianna highlighted the importance of 'lived experience and the value of including people with disabilities in these conversations at a high level and hear[ing] that no other experience can compare to that'.

Mental Health Protections and the CRPD

The challenges young people with cognitive disability have reported in accessing mental health services must be addressed. The CRPD provides a frame through which such interventions should be guided. The CRPD contains a right to non-discriminatory access to health. The greatest health innovation with the CRPD is transferring the power from the hands of the medical profession to persons with disability. This is a message that the participants in our research highlighted time and again.

The Right to Health in the CRPD

Out of the twenty-one substantive rights in the CRPD Article 25 focuses on health and Article 26 focuses on habilitation and rehabilitation. The chapeau to Article 25 recognises that persons with disability have a right to access the 'highest attainable standard of health without discrimination on the basis of disability'. Article 25(a) advances this right to health in six paragraphs, including ensuring their equal right to 'the same range, quality and standard of free or affordable health care' and related services provided to the non-disabled general population. These services include sexual and reproductive health, prevention of additional disabilities, and health-related rehabilitation. Article 26 is equally strong, requiring state parties to 'take effective and appropriate measures ... to enable persons with disabilities to attain and maintain maximum independence, full physical, mental, social and vocational ability, and full inclusion and participation in all aspects of life'.

Articles 25 and 26 reflect the general principles of the CRPD that focus on access, equality, full and effective participation and inclusion in society, and non-discrimination between people with and without disability. The principle of equality and non-discrimination is strengthened with the inclusion of Article 5, a stand-alone interpretive article in the CRPD. Article 5 explains that all discrimination on the basis of disability is prohibited, and that state parties 'guarantee to persons with disability equal and effective legal protection against discrimination on all grounds' in the convention. Within this interpretive context, the CRPD Committee in General Comment No. 6 has explained that the articles on health focus on ensuring that the provision of health interventions is not discriminatory, that persons with disability have equal access, and that the measures are appropriate for persons with disability (United Nations Committee on the Rights of Persons with Disabilities, 2018, Para. 89). To be accessible and appropriate, health facilities and services must, at a minimum, be available, adaptable, and include 'the support required by some persons with disabilities (for example those with complex communication requirements, psychosocial disabilities or intellectual disabilities ... during hospitalizations, surgeries and medical consultations)' (United Nations Committee on the Rights of Persons with Disabilities, 2018, Para. 89).

The CRPD and CRPD Committee on Human-Centred Approaches

The right to health is strongly connected with legal capacity and how society views people with a disability. The CRPD Committee has observed in General Comment No. 1 that the denial of legal capacity to persons with disability has, in many cases, led to their being 'deprived of many fundamental rights, including the right to ... found a family, reproductive rights, parental rights, the right to give consent for intimate relationships and medical treatment' (United Nations Committee on the Rights of Persons with Disabilities, 2014, Para. 8). Accordingly, the CRPD has profoundly shifted how law and society must approach young people with cognitive disability. The CRPD rejects all paternalistic approaches to persons with disability and explains that 'persons with disabilities enjoy legal capacity on an equal basis with others in all aspects of life'. The CRPD Committee and scholars have interpreted Article 12 to promote the concept of universal legal capacity (Dhanda, 2012). Essentially, CRPD Article 12 takes the social construct of legal status and establishes a universal right to recognition of subjecthood (Minkowitz, 2017). The CRPD posits in Article 12(2) that 'persons with disabilities enjoy legal capacity on an equal basis with others in all aspects of life'. Mechanisms to protect the legal capacity of persons with disability must 'respect the rights, will and preferences of the person, are free of conflicts of interest and undue influence, are proportional and tailored to the person's circumstances, apply for the shortest time possible and are subject to regular review by a competent, independent and impartial authority or judicial body' (Article 12(4)).

The first step in implementing Article 12 is to remove legal and social structures that deny people with disability rights because they are disabled. 'In order to fully recognize "universal legal capacity", whereby all persons, regardless of disability or decision-making skills, inherently possess legal capacity, States parties must abolish denials of legal capacity that are discriminatory on the basis of disability in purpose or effect' (Article 12). Under the CRPD paradigm, professionals are there to serve their clients and not remove the will of their clients, which was something that was highlighted as occurring in this research.

9.4 Conclusion

Transitioning into independent living is an exciting yet challenging time, for those with and without a disability. The young people with cognitive disability and practitioners in this study have highlighted the additional complexity involved with regard to fundamental rights regarding housing and living with a mental health issue. The young people have highlighted experiences of exploitation, trauma, and violence. Instead of being a fulfilling experience, young people with cognitive disability reported that their rights to live independently in the community and to access mental health supports are being denied. Key systemic-level or macro themes have emerged linked to the rights of the young people with cognitive disability to safe and secure housing reported in Section 9.2. Young people with cognitive disability were often deprived of choice about whom they live with, with choice being reliant on the judgement of professionals and family and constrained by funding. As such this removes the rights of the individual to decide who shares their intimate, personal lives. It is within such contexts that young people with cognitive disability can experience abuse, violence, and neglect. In addition, precarious housing can lead to further mental distress and retraumatise young people with cognitive disability. Living independently and in the community, and with the supports, including mental health supports, to realize this, is framed in the CRPD as a human right, yet this continues to remain elusive for many young people with cognitive disability.

CHAPTER 10

Young People's Experiences of the Child Protection and Criminal Justice Systems

Accessible Summary

- This chapter looks at the Department of Child Safety and the criminal justice system.
- Child Safety often didn't understand that a young person had a cognitive disability.
- Sometimes young people with cognitive disability were abused while they were in Child Safety.
- Young people with cognitive disability often did not get much help when they left Child Safety.
- Parents with cognitive disability often had their children removed from them by Child Safety.
- Some young people were abused by police.
- Young people with cognitive disability who went to prison didn't get much help. They also found it hard when they left prison.

10.1 Introduction

Violence and abuse have devastating consequences for individuals, families, and communities. This chapter examines the part played by professionals in the child protection and criminal justice systems in responding to violence against young people with cognitive disability. Young people and professionals who support them discuss the child protection system, the police, and corrective services, and the role these entities played in the young person's transition to adulthood, often being a central influence on the young person at times of crisis.

Section 10.2 of this chapter explores participants' experiences of the child protection system. Statutory child protection services have a vital function in providing assistance to children and young people who are at risk of, or have experienced, harm, abuse, and neglect. Section 10.3 considers young people's interactions within the criminal justice system. Young people's accounts of reporting violence and abuse to police officers are discussed, and practitioners share concerns regarding the capacity of correctional facilities to keep young people with cognitive disability safe from harm. Both the child protection system and the criminal justice system have overarching aims of individual and community safety, yet their response to young people with cognitive disability often failed to provide these protections.

10.2 Experiences of the Child Protection System

While there is little reliable evidence, at least within the Australian context, of the prevalence of children and young people with disability in the child protection system (Broadley, 2015), many authors both in Australia (e.g., Cheng et al., 2023) and internationally (e.g., Hill et al., 2017) report their over-representation in these systems. Child protection services have been criticised for their lack of adaptability towards children and young people with disability in their care, including children and young people with cognitive disability (Stalker et al., 2015). The findings of this research indicate that more could be done by child protection professionals in recognising and responding to young people with cognitive disability who are in care arrangements.

The Invisibility of Cognitive Disability

According to practitioners in this study, children and young people's cognitive disability were often not recognised or diagnosed by child protection services, which resulted in significant gaps in the level of support the young person was able to access, both while in care and then once they left care.

Lyn, a support coordinator, recalled working with a young man with cognitive disability. She spoke of child protection services 'refusing to acknowledge' the intellectual impairment of the young person, despite evidence, and instead seeing his behaviour as trauma-related due to his history of interaction with his mother. Lyn worked for eighteen months to have the young person reconnected with National Disability Insurance Scheme (NDIS) support, experiencing significant barriers from child protection staff who disregarded the impact of the young person's disability. Examples such as this highlight the systemic-level neglect of this young person and his parent, by not recognising and believing that he had a cognitive disability. Lyn explained:

> There's a lot of people who just make the assumption, 'Oh, it's because of trauma.' And I think everyone really needs to work in this area with a trauma-informed framework, but I think they also need to have an understanding of how disability impacts and creates trauma as well. Not just that the person has a trauma history, but sometimes there's a lot of other stuff underneath that you need to work really hard to identify.

The clear message from practitioners has been for child protection systems to listen to external clinicians in identification and recognition of cognitive disability rather than working on their own. Failing to utilise this expertise could lead to 'potentially subconscious bias' in child protection assessments, as commented by Brianna, another support coordinator.

G, a practitioner who supported young people with cognitive disability leaving care, reported working with several young people with cognitive disability who were self-placing and 'fell off the radar of Child Safety, and their disability . . . [was] never diagnosed officially, whether it had been observed at all'. These young people could find themselves homeless and living in poverty, with no resources to obtain disability assessments to access the NDIS.

Emma, another practitioner who worked with young people with cognitive disability, also identified the complexity for this group leaving care because they do not have access to their history, including formalised assessments, or have not been assessed formally. Emma, as others, identified that there are many young people with cognitive disability who do not understand their entitlements because of a lack of information recorded about their disability.

Failing to Protect

Sadly, the system designed to protect children and young people can sometimes fail in its primary purpose. G, a social work practitioner, talked about the risks of sexual assault to children and young people with cognitive disability in out-of-home care. G provided the example of a young Aboriginal man with cognitive disability she worked with recently who shared that he had been sexually assaulted by a kinship carer with whom he had been placed, over an extensive period. G highlighted the complexity involved in identifying safe people with whom young people can be placed, the importance of connection with community and kin, and the dilemma when the people who were identified as being safe end up harming the young person.

G also provided an example of child protection authorities failing to fully comprehend the world of a young person with cognitive disability:

> Here's a young person that I work with ... she's still in the care of Child Safety, and they are limiting her go card.[1] ... But part of her disability and how she communicates and connects with the world is through public transport. She's not currently engaged in school at the moment, so she can't get a student concession, she's not old enough to get on DSP [disability support pension], so she doesn't have an adult concession. So, she needs to be on an adult go card and Child Safety don't want to fund it for her to have the freedom that she needs to live her life. And it's a back and forth that we're trying to figure out.

These seemingly minor decisions could create a very negative impression for the young person and how they related to Child Safety officers, how they self-regulated their behaviours, and how they survived their young adulthood.

A lack of understanding of the young person can result in devastating consequences. TBone, a First Nations Australian young person with cognitive disability (aged nineteen), ended up in out-of-home care for about six weeks when he was a young child. His mother could not cope with his behaviour, which was triggered by sexual abuse. TBone, who was experiencing significant trauma, was placed in care. This propelled his anger and aggression, resulting in police being called out a few times to the group home in which he lived. The use of police as a form of behaviour management speaks to a common situation of the criminalisation of young people in care because of their trauma. The lack of appropriate supports to work with this highly traumatised child with cognitive disability led to feelings of despair in TBone's mother.

In contrast, there were some findings in this research that indicated positive experiences with the child protection system. For example, Darius, a practitioner who worked with families from culturally and linguistically

[1] A go card is an electronic smartcard ticketing system that is used to access public transport in South East Queensland.

diverse backgrounds, reported a positive response from Child Safety officers for a family he worked with where there was sexual abuse of the child with cognitive disability. The family was provided with a lot of support and were placed in a safe house. Both examples demonstrated that better outcomes were achieved when child protection officers communicated effectively with young people and families, and actively provided resources to ensure the young person's and family's safety.

Leaving Care: From Over-dependence to Being on Your Own

An important issue identified by several practitioners was how the child protection system 'institutionalised' children and young people with cognitive disability by constantly making decisions for them. This strong level of control could create a sense of 'over-dependence' for support – yet when the young person with cognitive disability moved out of this system, there was very little, if any, support. Only three of the young people interviewed in this research had experienced being placed in the out-of-home care system – Milly, Goldie, and TBone – however, for all three, they identified issues with care and support, and for Milly and Goldie, this was particularly related to leaving care and the lack of support. Practitioner Emma captured this when she said that

> for any young person transitioning, it's very instantaneous, unprepared, especially in the housing space because, depending on their circumstances, it's quite tough to get into stable accommodation . . . I think it's tricky to go from such an institutionalised, over-dependence from Child Safety, when change can already be such a challenge for a lot of people with cognitive disability.

In this regard, involvement in out-of-home care for young people with cognitive disability could thwart a young person's independent living skills and lead to greater vulnerabilities upon leaving care.

Brianna, a support coordinator, provided an example of a young person in Victoria who was in the child protection system who was expected to work out how to become independent on his own:

> He was a very, very angry young man when I met him because he had just been told that on his eighteenth birthday, he was going to literally be given a duffel bag of his possessions and be taken, basically, to a local homeless charity and that would be it. He didn't have a very effective case manager from the child protection space, or she found that he was support-resistant and said, 'Well look, if you're not going to invest in yourself, I'm not going to invest in you.' We did some really hard work together, really, really

> quickly using his NDIS support coordination funding. And one of his friends, who he was a co-tenant [with], didn't get linked to the NDIS and actually became homeless. Whereas my client was supported to actually find market rental with some other people with life[long] diagnosis and is still residing there with obviously adolescent challenges, but he's safe.

The input and advocacy from Brianna to assist the young person with cognitive disability to navigate the private rental market avoided the situation of the young person having to access a homeless shelter. This ultimately led to a more stable transition out of care.

A further challenge identified by several practitioners was that when young people with cognitive disability left care, like many young people who leave care, they were more vulnerable to returning to families of origin as a means of finding support and connection. This could lead to experiences of exploitation. Mary, a practitioner who worked with this group, talked about a young man with cognitive disability who returned to his family of origin – this consisted of a biological parent, a non-biological parent, and siblings. The young man was told he had to work and provide financial support to the family. Over time it became evident that the family were exploiting him – he had no money left over after paying rent and was responding to constant requests for money from other family members. Mary explained that the family would say:

> 'Give me some money for smokes or we'll throw you out.' Well, what are you going to do? You're going to give someone money for smokes because what do you do if you're homeless? You've got no one to turn to unless you've got someone to turn to. I think that broke down and then he moved with one of the siblings . . . and that got a bit interesting.. . . So, the sibling, [who] . . . was a brother and a partner, they were still doing financial exploitation. He was sharing that a lot more, but they were trying to drive a wedge with his supports.. . . Isolate him. So, there was a couple of things where he was like, 'I got in trouble because you came into the house.'

Intervention in these cases can involve careful consideration on the part of the worker as to how to navigate the relationships the young person has with extended family.

In many instances, it may be appropriate for a young person exiting the care of child protection services to return to their family of origin. It may be that the living situation in the family home has changed, and the issues that led to the young person entering care have improved or resolved (Mendes et al., 2012). Unfortunately, young people with cognitive disability may not have a choice other than to return to their family of origin, because of the lack of other supports available (Broadley, 2015). The above example illustrates that this may lead to further exploitation and isolation from disability supports.

Parents with Cognitive Disability

Discussions about the child protection system would be incomplete without some mention of the experiences of parents with cognitive disability. Practitioners in this study commented on the over-representation of this group of parents in child welfare matters. Amy, a mother with cognitive disability who had three children who were placed in out-of-home care, also shared her story. Amy's experiences verified practitioners' accounts that it is often the default position of child protection authorities to remove a child from birth when the parent has a cognitive disability.

The removal of children from parents with cognitive disability was referred to by practitioners as a cyclical process spanning several generations. A young person with cognitive disability, often a woman, could be faced with little support to parent her child, and the child is subsequently removed from her care by child protection authorities. This child may later become a parent, and the pattern is repeated. Emma, a practitioner, described this process:

> So we see those young people [with cognitive disability] go through the whole re-trauma, it's re-traumatising them through their own Child Safety experience of being removed.... And some of the limited family intervention services available, they're not even equipped to deal with young people who have disability themselves. And just the expectations in placement agreements and in initial orders of what they expect from the parents seem to be default for every parent, whether they have disability or not, which I don't think is fair.

According to Emma, accommodations were not made by the child protection system for parents with cognitive disability in terms of family intervention services, placement agreements, and initial orders.

Leanne, a social worker who almost exclusively works with parents with cognitive disability, reported that at one stage in her practice career she was working with ten parents, and eight of these had their children removed. She attributed these parents' over-representation to several factors, including the greater likelihood that persons with cognitive disability experience domestic and family violence, and are more likely to have mental health issues. Problematic substance use could also contribute to child safety involvement. Leanne also surmised that societal attitudes played a part in this pattern:

> I think a lot of people struggle with the concept that people with disability, particularly intellectual disability, have sex and that they have the right to have children. We're still in the generation where people were legally sterilised.... I have had two women say to me that when they were pregnant and Child Safety came on the scene, which is early, always, [they] offered to take them for an abortion, which the parents find extremely upsetting. They are made to have contraception. They are made to have those things in their arm [contraceptive injection], so they don't get pregnant again. And if they don't do it, it's used against them, that they're not being compliant and they're not working with Child Safety.

Leanne's account highlights eugenicist attitudes towards parents with cognitive disability, and undue pressure on this group of parents to conform to departmental expectations.

Leanne explained that for most of the parents she works with, child protection contacted them in hospital before the birth or at the birth of the baby. In talking about this, Leanne highlighted an attitude that she has seen where the mother is viewed as incompetent and incapable because of their disability. She provided the example of a young mother in her early twenties with cognitive disability. Leanne was asked to support this mother's access to the NDIS, but the hospital had also contacted child protection authorities who in turn were trying to appoint the Adult Guardian as her guardian, thus removing her independence in decision making.[2] Leanne explained that the mother had a Queensland Civil and Administrative Tribunal (QCAT)[3] hearing she was not even aware was happening. This example shows a denial of the person's rights to information, as well as discriminatory and ableist attitudes from the child protection system. Leanne added:

> The other thing Child Safety do too, because they've got an intellectual disability, they discredit everything they say. So if the person says something, they go, 'Oh no, she didn't know what she was talking about' or, 'She didn't say that.'

This discrediting of parents with cognitive disability was seen to permeate everyday interactions with child protection staff.

Emma shared the following story of a young woman with cognitive disability, which shows that ableist attitudes are present in other systems with regard to parenting capacity:

[2] Now referred to as the Public Guardian in Queensland, the Public Guardian can be appointed to make personal, health, and legal decisions for adults with impaired decision-making capacity.

[3] QCAT reviews decisions concerning adults with impaired capacity, as well as care decisions related to children and young people.

> I have a young mother who [has] ASD [autism spectrum disorder], ADHD [attention deficit hyperactivity disorder], BPD [borderline personality disorder]. She's become a mum in December 2020, her child has been removed. And how that came about was, in the initial six weeks of giving birth she was struggling at home, so she reached out for help through the public mental health system, and she went into a facility at [suburb] where they actually take in mothers and bubs to support them with their mental health issues at the time.

Even though the young woman voluntarily sought help, the professionals at the centre determined that her disability was 'too significant' and that she could not care for her child. The young woman reportedly responded, 'I don't know. I've never looked after a baby before. I don't have my parents around to role model. I would like help ... but there are no programs who will do it my style.'

Emma felt the young woman needed support that involved consistent repetition, and someone who understood her learning style:

> But no one could provide that. There [were] ... different nurses every night. They're just looking at the notes that are black and white of, 'She yelled at her child and got enraged.'... They're just looking at that and just saying, 'Oh, she's incapable. She has a disability.' But she has the capacity. I believe she has the capacity if she had the right supports, but it doesn't exist. So I can't even do a referral, and that's really heartbreaking.

This young person now has mental health issues and has a near impossible task of meeting the unrealistic expectations of the child protection system, which appears to not have made any allowances for her disability. Emma, as with others, highlighted the importance of prevention and early intervention, talking about how different this may have been if a robust NDIS plan could have provided her with consistent support workers and supported accommodation.

Amy (aged thirty) has three children in the care of the child protection system: a three-year-old whose father is incarcerated, a five-year-old (diagnosed with post-traumatic stress disorder (PTSD) and ADHD), and a six-year-old. Amy and her support worker identified that she has never had it explained to her why her children were removed; her experiences with the child protection system have been discriminatory and unhelpful. Amy reported that child protection authorities did not ever make the time to listen to her. Amy identified further discrimination when she said, 'And I know we're not a family they want to help and do anything and everything for. We're a family that are victims to the system.'

Amy talked about her current child protection workers being rude to her, cutting her off when she wanted to talk with them. Importantly, Amy stood up to this, telling the person that they were being rude and not listening to her. This would have taken considerable courage given how disempowered her position was. Amy talked about her contact visits with her children being moved back to the child protection office and the consequences of this:

> So I challenged the CSO [Child Safety Officer] a little bit and I said, 'What's your reason for putting this back in the office?' and she didn't give me a clear answer, and I just said, 'Being a CSO, you should be aware that you do not put a child, ADHD and a list miles long . . . in a closed room with absolutely nothing to do, for him to kick the walls and bounce off your walls.' And then because I spoke up for him and tried to advocate for him, they said all contact is suspended. So instead of trying to find somewhere in the community for him to go, that meets his needs and his challenging needs, they've decided, 'Well, we'll just cut contact and suspend it indefinitely.'

Speaking up against decisions made by CSOs appeared to lead to further punishment, victimisation, and barriers erected in contacting her children. Amy challenged this decision, taking it to QCAT, which was a significant step, demonstrating her determination and advocacy skills.

Matthew, a manager of a disability agency, pointed to the lack of a dedicated service to support parents with cognitive disability. His agency had made many attempts over several years to address the gap in service delivery, without much success. The agency has recently engaged with the relevant child protection department in their state to have further conversations about the issues. The agency has also created a parent educator/ family worker position to support parents in that space, which is funded through the NDIS. Matthew identified some of the challenges:

> Although even there, to do that, to put that in place, to try and build the referrals, all the rest of it, you've got a three-month investment before you actually have money to pay for the worker. And then it's just such a messy system that persuading support coordinators, going through, it's got to be in people's plans. It all doesn't match up at all.

For Matthew, creating specialised supports for parents with cognitive disability involved dedicated action and a willingness to work within an inflexible bureaucratic system.

Human Rights and Child Protection Services

The challenges young people experience with the child protection system should be framed within a human rights perspective. The experiences reported above by participants often amount to human rights violations. Children and young people with cognitive disability have a right to receive protection and support from the state to enable them to have an equal right to family. These rights can be divided into rights targeted at children with a disability and rights targeted at people with a disability who seek to start their own families.

Rights that protect children with a disability can be sourced in the Convention on the Rights of the Child, as well as in the CRPD. The Convention on the Rights of the Child is a United Nations specialist human rights convention which addresses children. Despite the relevance of disability to all rights in the Convention on the Rights of the Child, the particular vulnerability of children with a disability is referenced only in Article 23 (Harpur & Stein, 2019). Article 23 provides children with a disability an equal right to primary education; however, it does not address schooling beyond childhood. The committee governing the Convention on the Rights of the Child, the United Nations Committee on the Rights of the Child, has issued several General Comments relevant to where childhood interacts with state child support authorities. In particular, in General Comment No. 17 on the right of the child to rest, leisure, play, recreational activities, cultural life, and the arts (paragraph 31) (2013; www.refworld.org/legal/general/crc/2013/en/96090), the Committee on the Rights of the Child recognises the vulnerability of children with disability in residential institutions and requires the state to ensure such services are delivered in a non-discriminatory way. Further, General Comment No. 17 requires that the state enables children with a disability to engage in cultural and recreational activities on an equal basis as others.

Whereas the Convention on the Rights of the Child is a child-focused convention that recognises the particular vulnerability of children with a disability, the CRPD is a disability-specific convention that recognises the particular vulnerability of children with disability. In particular, the CRPD Article 7 is a cross-cutting article that requires states to take additional measures to protect and empower children with a disability when addressing all articles in the CRPD (Bantekas, 2018). The CRPD Committee, in its Concluding Observations on States, has illustrated how this duty operates. Illustratively, in its Concluding Observation on Australia, the CRPD Committee recommended that Australia ensure children with disability have access to quality and human rights-based early intervention mechanisms (United Nations Committee on the Rights of Persons with Disabilities, 2019, Paras. 14(b)–(d)). Where children with a disability were Indigenous, then this support must also include culturally suitable support in their local community (Para. 14(d)). Recognising the importance of hearing the voices of all children with a disability, the CRPD Committee also recommended that Australia provide age-appropriate support and accommodations to this cohort to enable them to express their views in all matters that affect their rights or interests (Para. 14(c)).

The focus in the CRPD on enabling persons with disability to voice and exercise family rights extends to a right to access reproductive services and have a family. Persons with disability have a sustained history of being subjected to forced abortions and sterilizations, and having their children forcibly removed (Fiala-Butora, 2018). As a consequence, the CRPD takes a strong position on mandating that states protect persons with disability's right to access reproduction services and to have a family. These obligations appear in the cross-cutting Article 6, on girls and women with a disability, as well as in other articles, including Article 16, on freedom from exploitation, violence, and abuse; Article 25, on health; and Article 23, on respect for home and the family. Article 23(1) states that persons with disability must have access to family planning information, retain their fertility, and be provided access to reproductive services. Further, the CRPD provides that in no case shall a child be separated from their parents on the basis of a disability of one or both of the parents (Article 25(4)). The CRPD Committee, in General Comment No. 3, has called upon states to combat eugenic stereotypes that hinder the rights of persons with disability in relation to producing and caring for their family (United Nations Committee on the Rights of Persons with Disabilities, 2016, Para. 39).

The next section of this chapter discusses the challenges young people with cognitive disability encounter with the criminal justice system.

10.3 Young People with Cognitive Disability and the Criminal Justice System

Young people with cognitive disability can encounter authorities from the criminal justice system for many reasons. Several Australian studies have identified a high incidence of police contact among people with cognitive disability as both offenders and victims (Dowse et al., 2021; Office of the Public Advocate, 2012). Young people with cognitive disability often begin this contact with the criminal justice system from an early age, and the likelihood of contact may be greater for those young people who have a history of child protection involvement (Baldry et al., 2016). Within the Australian context, Aboriginal and/or Torres Strait Islander young people with cognitive disability are significantly more likely to experience early and frequent contact with the criminal justice system (Baldry et al., 2015). Where people with cognitive disability do make contact with police, often their evidence is discounted and ignored (Douglas & Harpur, 2016). This section of the chapter discusses findings regarding the interactions of young people with cognitive disability with the police and practitioners' reports on how young people with cognitive disability fare in correctional settings. The involvement of criminal justice authorities in the lives of young people with cognitive disability often added further trauma and systemic abuse to their transition to adulthood.

Young People and the Police

A common recommendation by participants was the need for a better trained and more skilled police force for responding to young people with cognitive disability. The stories of participants demonstrated many examples of police responses that were unhelpful, traumatising, re-traumatising, judgemental, discriminatory, racist, and abusive.

There were several examples in this research where families have approached police to report abuse but have not been believed and, in some instances, treated disrespectfully. Being told no action would be taken against a charge of sexual abuse, for example, because the young person with cognitive disability would not make a reliable witness, denies the child or young person and family the right to justice.

A person and/or family not being believed by police that abuse has occurred is a systemic-level failing. TBone's mother spoke of the impact:

> I was shattered. I was absolutely shattered. And yeah, my husband was very shattered too. Just so shattered that we couldn't do more for TBone, and basically get justice. Because yeah, it was just all turned back in on us.

TBone and his family are First Nation Australians who are known to be over-represented in child protection and criminal justice systems. TBone's behaviour, exacerbated by his experiences of sexual abuse, became difficult to manage. His mother contacted the Department of Child Safety to ask for help, and TBone was then placed into care. This example shows how the systemic-level response contributed to the stressors on the family to cope with their child.

Amethyst, an Aboriginal young woman with cognitive disability, also experienced systemic-level abuse in her interactions with police. Her story, described in Chapter 4, showed how police offered her little protection from a perpetrator who horrifically abused her over three years. Her mother advocated and pleaded to authorities to no avail. Amethyst's mother recalled,

> On Boxing Day morning I got a phone call from somebody from the vulnerable adult unit, you'd think that's what their job is, a vulnerable adult. She rang me and she said, 'We went out. Covered in bruises from head to toe, but we asked her if she wanted to leave and she said, "No."'

Amethyst's mother felt the police had no understanding of Amethyst's disability and failed to keep her safe.

Mary, a practitioner, also described the difficulties for young people with cognitive disability where the police either dismiss the disability or do not recognise it. She shared an example where failing to follow procedure and arrange for a third person to be present at an interview could lead to exploitation of the young person with cognitive disability. Mary had approached the police officer concerned and said:

> 'You can't question him until there's someone there to support him because of his [cognitive disability].' He's like, 'Who do you think you are? What do you think . . ..' The police officer was trying to dress me down because I was pointing out to him . . . that he was going to do the wrong thing if he questioned him. We had police officers drive around another gentleman, who was highly suggestible, highly vulnerable, and he admitted to one break and enter he'd been involved in, they'd been driving around the area, to every single break and enter in the area and said, 'Did you do that one?' He's like, 'Yes.' 'Did you did [*sic*] that one?' 'Yeah.' 'Did you do . . .' Wasn't involved in the other one. So he then ended up with multiple charges out of all different areas. And he then told us, after the fact, what had happened, because we were a trusted people.

It is hard to determine whether the failure to include a support person was an oversight by police officers in this example. Yet it is also clear that there was much to be gained by not involving a third party, including greater expediency in the police officers' investigations and, as in the latter example, a compliant suspect who was willing to confess to multiple crimes. Chantal, a disability advocate, also referred to similar practices where a young person's cognitive disability was ignored or not considered by police. She felt that attending to the disability at an early intervention point would prevent the young person's further enmeshment within the criminal justice system.

Young People and the Prison System

Many young people with cognitive disability who enter the prison system have a history of trauma arising from histories of social disadvantage and discrimination (Ellem, Denton, & Davidson, 2020). Custodial environments can leave young people with cognitive disability susceptible to abuse, violence, and exploitation by other prisoners and in some instances prison staff (Eriksson et al., 2019). Annette, a solicitor who supported people in prison, conveyed how vulnerable young people with cognitive disability can be within the prison system. She provided an example of a young person with cognitive disability who was placed in solitary confinement because of their undiagnosed behaviours and the impact this had:

> The only way they can get out of solitary is to change that behaviour, but it's not possible without – it might be possible if they had like a twenty-four-hour support worker, but not in a prison environment. It's not going to be possible, and so it just makes the actual situation worse. And you get it with mental health as well or people with mental health conditions that can't be treated or aren't able to be treated in prison and they have to comply with things like certain behaviours, not do certain behaviours in prison, and it's just not going to happen. It's the same with cognitive disability, is that you can't expect people to behave in a certain way when they can't, and then they get treated worse because they'd get restrained, get put in solitary and that sort of thing.

Annette illustrates here that the response by the correctional system to behaviours that challenge may actually perpetuate those behaviours. Prolonged exposure to solitary confinement can have a lasting effect on the young person's mental health.

Transitioning into adulthood in the prison system brings unique challenges for young people with cognitive disability. Their daily life is so structured and predictable with limited choices to make. This structured environment can impede a young person's understanding of how things operate in the outside community, and the young person may struggle to develop appropriate life skills, for example, paying bills and living independently. Lorraine, another solicitor in this area, elaborated:

> I've worked with guys who are obviously quite significantly cognitively impaired, and they seem to be able to manage the prison environment quite well. Again, I think it's like there's that structure and they know it's very black and white, I suppose, you can do this, you can't do that. And they seem to be able to mostly manage that, or at least their prison records would suggest that, because I have worked with guys like that . . . perfect records in prison. They don't seem to step out of line while they're in jail, but the minute they get out of jail they can't cope.

The lack of programs in place to support young people with cognitive disability in prison and to support their re-entry into the community, including the development of independent living skills, is another form of systemic neglect.

CRPD and the Criminal Justice System

The neglect and failures that participants in this research have reported with the criminal justice system often amount to human rights violations. The CRPD framework recognises that persons with disability may interact with legal systems differently, and that they may require adjustments and support, but this does not diminish their right to full and equal participation in the justice system. CRPD Article 12 declares that persons with disability have a right to equal recognition before the law. Persons with disability enjoy legal capacity on an equal basis with others in all aspects of life (CRPD Article 12(2)). As declared by the CRPD Committee's first General Comment, this extends to full and effective participation in the criminal justice system, including as an accused, complainant, witness, juror, lawyer, or judge (United Nations Committee on the Rights of Persons with Disabilities, 2014, Para. 38). To ensure effective access to justice for persons with disability, state parties must promote appropriate training for those working in the field of administration of justice, including police and prison staff (CRPD Article 13(2)). CRPD Article 13(1) further explains that states must make adjustments and provide support to enable persons with disability to fully and effectively exercise their right to justice. In Concluding Observations on States, the CRPD Committee has raised concerns about failures to realize Article 13 for people with cognitive disability, and variously called for state parties to ensure this group are able to act as full parties in litigation (United Nations Committee on the Rights of Persons with Disabilities, 2022D, Para. 30(a)), can appear as witnesses (United Nations Committee on the Rights of Persons with Disabilities, 2023B, Para. 28(a)), and are provided the supports they need to participate in proceedings (United Nations Committee on the Rights of Persons with Disabilities, 2019E, 26(a)). Information should be provided in accessible formats, such as Easy Read (United Nations Committee on the Rights of Persons with Disabilities, 2021A, Para. 28(c); 2022J, Para. 28(a); 2023C, Para. 28(b)), and people with cognitive disability should be able to fully access all judicial premises (United Nations Committee on the Rights of Persons with Disabilities, 2019F, Para. 26(b)). Unfortunately, the experiences reported by participants in this section illustrates that more needs to be done to ensure human rights can be fully exercised.

10.4 Conclusion

This chapter has examined the part played by professionals in the child protection and criminal justice systems in responding to violence against young people with cognitive disability. First, this chapter analysed participants' experiences of the child protection system and considered these experiences within a human rights framework. Young people with cognitive disability who have experienced violence, abuse, and neglect can come into contact with the child protection system when they are children and also later as young adults who are trying to raise their own children. Despite being frequent users of this system, participants reported a lack of recognition, knowledge, and appropriate responses to young people with cognitive disability.

Lack of recognition of cognitive disability was reported to occur for children and young people under child protection orders, with an unconscious bias to understanding behaviour purely through a trauma-focused lens, rather than also taking into account the impact of cognitive disability on communication and learning. This lack of recognition of the additional needs of young people with cognitive disability was evident in the neglect experienced by young people leaving care. Conversely, the cognitive disability of young people who were parents was seen to be the defining factor in determinations by the system of fitness to parent. Practitioners spoke of patterns of reporting rather than supporting parents with cognitive disability, and professionals who sought to help parents with their parenting role faced further challenges in ensuring the NDIS system could provide appropriate resources. Section 10.2 analysed how the challenges experienced by participants should be understood as human rights violations.

Section 10.3 examined young people's experiences with the criminal justice system, and reported that young people's experiences of the criminal justice system were shaped by the system's lack of understanding of their cognitive disability and an absence of appropriate skills of authorities to respond effectively to this group. These failures were present in interactions with police, where young people with cognitive disability and family members felt their stories of abuse were not believed; the young person's disability was not recognised or ignored; and the appropriate procedure of accessing support was not followed. Practitioners reported that if a young person with cognitive disability were to enter prison, they could experience excessive periods of isolation and restrictive practices, as a result of the prison trying to manage the young person's behaviours. In addition, young people with cognitive disability in prison ran the risk of failing to develop appropriate life skills to live on the outside as young adults.

Experiences of violence and abuse can lead to young people with cognitive disability becoming enmeshed in the criminal justice system. While the police are vital stakeholders in the reporting of abuse, this research has found that they are not always reliable. The path from being a victim of abuse to an alleged offender appeared to be a common transition for some of the young people with cognitive disability in this research. Without an appropriate response from criminal justice authorities and the broader community, the cycle of violence and trauma can continue for young people with cognitive disability who become incarcerated. These failures amount to human rights failures, and more action is required to ensure that young people with cognitive disability are able to interact with the criminal justice system appropriately.

CHAPTER 11

Having Someone in Your Corner

Accessible Summary

- Family, friends, partners, and pets can help young people with cognitive disability as they become adults.
- Some young people with cognitive disability had families who spoke up for them and helped them when times were hard.
- Some young people with cognitive disability had partners who helped them feel good about themselves.
- Friends could help young people with cognitive disability leave abusive situations.
- Professionals can do more to help young people with cognitive disability make friends and be part of their community.

11.1 Introduction

Informal support networks, including family, friends, and intimate relationships, are influential in both protecting young people with cognitive disability from violence or, conversely, increasing the risks of young people experiencing abuse (Crowley, 2016; Johnson, 2020). For example, biological parents are often reported as the main perpetrators of abuse and neglect of children and young people with disability (Nyberg et al., 2021), yet parents also can play an essential role in advocating with or on behalf of young people with cognitive disability (Walmsley et al., 2017).

Section 11.2 of this chapter shares the accounts of young people with cognitive disability, family members, and professionals on the role of informal support networks in shaping the transition to adulthood. The advocacy efforts of and support from family members are acknowledged, as well as the positive influence of friendships, intimate relationships, and even pets in a young person's life. These experiences are juxtaposed with other personal accounts from young people of pain and hurt from unsafe and unsupportive relationships with informal networks.

Section 11.3 examines the CRPD in relation to family and other supports in the lives of young people with cognitive disability. Section 11.3 analyses the protection afforded by pets in the lives of young people with cognitive disability and how families are regarded as sources of both support and risk.

11.2 The Role of Informal Support Networks in Shaping the Transition to Adulthood

Family members can play an important role in the lives of young people with cognitive disability. Positive informal supports can contribute to feelings of safety, being heard, and happiness. Intimate relationships can have positive and negative impacts, depending on the nature of the relationship. Friendships and an informal support network outside the family are fundamental to the well-being of young people with cognitive disability. Pets can form part of an informal support network. The opposite to protective and positive informal support networks are negative, dysfunctional, or absent networks. Families can be unable or unwilling to support young people with cognitive disability. Practitioners identified the importance of assisting young people with cognitive disability to develop positive informal supports.

Family Advocacy

Family members can hold the most consistent roles in the lives of young people with cognitive disability over time (Walmsley et al., 2017). Families can become the authoritative witness to the performance of services and systems in a young person's life and can have a vested interest in the outcomes of any professional involvement (Kendrick, 1996). There were many instances in this research where family members advocated and protected the young person with cognitive disability. Negotiating complex systems such as Australia's primary disability support system, the National Disability Insurance Scheme (NDIS), and schools, disability agencies, health professionals, housing, criminal justice systems, and child protection systems have been a core part of this advocacy.

The knowledge and expertise of family members were clear assets to many young people with cognitive disability in this research to obtain much-needed resources and supports. The respective parents of Kim (aged sixteen) and Danni (aged twenty-two) had intimate knowledge of their young person's severe cognitive disability and were active in advocating for the right level of support. This included persistently fighting for assistive technology to support their young person's complex communicative support needs and to enable them to participate fully in society.

Family members can expend a lot of energy in fighting for their child's right to access justice following experiences of abuse. These efforts may not always be successful, but the fidelity and commitment of the family advocate endures. This was evident for Amethyst, a First Nations Australian young person with cognitive disability whose mother fought to obtain justice after Amethyst's first experience of sexual assault. The perpetrator of the violence was mandated to do 100 hours of community service. Amethyst's mother also explains that she played a part in ensuring some compensation for her daughter and other victims:

> We did get justice for that now. I know it's a long time ago. But he's just been given a victims of crime payment[1] for something that he shouldn't have gotten. But his victims have all had letters now. They've disbursed the money so he doesn't get it and his victims all share in the money that he's been awarded.

Amethyst's mother continued to persistently advocate to the police for Amethyst's safety when she was in an abusive relationship. These efforts continued for three years, despite multiple obstacles and levels of discrimination.

It is also important to acknowledge the hard work of TBone's family, in particular, that of his mother. TBone, also a First Nations Australian young person (aged nineteen), faced many challenges and received ongoing support by his family. The family supported him through times when he was highly traumatised and was subsequently acting out with aggression towards others. TBone's parents also had their own personal issues to resolve in terms of finding stable accommodation. When support was sought from the

[1] Financial assistance is provided to victims of violence committed in Queensland mostly from Queensland government funds. The amount of financial support is assessed according to individual circumstances and the nature of the crime (www.qld.gov.au/law/crime-and-police/victims-and-witnesses-of-crime/financial-assistance).

child protection system and TBone was placed in out-of-home care, the family remained vigilant about TBone's safety and whereabouts.

Sophie's mother was persistent in getting justice following Sophie's experiences of sexual abuse. At the time of being interviewed, Sophie (aged twenty) was required to testify in court, as the perpetrator of the abuse pleaded not guilty to the charges. Sophie's mother was paying for a lawyer to fight this, ensuring Sophie had legal representation and that she would not have to confront the perpetrator in court. Sophie's mother also advocated strongly for Sophie's right to inclusive education at the private Catholic school Sophie attended for about four years. During this time, when Sophie became distressed and had 'meltdowns', the school would isolate her for hours in a mirrored room. Sophie was later expelled. Her mother followed up with the principal, who provided this decision in writing, and she then went to the director of Catholic Education. This advocacy resulted in Sophie being readmitted to the school. However, her mother said she had to provide extraordinary support to the school, which included recommending training, providing books, and writing a behaviour management plan. Eventually, the school advised they were unable to cater to Sophie's needs and Sophie was forced to leave. While Sophie lost her place in this school, her mother's advocacy shed light on discriminatory school practices.

Many of these examples show that supportive family may not always be able to prevent abuse from occurring, but that families can play an important role in redressing the impact of abuse. Providing support and believing in the young person with cognitive disability are all vital to validating their experiences and supporting them through their trauma recovery.

Feeling Safe and Supported by Family

The young people with cognitive disability who had positive informal supports through their family were able to identify times when they felt safe, heard, and experienced happiness. Both April (aged twenty-four) and Milly (aged twenty-one) identified supportive family networks that helped them to recover from abuse. This was also highlighted by practitioners, who recognised the important protective buffer a supportive family can provide to a young person with cognitive disability.

David's mother was very invested in supporting him as he transitioned out of school. This involved researching support options, managing David's support workers, and ensuring they were trained to understand his needs. David's mother, like many dedicated family members, structured her hours of employment so she could be there to support David.

Parents could fill the void created by services that did not always provide adequate supports. Angela, stepparent to Danni (aged twenty-two), shared how she needed to be present during the day when Danni attended a disability service:

> [Centre 1], where she went, didn't have a disabled toilet that allowed her to be changed. When she went to the bathroom and required changing, I would have to pick her up and bring her home and change her and then bring her back.

Angela was willing to provide this support to ensure Danni could access the disability service.

Cooper (aged twenty-three) was supported by his mother, who negotiated and navigated many systems on his behalf, including health services and schools. Cooper noted that when he 'struggled to figure out information, my mum's always been there like that for me and stuff. So, she does a good job.' It appears that this support provided a strong safety net and allowed Cooper the confidence and the time to be a young person and to socialise with his friends.

Having a protective and supportive family is so important, yet it also raises the issue of what happens where the circle of support for the young person is limited to family members. In addition, young people are likely to outlive their parents. Cody (aged twenty-two) spoke of his fears regarding this: 'And I'm petrified when my family have passed, that when my family are no longer there, I will have no one to back me in my corner or anything.' This issue was also highlighted by practitioners, who talked about the importance of supporting young people with cognitive disability to develop positive informal networks outside family, to create long-term supports into the future.

Intimate Relationships and Safety

Some of the participants talked about the positive nature of intimate relationships, which acted as a further support network to young people with cognitive disability. Amethyst (aged twenty-nine) talked about her current partner whom she and her mother described as being lovely and treating her well, with lovely manners. The importance of reciprocity is highlighted here when Amethyst said, 'Every time he has anxiety, I keep telling him that he's stronger than he thinks he is and to start proving that. Because he calls me, and I soothe him like he soothes me.'

Milly (aged twenty-one) talked about her positive relationship while also highlighting that her past relationships have tended to be abusive and negative:

> I've only been with him for a year. But he helps. He's probably the first relationship that's actually helped me with my child and actually been there for me. I have a habit of going to red flag, toxic relationships, so that comes under the scary part of my life.... I've been in domestic, like domestic [violence] relationship[s] before, and that's scared the hell out of me.

Milly's personal insight into previous abusive relationships allowed her to evaluate and appreciate her current intimate relationship and the benefits it brought her.

T, a young man with cognitive disability who had to become independent at a young age after his mother experienced mental health issues, talked about the importance of his relationship with his girlfriend when he was seventeen. Her parents let him move into their house and set up his caravan in their backyard, describing this as positive as it provided him with security and connection.

The opportunity to develop and engage in intimate relationships is important for any young person, yet often denied to young people with cognitive disability (Puyaltó et al., 2022). The findings of this research align with previous research, showing that some intimate relationships can also involve abuse and exploitation, but this is not the case for all relationships. Young people with cognitive disability have a human right to seek intimacy as any other person. If they are supported to make such choices, they can experience many benefits, including joy, love, and connection, all of which are central to a good life. Those relationships can also serve as an anchor and haven from violence and abuse.

Friendships and Well-Being

Friendships and an informal support network outside the family are also fundamental to the well-being of young people with cognitive disability. Cooper (aged twenty-three) identified the importance of friendships and his goal to 'friend everyone', suggesting the importance of these relationships in his life. Similarly, Becky (aged twenty-five) talked about having a few close friends who believed in her and understood her, which was important to her sense of self-worth.

The memory of friendship can be something that a young person carries with them through difficult times. Goldie, a First Nations Australian young person with cognitive disability, recalled a happy time as a young child playing with the children in her neighbourhood, particularly as this seems to have countered the experiences of being bullied at school. However, Goldie's life appears to have been full of sad times in terms of the support she received from her family, and she could only name the time when she played with her childhood friends as being a safe time.

Hilde (aged eighteen) also reflected fondly on the time when she made her first friend at school:

> When I was in grade 5, something very special happened to me. I got a friend. Obviously, it's terribly depressing that I hadn't had any friends up till then, but it was amazing. And the way I made the friend is very typically me. The teacher says, 'We've got a new student. Does anyone want to show her around?' I go, 'Me, me, me.'. . . Well, now I have four. I mean, I have a network of other people. I would be in a very bad place if I didn't have four very lovely people that I have now. Unfortunately, they're only online, because three are in the US and one lives a reachable distance but has a very abusive, controlling mother. We all have the same model of mother, amazingly. It's like finding three people you get along with, finding out you are the same make of car.

Friendships for Hilde include connections online. These online friends have provided a safe space for Hilde to work through her feelings about the strained relationship with her mother, as her friends are able to share and discuss similar experiences.

Friends can also assist a young person to leave abusive situations. After Milly experienced domestic violence from her partner, it was her friends who supported her as she had no family that she felt safe to turn to. However, this was not always the case, as she described how difficult it was to get friends at school because she was always segregated in the Special Education Unit.[2] Milly has been able to develop friends in her later years, and the importance of these relationships in her life is evident: 'But I had friends, I had like maybe one or two close people that helped me, sort of tell me to get out.'

Friendships have emerged as valuable supports for the young people with cognitive disability in this research. They provided a sense of safety, belonging, and connection during the transition to adulthood, a time when many young people with cognitive disability can experience

[2] Special Education Units are purpose-built classrooms for students with disability to provide tailored education to these students. Unfortunately, students in these classrooms could be segregated from their peers without disability.

loneliness (Garolera et al., 2021). Friends could step in when there was an absence of family support and were an important resource within the micro and meso systems for the young people.

The Valuable Role of Pets

Pets were also identified as part of the informal support networks of young people with cognitive disability. Young people became excited and happy when they talked about their pets and often relayed what an important part of their lives they were. Sophie talked about the importance of her pets, which provided another level of informal support; Goldie talked about her dog Bob whom she has had since 2007 who was special in her life; Ben talked about his dog Gemma, who made him feel safe. Milly shared, 'Oh, my cats make me happy. I have cats. I've always had cats. I've had cats since I moved out.... I'm a cat lady apparently.... It makes you calm and support[ed] and secure.'

There has been increased recognition of the benefits of assistance animals to people with disability (Chan et al., 2022). This study has found that animals can also play a valuable role in helping young people with cognitive disability to feel safe in their communities.

Lack of Informal Support

The opposite to protective and positive informal support networks is negative and dysfunctional networks, or a lack of networks, creating additional risks for young people with cognitive disability. The research identified common themes of the link between negative informal support networks and violence and abuse.

'I Knew I Wasn't Loved'

Milly (aged twenty-one) experienced a lack of love and support from her family. As a result, Milly would either reach out for other supports or isolate herself from further harm:

> Oh, so when I was living at home throughout my teenage years I really isolated myself.... I was either in my room half of the time or at a friend's or a boyfriend's house or something like that.... I don't remember if I was scared or not, but I knew I wasn't loved.... If you get what I mean. I realise now, 'Oh, that's the reason why I isolated myself and stuff,' because no one

> was really helping me. I felt no one was there for me ... she [her mother] just never cared. She didn't really seem to care for me.

Goldie (aged twenty-two) shared a similar experience of feeling unsupported by her mother:

> If I have a problem she just doesn't want to know. If something good happens, she still doesn't want to know. When I learnt how to ride a bike, she was allegedly too busy to watch me riding the bike, she just didn't care. She just didn't want to know.... They're not little [things]. That's actually big things. It's actually just times when I was growing up and she just didn't care, didn't want to know, didn't want to be there.

Goldie ended up in the child protection system, and the lack of family support continued. She described that after leaving care at sixteen her mother would not have her back and she ended up in homeless shelters until the age of eighteen. What is evident is that Goldie learnt to fend for herself, showing remarkable resilience.

Managing on Your Own

Not all young people with cognitive disability felt unloved by their family, but some young people came to the realisation that their family was unable to provide them the support they needed. T experienced an abusive relationship with his father, whom he described as 'not the best person', resulting in his mother leaving with his siblings. In describing his life with his mother, T was very focused on sharing her experiences with relationships and depression, and so what was missing here was any real narrative about his own experiences of being loved. T appears to have grown up quickly and taken responsibility for himself at a very early age.

Angel (aged twenty-four) described growing up in a family where he felt constant sadness and a lack of safety:

> I was always treated like there was nothing wrong with me [in relation to his learning difficulties], so my parents worked very hard to really gaslight me into thinking that, 'You're the problem. There's nothing wrong with you. If you can't do it, it's because you don't want to do it.' So, I always had that mental barrier of, 'I don't understand why I can't do it because my brother can do it, my sister can do it. I can't understand why I'm not doing it.'

Angel's story appeared to be in part a struggle to overcome the unrealistic expectations of his parents and forge his own identity as a young adult.

How Practitioners Can Support Informal Networks

Practitioners identified the importance of assisting young people with cognitive disability to develop positive informal supports. This was emphasised for young people with cognitive disability who have been in out-of-home care who have been reliant on formal supports, which can end when they turn eighteen. A lack of positive and protective informal supports was seen by professionals as increasing the risk for abuse, neglect, and exploitation.

Emma, a practitioner who worked with children, young people, and families, talked about a new Australian program called Next Steps, which is focused on identifying mentors who can act as informal supports for young people. However, the work of building supportive, freely given relationships in the lives of young people with cognitive disability should not be constrained to isolated programs. To be effective, it is suggested that young people need to be supported to maintain and develop informal family and friendship networks throughout their lives.

11.3 The CRPD on Family and Supports and Protection from Those Who Should Give Support

Through their connection with people with a disability, pets and service animals have protection under the CRPD. The CRPD framework responds to families as sources of support and sources of abuse.

The Support of Pets

Some young people in this research shared the important role that having a pet played in supporting their transition to adulthood. The CRPD empowers persons with disability to access supports they need to advocate and protect themselves, as well as including mechanisms to protect persons with disability against those who cause them harm instead of support. The supports in the CRPD are not limited to human supports. In particular, persons with disability have a right to use assistance and guide dogs as well as pets in other circumstances (Harpur, 2010). Whereas assistance and guide dogs provide specific disability protections and are addressed by the CRPD Committee in Concluding Observations (United Nations Committee on the Rights of Persons with Disabilities, 2021A, Para. 43 (a); 2022L, Para. 43(a); 2023A, Para. 42(a)), and thus receive higher protection, the CRPD also recognises that persons with disability have a right to have a pet. Illustratively, in its General Comment No. 5, the CRPD Committee explains that the right to independent living in CRPD Article 19 means that individuals with disability are provided with all necessary means to enable them to exercise choice and control over their lives and make all decisions concerning their lives (United Nations Committee on the Rights of Persons with Disabilities, 2017, Para. 16 (a)). Exercising such rights includes the choice to have pets or not.

Unfortunately, assistance animals, guide dogs, and pets can be targeted by those seeking to harm people with disability (Harpur & Douglas, 2014). Reflecting this position, the CRPD Committee General Comment No. 3 explains that acts of violence, exploitation, and/or abuse against women with disability that violate Article 16 include 'harming or threatening to harm, removing or killing pets or assistance dogs.' Thus, states have obligations to protect people with disability against such harm by virtue of CRPD Article 16.

Responding to the Supports from Families

Even though the CRPD includes non-human supports, human advocates and supports are more common. This research has given many examples in which families can support young people with cognitive disability to transition to adulthood. While the CRPD focuses on advancing individual rights, the convention does recognise the value people with disability glean from being part of a community and families. The Preamble of the CRPD reflects the importance of families for enabling people with disability to exercise their rights: the Preamble recognises that 'the family is the natural and fundamental group unit of society and is entitled to protection by society and the State, and that people with disabilities and their family members should receive the necessary protection and assistance to enable families to contribute towards the full and equal enjoyment of the rights of persons with disabilities' (Preamble, (x)). The CRPD directly links family supports with protection from freedom from exploitation, violence, and abuse in several articles. For example, CRPD Article 16(2) requires states to take all appropriate measures to prevent all forms of exploitation, violence, and abuse by ensuring, inter alia, support for people with disability and their families and caregivers, including through the provision of information and education on how to avoid, recognise, and report instances of exploitation, violence, and abuse.

The CRPD draws a distinction between the situation where a family member substitutes their own will for that of a person with a disability, as opposed to when a family member acts as a support to enable the will of a person with a disability to be realised. The concept of substituted decision making is expressly rejected by the CRPD in Article 12 and in CRPD Committee jurisprudence as it applies to people with intellectual and psychosocial disability (United Nations Committee on the Rights of Persons with Disabilities, 2022J, Para. 26(a); 2023A, Para. 26(d); 2023D, Para. 26(a); 2023F, Para. 20). The CRPD Committee in General Comment No. 1 has explained how guardianship and substituted decision making are contrary to disability human rights norms (United Nations Committee on the Rights of Persons with Disabilities, 2014, Para. 26). To realise this paradigm shift, the CRPD Committee requires states to advance a universal legal capacity paradigm, where all people, regardless of disability or decision-making skills, inherently possess legal capacity (United Nations Committee on the Rights of Persons with Disabilities, 2014, Para. 25). To realise supported decision making, the CRPD Committee adjures state parties in General Comment No. 1 to 'recognise the social networks and naturally occurring community support (including friends, family and schools) of persons with disability as key to supported decision-making' (United Nations Committee on the Rights of Persons with Disabilities, 2014, Para. 45).

The capacity of families to intervene in different domains is supported by other articles and CRPD Committee jurisprudence. Illustratively, Article 4(3) empowers people with disability and their representatives to be closely consulted in all decision-making processes under the CRPD. The CRPD Committee's General Comment No. 4 on education explains that families have a right to be involved in the educational decisions of people with disability, by virtue of Articles 4(3) and 24(2)(c) (General Comment No. 4, Paras. 7 and 29). With respect to Article 4(3), General Comment No. 4 explains that people with disability and, when appropriate, their families, must be recognised as partners and not merely recipients of education (General Comment No. 4, Para. 7). To enable the families of people with disability to advocate and support them, the CRPD includes measures to foster this protective arrangement. This includes access to information. Illustratively, Article 23(3) requires state parties provide early and comprehensive information, services, and support to children with disability and their families to help 'prevent concealment, abandonment, neglect and segregation of children with disabilities'. Relatedly, Article 28 (1) supports people with disability and their families to an adequate standard of living and social protection.

The CRPD also acknowledges that violence and abuse of people with disability can occur within families. Related to contacting and engaging with family, Article 22(2) grants people with disability a right not to have their privacy or their family's privacy interfered with by the state or others. For instance, the CRPD Committee has explained the need to ensure the privacy of people with disability, including the confidentiality of information and of their personal medical records, in institutions and mental health systems and services (United Nations Committee on the Rights of Persons with Disabilities, 2019D, Para. 42; 2023, Para. 50; 2023F, Para. 46). This right of privacy, however, is balanced by measures in the CRPD seeking to reduce the instances where people with disability are exploited by their families. Some measures are less likely to interfere with their rights to privacy. Some measures require states to raise awareness throughout society, including at the family level, regarding people with disability, and to foster respect for the rights and dignity of people with disability (CRPD Article 8(a)).

11.4 Conclusion

Having access to a positive, supportive, and responsive informal support network within a person's micro and meso system is vital to a sense of safety, belonging, and connection. This section has highlighted the importance of having positive and helpful informal support networks for the young people. Where this was present, it created a sense of 'having someone in my corner', someone to advocate for the young person and to provide them with the unconditional positive regard everyone needs. It also provided support in enabling the young person with cognitive disability to navigate the complexities of multiple systems such as schools, police, and formal supports. However, when these informal networks have not been present or where they have been negative or abusive, the need for formal support services to step in and scaffold the young person has been necessary.

These findings show the need for further research into how we can support families, kin, and carers of children and young people with cognitive disability to keep them from harm and exploitation. Furthermore, consideration also needs to be given to ensuring that service providers consider informal networks and look to ways of fostering resilience in young people by connecting them to others in their community.

CHAPTER 12

In the Voices of Participants
What Needs to Change

Accessible Summary

- Violence can happen anywhere in the lives of young people with cognitive disability.
- Young people with cognitive disability, family members, and workers talk about what needs to change.
- Services need to work together to help young people with cognitive disability.
- Others need to know about and respect the culture of young people with cognitive disability.
- Others need to respect young people's choices on whom they want to love.
- Young people with cognitive disability can be helped to understand what is violence.
- Services can change what they do so that they can keep young people with cognitive disability safe.
- Young people with cognitive disability say there should be 'nothing about us unless it is led by us'.

12.1 Introduction

Throughout this book we have reported how young people with cognitive disability have overcome violence in their journeys to adulthood. The experiences reported often fell short of expectations under the CRPD.

The Disability Royal Commission has noted the importance of adopting a disability rights approach, informed by the CRPD, to disability responses (DRC, 2023D, p. 13) and to enhancing national strategic approaches and governance on disability and specific disability issues (DRC, 2023, pp. 78–184). This chapter embraces this approach through providing a voice to the participants in our study and positioning the call for developing national strategic responses in accordance with the CRPD.

In this chapter, first, we revisit the intersectional ecological systems lens to summarise the transition experiences of young people with cognitive disability. The findings on transition to adulthood for young people with cognitive disability presented in this book illustrate how there are many influences on a young person's experience, spanning from the relationships a young person has with family and intimate partners to broader overarching values and beliefs of the society in which young people live. This research has adopted an intersectional ecological systems approach to explain the complexity of this experience and to provide a holistic framework for understanding the multitude of factors that both lead to, and prevent, violence in all its forms. The context of the young people's experiences is explained in terms of microsystem, mesosystem, exosystem, macrosystem, and chronosystem influences.

The research team has asked for, and listened to, the voices of stakeholders about experiences of abuse, neglect, discrimination, and exploitation. In Section 12.3, we honour the voices of the young people with cognitive disability, their parents, and practitioner stakeholders, by providing their responses to the question about what they believe would reduce the violence experienced by young people raised in this book. We report on the voices of participants and draw out how they believe an integrated strategic approach should operate. Finally, in Section 12.4 we frame the need for an overarching strategic approach within a CRPD context.

12.2 Understanding Transition through an Intersectional Ecological Systems Lens

This book has adopted an intersectional ecological systems lens to understanding youth transition for young people with cognitive disability and their experiences of violence and abuse. This frame considers the social, cultural, economic, and structural forces impacting on young people's lives (Hollomotz, 2009). Violence and abuse are considered at the micro, meso, exo, macro, and chrono systems levels. Yet each level cannot be understood in isolation. Changes in one system can influence changes in other systems. By considering these systems as intersecting, it is hoped that further understanding can be achieved as to what leads to violence and harm to young people with cognitive disability.

Micro-System Influences

As previously discussed, the micro system involves the immediate relationships in a young person's life. While this sphere of interaction may appear to focus on a young person's direct experiences of violence, such events are influenced by the other systems in the young person's life, as demonstrated in this research.

The stories of transition to adulthood have shown that young people with cognitive disability want all aspects of their identity, including their cultural background, gender, and sexuality, to be acknowledged and accepted by others. Young people with cognitive disability, as with any young person, want others to understand the support communities that are important to them. These support communities can play an important part in facilitating the young person's transition to adulthood. By virtue of knowing and caring for the young person, family members could provide that young person with the safety and space to navigate adulthood in their own time and at their own pace. However, not all communities in this research were truly supportive. Young people with cognitive disability could become enmeshed in intimate relationships that were horrifically abusive. Parents or substitute carers could be challenged by the young person's behaviour and seek to control this through inappropriate use of medication. Sometimes family members were in need of their own healing from trauma and abuse and did not have capacity to provide the support the young person needed.

Some young people with cognitive disability needed to create their own micro system as emerging adults. For these young people, family was often absent, and the young person was reliant on services and systems such as statutory child protection services to help them gain their independence. These services and systems were often poor substitutes for family. The young people we spoke to have had to develop resilience quickly, but also through experiences, can became more vulnerable to violence. These findings reflect the challenges and need for balance in allowing young people with cognitive disability to self-direct their transition to adulthood, and at the same time ensuring that they have the right supports to safeguard them from violence.

Understanding the impact of normative constructions of young people have been highlighted as important, as is the need to challenge these. The unique experiences of the young people with cognitive disability were not always recognised by those around them in terms of expectations and supports available based on these dominant normative constructions of development and heteronormative sexuality. An additional challenge was the intersection of co-occurring mental health conditions, which further complicated the path to independence. Our research highlighted the impact of this, creating additional barriers for the young person's transition to independence. Again, this was not always recognised and thus supported within the microsystems.

The violence that could occur within a young person's micro system indicates that families need resourcing to provide appropriate caring support to their young person with cognitive disability. Families can be under intense pressure for many reasons, as was identified in our research. This includes needing support to manage the complex behaviours of their young person. Pressure also comes from the lack of appropriate supports and services, and the onus on families to advocate for basic needs and rights for their children. Violence also arose when a young person with cognitive disability sought connection with others who were exploitative, out of a human need to overcome loneliness. The need for human connection also included young people seeking to build their own family. However, as seen, exploitation and violence also emerged from some of these new families, such as experiences of physical and sexual abuse, coercion, and control from an intimate partner.

When violence was perpetrated by someone outside the family, the role of families to support a young person with cognitive disability to recover and heal was vital. Families could feel alone in their efforts to ameliorate the harm that occurred to young people. In many of these situations the young person was let down by education, child protection, and criminal justice systems, and the family was the only helpful resource available.

At the micro-system level, the research highlighted the importance of culturally appropriate responses and supports to facilitate and enable First Nations Australian families and culturally and linguistically diverse families to best support their child. Added to this is the need for support beyond the child, as quite often the families are also dealing with their own traumas related to colonisation, migration, racism and discrimination. As demonstrated, without appropriate support, the intersection of these factors creates further barriers and challenges for young people with cognitive disability as they transition to adulthood.

Meso-System Influences

The meso system examines the interplay between two or more settings the person participates in, for example, home, education, and work. There were many examples in this research of how services responded to the transition needs of the young person with cognitive disability through an ableist and ill-informed lens. The experiences of participants indicated that the failure of services and others to be responsive to a young person's emotional, social, and cognitive development, along with cultural and/or sexual identities, was linked to an increased risk for violence to occur. In addition, young people with cognitive disability were at times excluded from support, or a service provider neglected to provide adequate support on the basis that the young person did not 'fit' the service's definitions of young adulthood or cognitive disability. The lack of support thus impacted on the young person's transition to adulthood.

Dignity of risk for young people with cognitive disability was also denied by some services settings where they provided surveillance and over-regulation of young people's lives. Extreme examples of this were reported within child protection and criminal justice settings, where young people with cognitive disability were 'involuntary' clients. These settings were often highly structured, centred around institutional routines and procedures, and failed to provide young people the opportunity to develop independence and attain appropriate life skills to live outside these environments.

The research highlighted the need for services to focus on the young person's connection to their family and local community. Helping young people with cognitive disability to develop supportive, natural, or informal relationships has emerged as a key area for services to focus on. Assisting young people to develop these rather than just focusing on formal supports is important for all young people, but especially for First Nations Australian young people and young people from culturally and linguistically diverse communities. This research identified examples where services not only failed to consider the community of a young person with cognitive disability, but further isolated the young person from family, friends, and culture by not paying attention to the importance of supporting the development of informal support systems. The research has further highlighted the need to balance informal support with appropriate formal support systems, which is discussed below.

Exo-System Influences

The exo system refers to the cultural institutions and structures that function independently of the young person with cognitive disability but nevertheless impact their lives. This involves legislative and policy frameworks and associated resourcing that affect young people with cognitive disability.

A key finding from this research has been the increasing 'responsibilisation' of young people with cognitive disability and their families to ensure their own well-being and safety. Responsibilisation refers to the process in which the neoliberal state transfers responsibilities to individuals and communities to solve their own problems (Pyysiäinen et al., 2017). This was manifest in policy and resourcing decisions that left young people and/or their families with little choice but to make do with what inadequate formal services were on offer.

Examples of responsibilisation were evident in the resourcing of disability supports and what was prioritised. The support needs of young people with severe or profound cognitive disability were often deemed too costly to the system. Formal systems relied too heavily on the informal care of families. Families of young people with profound cognitive disability needed to create their own supports for their loved one and were continually engaged in advocacy to improve the young person's situation and access to their rights.

Practitioners also reported a narrow, time-limited scope of support under the National Disability Insurance Scheme (NDIS) for young people, where it appeared that decisions were made to address fiscal concerns, rather than the long-term well-being of the young person. The NDIS has a strong emphasis on supporting participants on the scheme to become 'self-actualising' and fostering social and economic independence (Cortese et al., 2021). However, there is insufficient attention given to many of the daily complexities facing young people with cognitive disability. For example, young people with cognitive disability who had been in the care of the statutory child protection system were often thrust into independence after leaving care, with a myriad of assumptions from service providers that life skills would be learnt without too much assistance.

Young people with cognitive disability were also often left to find their own ways out of situations of vulnerability if they did not meet the conditions set by service policies, which increased the risk of experiencing violence. Conditional support was provided to young people with cognitive disability based on whether they met the service's eligibility criteria and were compliant with the program requirements set by the agency. This conditional support was most pronounced for First Nations Australian and culturally and linguistically diverse young people, as systems and services often failed to adjust their practices to support differences in language and culture, and the impacts of intergenerational trauma, racism, and poverty.

Transitions between services were also often left to young people with cognitive disability and families to navigate effectively; thus, some young people were reliant on their family's access to information and resources. This led to inequitable outcomes, with some young people faring better than others, depending on the degree of stability and resources in their family situation. Service transitions included moving from child services to adult services, child protection services to disability services, and correctional facilities to disability services. As other studies have found (e.g., Baker Collins et al., 2018; Dowse et al., 2014), each service system had their own practice frameworks and priorities, and professionals within each system assessed young people through a particular practice lens. These assessments were therefore narrow in their understanding of the young people and their particular needs, and there was a lack of wraparound support to facilitate these transitions.

This research supports the importance of greater collaboration between systems to respond effectively to young people with cognitive disability who experience violence if we are to meet the human rights of each young person. Equity is required in access to consistent and appropriate support, which accounts for the individual needs of each young person.

Macro-System Influences

The macro system is the larger culture in which a person belongs. It refers to the broader cultural values and discourses that permeate a young person's life.

Cultural values of what constitutes successful adulthood in Australian society impacted on young people with cognitive disability in this research. Many of the young people experienced numerous barriers to achieving the so-called markers of success in adulthood. There were many examples of young people with cognitive disability struggling to achieve further education and employment due to ableist discourses.

Supports were provided to young people with cognitive disability within the context of a neoliberal state. A system of competition between and compartmentalisation of services often meant that supports around young people with cognitive disability were poorly coordinated. Transition to adulthood was therefore further complicated by a lack of continuity in care; narrow understandings of young people's needs, culture, and experiences; and failure to consider long-term goals for the young person.

Ableist understandings of social, emotional, and cognitive development led to neglect of young people with cognitive disability when the system failed to recognise their developmental needs. As reported in this research, ableist expectations led to young people with cognitive disability feeling dehumanised, as if they did not belong, and experiencing loneliness and disconnection from their peers. Other social identities related to gender and sexual orientation and culture were also relegated to the category of 'other' by services, systems, and society, setting the background context for violence.

Chrono-System Influences

The chrono system examines the changes and continuities occurring over time that influence a young person's experience. These changes can include environmental events and shifts over the life course.

The transition to adulthood has become more complex and varied for all young people in the twenty-first century. Many of the expectations placed on young people with cognitive disability may be equally problematic for other groups of young people. For example, finding meaningful employment may also escape the reach of many able-bodied young people. However, as indicated by the experiences of the research participants, there are likely to be greater challenges for young people with cognitive disability due to an inherent social devaluation because of their disability, resulting in less social, economic, and cognitive resources.

The research took place at a time when the NDIS has become more established in Australia. The NDIS has represented a massive and rapid change in disability policy and programmes (Henderson & Bigby, 2021). While an important initiative, this research has emphasised some of the challenges for young people with cognitive disability in accessing and receiving appropriate support through NDIS. The NDIS, at the time of writing, is under review by the Australian government, in part to examine the design, operations, and sustainability of the scheme (www.ndisreview.gov.au/about/terms-of-reference). This is likely to result in further change to supports to young people with cognitive disability, which is likely to have implications for their transition to adulthood.

12.3 What Needs to Change

Experiences of Transition and the Need for an Integrated Strategic Response

Participants have called for an integrated strategic response to empowering and supporting young people with cognitive disability in their transition to adulthood. These interventions must be culturally safe. Participants called for their voices to be heard in the implementation of policies that impact them. Participants called for accountability measures to ensure responses are realised. Participants echoed the disability rights movement and called for 'nothing about us unless it is led by us'. Education is required to realise empowerment. Overall, more needs to be done to address systemic abuse against young people with cognitive disability. This must include increased data collection and research.

When services and supports actively seek to understand the individual needs of young people with cognitive disability, this sets the context for addressing the exo- and macro-level system practices and structures that lead to violence and abuse. Addressing violence, like supporting transition to adulthood, involves a systematic approach that is holistic and accounts for the complex tapestry of interrelated individual, social, community, organisational, and systemic factors that enable or prevent abuse (Ottmann et al., 2017).

In the Words of Participants: The Need for Integrated and Holistic Strategies

Parent and practitioner stakeholders consistently identified the need for collaboration and integrated service systems that see the young person with cognitive disability holistically in their environment. The current siloed approach to services has been consistently criticised by participants in our study for failing to afford appropriate resources and safety to young people. The need for an increased strategic focus on integrating services was illustratively raised by Chantelle, a practitioner who led a disability advocacy service:

> Integrated responses are happening in all communities now around Australia, where it brings together the police, the courts, the domestic violence service, the corrections service. All the players are working together in a localised response model that focuses on the individual and brings together their pieces of the support to be to provided and focus on safety and outcomes.... We need to get better at [collaboration and information

> sharing] . . . because it's only when there is some kind of integration and sharing of information and responsibility to support someone in their trajectory and in their interactions with the different service systems – that means that people can be safer.

Rod, an occupational therapist, also emphasised the need for a community and government response that works collaboratively to provide continuity of care and to ensure practitioners are equipped with appropriate information to respond effectively to incidents of violence against young people. This involves:

> local, state, federal organisations to help address the issues of neglect, exploitation, violence, and abuse . . . [and] consultation bodies to help on-the-ground clinicians.. . . 'I hear that this child is being abused and neglected or something, I don't know who to call.. . . Is there someone I can consult with that sort of information? I don't know what those numbers are.'. . . And I guess but just a nice information of what is neglect, what is exploitation, what is violence and abuse, examples of it, so that when I'm working I'm like, 'Oh, actually what I'm witnessing is that.' And then just, I don't know, helplines or NGOs [non-governmental organisations] or some organisations that I can actually call.. . . Maybe sort of pathways to what I can refer to my client, what referral services I can give to them if I'm witnessing this.

While Rod saw the benefit in establishing formal pathways of information exchange to safeguard young people with cognitive disability, Peter, father of Kim, felt that young people with cognitive disability would be assisted by having a key worker or advocate to navigate different systems. For example, a young person with cognitive disability who has critical need for medical intervention could be supported by a worker or advocate who understands the person's history, means of communication, and personal wishes.

Cody (aged twenty-two) argued that the time for 'buck passing' needs to end:

> Disabilities can cause health issues and vice versa. So . . . to me . . . the health ministers are passing the buck, the health teams are passing the buck to the NDIS staff bureaucracy, and even that's just passing it onto the health bureaucracy.

Cody contends, like many other participants in this study, that collaboration and coordination between services and systems is a collective responsibility. Different sectors who work together can facilitate better outcomes for young people with cognitive disability as they transition to adulthood.

In the Words of Participants: The Importance of Culturally Safe Approaches

Cultural Safety for Aboriginal and/or Torres Strait Islander Young People with Cognitive Disability

Practitioners were clear about the need for culturally specific services for Aboriginal and/or Torres Strait Islander young people with cognitive disability. Such services needed to be accessible and 'friendly', as, according to John, a First Nations practitioner, when 'Mob' find out that a service is not supportive, they stop attending. Services that were culturally appropriate were able to identity the 'little wins' for young people:

> For me, you get a young person, they might have a few things going on at the moment and then working with them and building up their confidence and linking them in with youth groups and stuff. And then just watch them go from a really shy person to like almost a leader within the group and building them up to be proud, young Indigenous males. And yeah, it's awesome to see that sort of transition.

The importance of connecting with a culturally appropriate service was expressed by TBone's mother, who spoke about the effectiveness of TBone's current service provider, which was a First Nations organisation. The family had received limited positive support from previous organisations. TBone's mother described seeing the Aboriginal and/or Torres Strait Islander service as being honest, and really focusing on his needs and his culture:

> And he's actually a special client because they're more family well-being now. But because they know TBone very well and they see him as family, ... we've become quite close with the workers. A few of them know us quite well. They've become friends with TBone.

The service the family accessed clearly prioritised their relationship with TBone as well as showing a long-term commitment to the family, even when the nature of their work changed. TBone's mother placed trust in this service, an important element also raised by First Nations practitioners, who saw their work as developing trust with young people and with other services.

Practitioners identified other elements that make for supportive services for First Nations Australian young people with cognitive disability. These include adopting an ecological and holistic approach to young people's needs. Annette, a lawyer who worked with Aboriginal and/or Torres Strait Islander young people, explained:

> I think often it needs to be looked at as a whole family and community problem. And when I have success with my clients, it's when I've connected with their family and their community and say, 'Okay, so this "sister's"[1] the one who's going to help you, so let's connect with her. Let's support her to do it. Let's make sure she has all the services she needs to be able to support you.' Often it's about not just seeing it as the individual. It's in community; what do they need to help to support the child? I think you can get better results if you do it that way, especially for Indigenous clients. And then what other ones? It can be just about what supports do the family need. If the child's got a disability, maybe they can't handle the complexities of that. Because of their own traumas in life and things going on, they need support as well. It's about recognising the family, to support the family.

In addition, proactive, early intervention for young people was considered vital so that they did not 'fall through the cracks'. Support also needed to be of an unconditional nature, not predicated on rules governed by the agency. This meant allowing young people to come in and out of programs and services, engaging in outreach, and providing consistency to young people who may lead chaotic, unstable lives due to a history of trauma. For all these elements to be present, there also needed to be a concerted effort on the part of governments to invest in such services.

Cultural Safety for Culturally and Linguistically Diverse Young People with Cognitive Disability

There is a substantial need for culturally appropriate advocacy services for persons with disability from culturally and linguistically diverse backgrounds. Access to supports may not be possible for many young people with cognitive disability without the outreach initiatives by advocacy agencies. Monica, an advocacy worker for this group of young people, explained that her agency has recruited workers from different cultural backgrounds to be able to reach more diverse communities:

> We've got someone from Burundi, Vietnam, Afghanistan, Syria, and now from Iran, who are all looking for people from community who have disabilities. So, they've been out just getting the word out to just everybody and anyone they can possibly think of, all the multicultural services, GPs [general practitioners], hospitals, child health services, et cetera, to try and find where those people are.

[1] In First Nations Australian culture, the use of the word 'sister' in this context refers to a First Nations worker. Similarly, the use of the word 'brother' also refers to a worker.

Practitioners in this study also highlighted the need for services to be culturally aware and work towards reducing the additional barriers of language so that the young people can receive the services they need and have a right to. The ongoing issue of cultural barriers remains a significant challenge, yet much can be achieved through access to appropriately qualified interpreters, translations, and practitioners who work from a culturally sensitive framework. These findings are consistent with research in this area, which highlights the need for greater systemic-level change to address these issues (King et al., 2016A).

In the Words of Participants: Empowering Young People Who Identify as LGBTIQA+ to Access Services and Engage in Self-Advocacy

Formal supports could also recognise the contribution LGBTIQA+ young people with cognitive disability can make in terms of peer mentorship to other LGBTIQA+ young people. Becky was eager to support other LGBTIQA+ young people:

> I would love to talk to some young people and tell them, if they're transitioning or if they're gay or they're bisexual or if they're lesbian, I'd actually love to go and talk to someone and say, 'Yes, your parents might not accept you for what you are, but I'll tell you one thing, you are who you are and don't let anyone tell you anything different. Be proud of who you are.. . . I'm more than happy to talk to you and help you get through those hard times.'

At the time of conducting the research, there was a growing interest in the Australian disability sector to develop better responses to LGBTIQA+ young people with disability. One of the practitioner participants, Riley, had been instrumental in creating a stakeholder group to improve practice and service outcomes. Riley outlined the need for services to recognise the intersection of gender, sexuality, and disability:

> So, LGBTIQA+ people might not be getting their needs met by disability service providers, and by the same token, there is the same lack of understanding and unmet need for queer health services for people with disability. So, trying to start a little bit of a process in Brisbane and wider Queensland area to look at improving, but also just have better connections and access points, for community members. Because I think what people are saying within organisations is 'Yes, we want to do better, but we're not getting any referrals.' So, what is the thing that's preventing those points of referral and connectivity as well?

Riley's comments also suggest that LGBTIQA+ young people and their families may lack information about what services are available.

Another practitioner in Victoria shared how she helped support the only LGBTIQA+ self-advocacy group for persons with intellectual disability in Australia. In this work there was a commitment to strengthening the group of young people, ensuring that they controlled the agenda and work. This demonstrated what can be achieved through targeted support for this group of young people.

In the Words of Participants: Nothing about Us without Us

Reflecting the 'nothing about us without us' mantra, participants called for young people with cognitive disability to be heard in the development, implementation, and monitoring of policies and services that impact upon them. Illustratively, Hilde (aged eighteen) called for full participation in decision making:

> I think the only short-term solution is to involve disabled people in everything, because otherwise we're not going to get those long-term solutions going.... The only thing to do, truly, is to break down the harmful power structures and make everything, absolutely everything, not about people having things decided for them, but about people being supported to make their own decisions.

Our study has shown that young people with cognitive disability act as the authoritative witnesses to the performance of professionals and systems. They are able to identify and comment on the effects of violence, and highlight when support is not forthcoming (Hollomotz, 2012). Addressing violence involves ensuring young people with cognitive disability are empowered to speak up, share their views, and be instigators of change.

In the Words of Participants: Action to Support Young People to Understand Exploitation

Practitioners talked about the importance of education in supporting young people with cognitive disability to understand exploitative relationships and what are safe and appropriately respectful relationships. Being able to offer support and assessing the full depth of the exploitation and violence is only possible when the young person feels safe to do so. Practitioners highlighted that trying to work through this while the young person is experiencing other forms of violence, insecurity, and lack of safety can be challenging. Long-term support is needed to respond to the multiple forms of violence and their after-effects in young people's lives.

G, a disability practitioner, explained how challenging it can be to say to a young person, 'Hey, that one person that you really respect, who supports you, may actually not be treating you very nicely.' Such discussions potentially could undermine the worker's rapport with the young person with cognitive disability, and subsequently further isolate the young person from support. G described her work as often 'just keeping our eyes on it and seeing what happens, and then supporting the young person to do whatever they want to do with that information'.

Emma, a practitioner who worked with children, young people, and families, also spoke of the importance of building trusting relationships:

> So, until they have those discussions that come out naturally with us when we're engaging with them and build that rapport, it's only that moment that I'm able to do like a natural kind of role modelling and talk through to unpack it and to let them know that that is not the norm and they have rights and it should be delivered differently and they shouldn't be giving their real estate agent that extra $20 cash in hand that's outside of the bank transfer.

Educating and empowering young people with cognitive disability can involve practitioners grappling with many ethical questions and uncertainties. For example, managers from an employment service pointed to questions as to the scope of the role of their organisation to intervene in matters of exploitation, particularly in incidents where the young person with cognitive disability is a legal adult, has no guardian, and chooses not to report the abuse. Practitioners require their own professional development and education in deciding who should intervene, how to intervene, and whom to report the matter to. Practitioners in this study confirmed that addressing exploitation of young people with cognitive disability involves assessing and balancing dignity of risk, duty of care, and self-determination of young people.

In the Words of Participants: Addressing Systemic Abuse against Young People with Cognitive Disability

This study has outlined the numerous ways in which service systems can fail to consider the needs of young people with cognitive disability and thereby create harm and disadvantage. To list all the various forms of macro-level systemic abuse is beyond the scope of this final chapter. One example for change are the suggestions made by participants to improve the child protection system for parents with cognitive disability:

- The need to collect data in statutory child protection services about the number of parents with cognitive disability in the system
- Addressing resourcing gaps to the current legal aid services, as parents with cognitive disability often need more time with lawyers to be able to discuss and ensure their understanding
- A more transparent and independent system for making complaints where there is poor practice
- Targeted and specific training for child protection workers and others who work with parents with cognitive disability.

These suggestions have applicability to other jurisdictions outside Australia, and to some extent speak to broader principles in systems change. These broader principles include:

- Making visible the presence of young people with cognitive disability within systems
- Adapting practices so that the specific communicative and learning needs of young people with cognitive disability are catered for within systems
- Ensuring systems provide appropriate mechanisms to enable young people with cognitive disability to report abuse and exercise control over the supports they receive (Collins & Murphy, 2022)
- Considering how to promote a culture of safety 'downstream' through appropriate education and training of frontline staff (Shier et al., 2019).

In the Words of Participants: A Need for Improved Identification, Data Collection, and Research

Data collection on young people with cognitive disability can only occur once there is universal access to appropriate diagnostic screening and functional assessment of young people's developmental needs. These assessment processes must be conducted within a disability human rights paradigm in line with the CRPD, and outcomes appropriately evaluated to ensure the best interests of young people with cognitive disability.

Practitioners often commented that systems failed to collect data on the prevalence of people with cognitive disability within their operations. Chantal, a disability advocate, cited anecdotal evidence from the

Department of Justice and Attorney-General[2] that 50 per cent of people coming into the criminal justice system have a cognitive or intellectual disability, yet this data was not being systematically gathered. This data failure is caused, in part, by challenges in accessing appropriate professional services to identify the person's disability and understand their support needs. Lorraine, a legal practitioner, also argued for the need for earlier and affordable assessments:

> I think there needs to be a lot more assessments happening for young people who might be identified as not functioning in the same way or having behavioural issues, to see whether there is something more going on than just this person's bad or naughty, to try and identify and work with those issues at an earlier stage, rather than waiting until someone's in their twenties or thirties.... There's adjustments and therapies that need to be used or utilised to try and help this person be able to, I guess, work within the community so they're not just constantly within the criminal justice system....
>
> It would be good if some of those assessments were free. Because, I mean, obviously paying for assessments is a pretty big barrier for anyone, because most of those people obviously don't have huge resources.

Chantal linked individual assessment and diagnosis as being closely aligned with gathering evidence of where support is needed for young people with cognitive disability:

> Unless each of the systems are starting to collect and measure where people are and who they are and the outcomes that they're experiencing, then we can keep going around in circles. Because without the evidence and the data, we don't understand the true realm of the needs.

She elaborated that without robust measures of prevalence of young people with cognitive disability within systems, governments would not provide appropriate funding mechanisms in place to improve outcomes for this group of young people.

12.4 The CRPD and an Integrated Strategic Approach to Protecting Young Persons with Cognitive Disability from Violence

The CRPD has granted persons with disability a right to be heard in national and international policy development, implementation, and

[2] The Department of Justice and Attorney-General is a Queensland government department that provides a range of services related to justice for all.

monitoring. The CRPD requires states to reflect the participatory dynamic in its development, adoption, implementation, and monitoring of strategic and integrated responses.

Disability Empowerment: Nothing about Us without Us

The CRPD provides the overarching value framework that must drive cultural values and discourses regarding supporting young people with cognitive disability and their transition to adulthood rights. The aphorism of 'nothing about us without us' was central to the drafting of the CRPD (Harpur, 2017). This manifested with people with disability directly participating in the drafting of the Convention and then its implementation and monitoring (Harpur & Stein, 2022). Disabled persons organisations (DPO) are organisations of people with a disability that are led and governed by people with a disability (United Nations Committee on the Rights of Persons with Disabilities, 2018A, Para. 14). The importance of DPO involvement is emphasised in General Comment No. 7, where the CRPD Committee explains that the 'close consultation and active involvement of persons with disabilities, through disabled persons organisations (DPOs)/organisations of persons with disabilities (OPDs), in the negotiations, development and drafting of the Convention on the Rights of Persons with Disabilities, had a positive impact on its quality and relevance for persons with disabilities and also showed the power possessed by persons with disabilities' (United Nations Committee on the Rights of Persons with Disabilities, 2018A, Para. 1). Indeed, the participation of persons with disability during the drafting of the Convention represented a tipping point in how persons with disability are included in decision-making processes that impact upon them (Harpur & Stein, 2022A). When it comes to implementation, the 'nothing about us without us' approach is increasingly merging into the more empowered, 'nothing about us unless it is led by us' (Harpur & Stein, 2022).

The CRPD most trenchantly advances the participatory dynamic in Articles 4(3), 7(3), and 33(3). Articles 4(3) and 33(3) combined create over-arching obligations upon states to actively support and engage with persons with disability in advancing the disability human rights paradigm. Article 4(3) requires states to closely consult with and actively involve persons with disability, through their representative organisations, in the development and implementation of legislation and policies to implement the convention, and in other decision-making processes concerning issues relating to persons with disability. Article 33(3) takes this obligation further by mandating that persons with disability, and their representative organisations, are involved and are fully able to effectively participate in the monitoring process of the convention.

The visible role that DPOs played during the drafting of the CRPD is reflected in General Comment No. 7, where the CRPD Committee explained that participation with disability-led representative groups represents an efficient and effective means of advancing the CRPD (United Nations Committee on the Rights of Persons with Disabilities, 2018A, Para. 24).

In addition to such engagement, the CRPD Committee has emphasised that Articles 4(3) and 33(3) necessitate genuine inclusion of people with a disability in different decision-making bodies 'both at local, regional, national and international level as well as in the National Human Rights Institutions ... ad-hoc committees, councils, regional or municipality organisations, as well as to be nominated or elected to any such democratic and representative forums' (United Nations Committee on the Rights of Persons with Disabilities, 2018A, Para. 24). As well as being present, the CRPD Committee has explained that this participation must take part throughout the decision-making process. Thus, General Comment No. 7 requires participation at all stages of public decision making, including before the adoption of legislation, policies, and programmes that affect persons with disability (United Nations Committee on the Rights of Persons with Disabilities, 2018A, Para. 19).

The CRPD requires that states alter their practices and funding to realise this new participatory dynamic (Harpur & Szucs, 2023; Stein & Stein, 2022). With respect to funding, in General Comment No. 7, the CRPD Committee explains that state parties should support DPOs through 'non-conditional and sufficient funding and technical capacity-building' (United Nations Committee on the Rights of Persons with Disabilities, 2018A, Para. 42). These capacity-building obligations extend beyond simply funding attendance at meetings. The CRPD Committee explains in General Comment No. 7 that the capacity building requires the development of technical, administrative, and communication skills in the disability community, as well as the facilitation of access to information, education, tools, and work opportunities so that people with a disability can devote time and effort to realising the participatory dynamic (United Nations Committee on the Rights of Persons with Disabilities, 2018A, Para. 42).

The CRPD Committee has applied the participatory dynamic expressly to people with cognitive disability in its General Comment No. 5 on Article 19 on Independent Living (United Nations Committee on the Rights of Persons with Disabilities, 2017, Para. 70). In General Comment

No. 7, the CRPD Committee observed that Article 4(3) of the CRPD requires decision makers to 'actively involve and consult the full range of persons with disabilities including organisations of . . . persons with psychosocial disabilities and persons with intellectual disabilities' (United Nations Committee on the Rights of Persons with Disabilities, 2017, Para. 70). Similarly, there are examples where the CRPD Committee has applied the participatory dynamic to people with cognitive disability through its Concluding Observations on state parties across a range of articles. Illustratively, when addressing General Obligations in Articles 1–4, the CRPD Committee raised concerns with the lack of measures to recognise 'organisations of persons with intellectual disabilities and involve them in decision-making forums' (United Nations Committee on the Rights of Persons with Disabilities, 2023E, Para. 9(b)). Similarly, when addressing Article 9 in its Concluding Observation on Mongolia, the CRPD Committee called for the meaningful participation with groups, including persons with 'intellectual and/or psychosocial disabilities, . . . autistic persons . . . and persons with disabilities requiring higher levels of support' (United Nations Committee on the Rights of Persons with Disabilities, 2023C, Para. 10). Further, in its Concluding Observation on Malawi, the CRPD Committee raised concerns with 'the underrepresentation of organisations of persons with intellectual disabilities' in consultations under Article 9, and adjured the state party to 'strengthen consultation with and the effective and meaningful participation of persons with disabilities through their representative organisations, including those that represent . . . persons with intellectual or psychosocial disabilities' (United Nations Committee on the Rights of Persons with Disabilities, 2023B, Paras. 9(a) and 64(c)). Even though it is not always necessary to specifically identify every disability group, this does become more important where a group is especially impacted. Accordingly, when the CRPD Committee advised Venezuela to amend its criminal and mental health laws, the Concluding Observation required the state party to do so 'in close consultation with organisations of persons with psychosocial or intellectual disabilities' (United Nations Committee on the Rights of Persons with Disabilities, 2022L, Para. 27(a)).

The CRPD and CRPD Committee on the Need for a Strategic Integrated Approach to Transition Rights

The CRPD framework requires that states have integrated disability strategies at the national level, along with supporting strategies that deal with individual rights in the Convention and then specific issues, such as national strategies to raise awareness throughout society by eliminating negative stereotypes and prejudice towards people who have a disability described in the Concluding Observations, as with intellectual and/or psychosocial disability (United Nations Committee on the Rights of Persons with Disabilities, 2022J, Para. 18(a); 2022K, Para. 16(a); 2023F, Para. 18(a); 2023G, Para. 16(a)).

The CRPD Committee has demonstrated the interconnectedness of disability strategies in its General Comment No. 4 on education (United Nations Committee on the Rights of Persons with Disabilities, 2016A). To advance the measures addressed in Article 24 and General Comment No. 4, the CRPD Committee requires that state parties 'adopt and implement a national educational strategy which includes provision of education at all levels for all learners, on the basis of inclusion and equality of opportunity' (United Nations Committee on the Rights of Persons with Disabilities, 2016A, Para. 40(c)). In addition to this national lifelong education strategy covering early childhood, through K-12, and into university and beyond, General Comment No. 4 also requires strategic responses to link other rights in the CRPD to education. For example, the CRPD links the right to education in Article 24 with Article 11 on situations of risk and humanitarian emergencies, where General Comment No. 4 requires state parties to adopt inclusive Disaster Risk Reduction strategies for comprehensive school safety and security in emergencies (United Nations Committee on the Rights of Persons with Disabilities, 2016A, Para. 14). Similarly, the CRPD Committee links the right to education with the right to live in the community in Article 19, through requiring in General Comment No. 4 that inclusive education in the local community must take place alongside a strategic commitment to the ending of institutions for persons with disability (United Nations Committee on the Rights of Persons with Disabilities, 2016A, Para. 50).

12.5 Conclusion

This book has reported profound human rights violations against young people with cognitive disability. Participants to this book have depicted a damning portrayal of how Australian policies and corresponding service systems have let young people with cognitive disability experience physical, emotional, and sexual assault; individual and systemic neglect; denial of decision-making rights; denial of parenting rights; disability discrimination; domestic and family violence; economic exploitation; exclusion from work and employment as well as safe and secure housing; refusal of medical treatment; and other forms of abuse and violence. It goes without saying that Australian policies and the underlying discourses must change so that rights can be realised and not denied.

Our overarching observation is that the violence experienced by young people with cognitive disability in transition cannot be framed as a housing problem, or a criminal justice problem, or an education problem, or through any other single silo. The causes of the violence are strongly interconnected across all domains of life. Accordingly, we recommend, in line with our CRPD obligations, that an integrated strategy across life stages and government agencies is critical to redressing the human rights violations experienced by young people with cognitive disability transitioning to adulthood.

Business as usual will not achieve equality. The CRPD, scholarship, and the participants in our book have highlighted that a conceptual shift is required so that persons with disability in Australia (and elsewhere) can realise equality. The absence of abuse, exploitation, neglect, and violence will not achieve this. Persons with disability have a right to equality in all walks of life: equal access to housing, health care, education, and work, and a voice in public affairs. The voices of young people, family members, and practitioners in this book have strongly called and fought for young people's right to exercise all their human rights on an equal basis as others.

Persons with disability all experience their disability differently. Young people with cognitive disability encounter different disabling barriers than persons who have mobility or sensory disabilities. Severity levels alter how barriers are experienced, and some people have multiple disabilities. Equally, people who have other attributes, such as First Nations Australians, people from culturally and linguistically diverse backgrounds, women overall, and those who identify as LGBTIQA+, experience intersecting vulnerabilities that impact how disablement is lived. We suggest that the reform agenda address all the causes of disablement, which will require situating disability within a broader concept of disadvantage. It also requires real and meaningful action and investment in challenging hegemonic ideology that results in ongoing social disadvantage: gender inequality and the corresponding unacceptable levels of gender-based violence, the ongoing impacts of colonisation on our First Nations Australian people, and systemic and ingrained racist discourses.

Our book was guided by young people with cognitive disability and led by people with both lived experience of disability and those with children with cognitive disability. The CRPD is based on 'nothing about us without us', and young people in this book repeatedly sought to have their voices heard. To realise equality and equity, and to fulfil Australia's obligations under international human rights law, it is critical to ensure persons with disability have representative access to the halls of power. This requires that persons with disability are leading the development, implementation, and monitoring of disability interventions.

Fundamentally, this book has demonstrated the need for a significant cultural shift in the discourse of disability, and how this is created and perpetuated, systemically and structurally. Without significant cultural reform in terms of dominant and hegemonic discourses, we will continue to have business as usual, yet this is not good enough. Society creates the barriers and constructs the vulnerabilities that result in abuse, harm, and exploitation; it is up to us collectively, both in Australia and internationally, to pull these down and create a society that values every single person.

References

Algood, C. L., Hong, J. S., Gourdine, R. M., & Williams, A. B. (2011). Maltreatment of children with developmental disabilities: An ecological systems analysis. *Children and Youth Services Review*, 33(7), 1142–1148. https://doi.org/10.1016/j.childyouth.2011.02.003

American Psychiatric Association. (2013). *Diagnostic and statistical manual of mental disorders: DSM-5* (5th ed.). American Psychiatric Association.

(2022). *Diagnostic and statistical manual of mental disorders: DSM-5-TR* (5th ed., text revision ed.). American Psychiatric Association Publishing.

Amparo Advocacy. (2016). The NDIS and culturally and linguistically diverse communities: Aiming high for equitable access in Queensland. www.amparo.org.au/wp/wp-content/uploads/2016/11/AMPARO-report-for-CALD-NDIS-hr-003.pdf

Anderson, J., McVilly, K., Koritsas, S., Johnson, H., Wiese, M., Stancliffe, R., Lyon, K., & Rezzani, N. (2017). Accessible written information resources for adults with intellectual disability: Compiling the evidence to inform good practice. www.scopeaust.org.au/news-event/accessible-written-information-resources-adults-intellectual-disability/

Armitage R. (2021). Bullying in children: Impact on child health. *BMJ Paediatrics Open*, 5(1), e000939. https://10.1136/bmjpo-2020-000939

Arstein-Kerslake, A. (2019). Gendered denials: Vulnerability created by barriers to legal capacity for women and disabled women. *International Journal of Law and Psychiatry*, 66(September–October), 101501. https://doi.org/10.1136/bmjpo-2020-000939

Aspinal, F., Stevens, M., Manthorpe, J., Woolham, J., Samsi, K., Baxter, K., Hussein, S., & Ismail, M. (2019). Safeguarding and personal budgets: The experiences of adults at risk. *Journal of Adult Protection*, 21(3), 157–168. https://doi.org/10.1108/jap-12-2018-0030

Australian Bureau of Statistics (ABS). (2016). Personal Safety Survey, Australia. www.abs.gov.au/statistics/people/crime-and-justice/personal-safety-australia/2016

Australian Institute of Health and Welfare (AIHW). (2007). Disability in Australia: Acquired brain injury. *Bulletin* 55, 1–28.

(2018). Aboriginal and Torres Strait Islander adolescent and youth health and wellbeing. aihw.gov.au/getmedia/b40149b6-d133-4f16-a1e8-5a98617b8488/aihw-ihw-202.pdf?v=20230605181520&inline=true

(2022). People with disability in Australia. www.aihw.gov.au/reports/disability/people-with-disability-in-australia/contents/justice-and-safety/violence-against-people-with-disability

(2023). Family, domestic and sexual violence. www.aihw.gov.au/reports/domestic-violence/family-domestic-and-sexual-violence

Australian Research Centre in Sex, Health and Society, & Living with Disability Research Centre, La Trobe University. (2022). Violence, abuse, neglect, and exploitation of LGBTQA+ people with disability: Report prepared for the Royal Commission into Violence, Abuse, Neglect and Exploitation of People with Disability.

Baidawi, S., Sheehan, R., & Flynn, C. (2020). Criminal exploitation of child protection-involved youth. *Children and Youth Services Review*, 118(15), 105396. https://doi.org/10.1016/j.childyouth.2020.105396

Bailey, C. A. (2018). *A guide to qualitative field research* (3rd ed.). SAGE Publications.

Baker Collins, S., Schormans, A. F., Watt, L., Idems, B., & Wilson, T. (2018). The invisibility of disability for homeless youth. *Journal of Social Distress and Homeless*, 27(2), 99–109. https://doi.org/10.1080/10530789.2018.1480892

Baldry, E., Clarence, M., Dowse, L., & Trollor, J. (2013). Reducing vulnerability to harm in adults with cognitive disabilities in the Australian criminal justice system. *Journal of Policy and Practice in Intellectual Disabilities*, 10(3), 222–229. https://doi.org/10.1111/jppi.12039

Baldry, E., McCausland, R., Dowse, L., & McEntyre, E. (2015). A predictable and preventable path: Aboriginal people with mental and cognitive disabilities in the criminal justice system. www.mhdcd.unsw.edu.au/a-predictable-and-preventable-path-iamhdcd-report.html

Baldry, E., McCausland, R., Dowse, L., McEntyre, E., & MacGillivray, P. (2016). 'It's just a big vicious cycle that swallows them up': Indigenous people with mental and cognitive disabilities in the criminal justice system. *Indigenous Law Bulletin*. https://doi.org/10.3316/ielapa.896305946383264

Bantekas, I. (2018). Article 7: Children with disabilities. In I. Bantekas, M. A. Stein, & D. Anastasiou (Eds.), *The UN Convention on the Rights of Persons with Disabilities: A commentary*, pp. 198–228. Oxford University Press.

Bantekas, I. Pennilas, F., & Trömel, S. (2018). Article 27: Work and employment. In I. Bantekas, M. A. Stein, & D. Anastasiou (Eds.), *The UN Convention on the Rights of Persons with Disabilities: A commentary*, pp. 764–800. Oxford University Press.

Bantekas, I., Stein, M. A., & Anastasiou, D. (Eds.). (2018). *The UN Convention on the Rights of Persons with Disabilities: A commentary*. Oxford University Press. https://doi.org/10.1093/law/9780198810667.001.0001

Barron, I., Allardyce, S., Young, H., & Levit, R. (2019). Exploration of the relationship between severe and complex disabilities and child sexual abuse: A call for relevant research. *Journal of Child Sexual Abuse*, 28(7), 759–780. https://doi.org/10.1080/10538712.2019.1645782

Basterfield, C. (2019). Plain language easy English. What does it all mean? *Intellectual Disability Australasia*, 40(2), 15–18.

Bates, C. (2020). 'It's nothing to be ashamed of, I'm like, I'm bisexual and I love women, I like men': Being a bisexual person with an intellectual disability. *Journal of Bisexuality*, 20(4), 493–513. https://doi.org/10.1080/15299716.2020.1836544

Beadle-Brown, J., Mansell, J., Cambridge, P., Milne, A., & Whelton, B. (2010). Adult protection of people with intellectual disabilities: Incidence, nature and responses. *Journal of Applied Research in Intellectual Disabilities*, 23(6), 573–584.

Beckene, T., Forrester-Jones, R., & Murphy, G. H. (2020). Experiences of going to court: Witnesses with intellectual disabilities and their carers speak up. *Journal of Applied Research in Intellectual Disabilities*, 33(1), 67–78. https://doi.org/10.1111/jar.12334

Bekken, W. (2020). Negotiating embodied knowledge in the transition to adulthood: A social model of human rights. *Disability & Society*, n.p. https://doi.org/10.1080/09687599.2020.1816902

(2022). Negotiating embodied knowledge in the transition to adulthood: A social model of human rights. *Disability & Society*, 37(2), 163–182. https://doi.org/10.1080/09687599.2020.1816902

Bennett, B. (2013). The importance of Aboriginal and Torres Strait Islander history for social work students and graduates. In B. Bennett, S. Green, S. Gilbert, & D. Bessarab (Eds.), *Our voices: Aboriginal and Torres Strait Islander social work*, pp. 1–25. Palgrave Macmillan.

Bigby, C. (2014). Is the National Disability Insurance Scheme taking account of people with intellectual disabilities? *Research and Practice in Intellectual and Developmental Disabilities*, 1(2), 93–97. https://doi.org/10.1080/23297018.2014.974484

(2021). 'The scheme was designed with a very different idea in mind of who a disabled person is': The National Disability Insurance Scheme and people with intellectual disability. In M. Cowden & C. McCullagh (Eds.), *The National Disability Insurance Scheme: An Australian public policy experiment*, pp. 257–283. Palgrave Macmillan.

Bigby, C., Knox, M., Beadle-Brown, J., Clement, T., & Mansell, J. (2012). Uncovering dimensions of culture in underperforming group homes for people with severe intellectual disability. *Intellectual and Developmental Disabilities*, 50(6), 452–467. https://doi.org/10.1352/1934-9556-50.06.452

Boodle, A., Ellem, K., & Chenoweth, L. (2014). Anna's story of life in prison. *British Journal of Learning Disabilities*, 42(2), 117–124. https://doi.org/10.1111/bld.12015

Braun, V., & Clarke, V. (2022). *Thematic analysis: A practical guide*. SAGE Publications.

Brendli, K., Broda, M., & Brown, R. (2021). Children with intellectual disability and victimization: A logistic regression analysis. *Child Maltreatment*, 1–5, Article 1077559521994177. https://doi.org/10.1177/1077559521994177

Brennan-Krohn, Z. (2016). Employment for people with disabilities: A role for anti-subordination. *Harvard Civil Rights-Civil Liberties Law Review*, 51, 239–272.

Brenner, J., Pan, Z., Mazefsky, C., Smith, K. A., & Gabriels, R. (2018). Behavioral symptoms of reported abuse in children and adolescents with autism spectrum disorder in inpatient settings. *Journal of Autism and Developmental Disorders*, 48(11), 3727–3735. https://doi.org/10.1007/s10803-017-3183-4

Broadley, K. (2015). Is there a role for adult protection services in the lives of young people with disabilities transitioning from out-of-home care? *Australian Social Work*, 68(1), 84–98. https://doi.org/10.1080/0312407X.2014.932400

Bronfenbrenner, U. (1986). Ecology of the family as a context for human development: Research perspectives. *Developmental Psychology*, 22(6), 723–742. https://doi.org/10.1037/0012-1649.22.6.723

Brookes, L., & Ballantyne, T. (2019). Review and appeal rights in the NDIS. Precedent (Sydney, N.S.W.), (154), 8–11.

Brown, H. (1994). 'An ordinary sexual life?': A review of the normalisation principle as it applies to the sexual options of people with learning disabilities. *Disability & Society*, 9(2), 123–144. https://doi.org/10.1080/09687599466780181

Buijs, P. C. M., Boot, E., Shugar, A., Fung, W. L. A., & Bassett, A. S. (2017). Internet safety issues for adolescents and adults with intellectual disabilities. *Journal of Applied Research in Intellectual Disabilities*, 30(2), 416–418. https://doi.org/10.1111/jar.12250

Buljevac, M., Milić Babić, M., & Leutar, Z. (2022). 'You don't have to tell me in person I'm not to your liking': Experiences of discrimination of people with intellectual disabilities. *International Journal of Disability, Development, and Education*, 69(3), 837–852. https://doi.org/10.1080/1034912X.2020.1736522

Burch, L. (2021). *Understanding disability and everyday hate* (1st ed.). Palgrave Macmillan.

Burns, N. (2020). Boundary maintenance: Exploring the intersections of disability and migration. In N. Watson & S. Vehmas (Eds.), *Routledge handbook of disability studies* (2nd ed.), pp. 305–320. Routledge.

Cantor, J., McBain, R. K., Kofner, A., Stein, B. D., & Yu, H. (2020). Fewer than half of US mental health treatment facilities provide services for children with autism spectrum disorder: Results from a survey of US mental health treatment facilities on the availability of behavioral health care services for children with autism spectrum disorder. *Health Affairs*, 39(6), 968–974. https://doi.org/10.1377/hlthaff.2019.01557

Carey, G., Malbon, E., Olney, S., & Reeders, D. (2018). The personalisation agenda: The case of the Australian National Disability Insurance Scheme. *International Review of Sociology*, 28(1), 20–34. https://doi.org/10.1080/03906701.2018.1425084

Chan, K. W., Young, J., Williams, L. J., & Nottle, C. (2022). Assistance dogs in occupational therapy practice: A survey of Australian occupational therapists' experiences and recommendations. *Australian Occupational Therapy Journal*, 69(2), 129–139. https://doi.org/10.1111/1440-1630.12775

Cheng, Z. M., Tani, M., & Katz, I. (2023). Outcomes for children with disability in out-of-home care: Evidence from the pathways of care longitudinal study in Australia. *Child Abuse & Neglect*, 143(106246), 1–16. https://doi.org/10.1016/j.chiabu.2023.106246

Chowdhury, P. R. (2011). The right to inclusive education of persons with disabilities: The policy and practice implications. *Asia Pacific Journal on Human Rights and Law,* (1), 1–36. www.rodra.co.za/images/documents/inclusive_education/The%20Right%20to%20Inclusive%20Education%20of%20Persons%20with%20Disabilities%20The%20Policy%20and%20Practice.pdf

Chung, E. (2018). The child welfare and education gap. *Yale Law & Policy Review*, 36(2), 365–418.

Cocks, E., Thoresen, S. H., O'Brien, P., McVilly, K., Thomson, A., Gadow, F., & Prain, M. (2016). Examples of individual supported living for adults with intellectual disability. *Journal of Intellectual Disabilities*, 20(2), 100–108. https://doi.org/10.1177/1744629516629854

Collings, S., Dew, A., & Dowse, L. (2019). 'They need to be able to have walked in our shoes': What people with intellectual disability say about National Disability Insurance Scheme planning. *Journal of Intellectual & Developmental Disability*, 44(1), 1–12. https://doi.org/10.3109/13668250.2017.1287887

Collings, S., Spencer, M., Dew, A., & Dowse, L. (2018). 'She was there if I needed to talk or to try and get my point across': Specialist advocacy for parents with intellectual disability in the Australian child protection system. *Australian Journal of Human Rights*, 24(2), 162–181. https://doi.org/10.1080/1323238X.2018.1478595

Collins, J., & Murphy, G. H. (2022). Detection and prevention of abuse of adults with intellectual and other developmental disabilities in care services: A systematic review. *Journal of Applied Research in Intellectual Disabilities*, 35(2), 338–373. https://doi.org/10.1111/jar.12954

Corr, C., Miller, D., Spence, C., Marshall, A. A., Mott, K., & Kretzer, J. (2019). 'It's never black and white': Early interventionists' experiences supporting abused children and their families. *Psychological Services*, 16(1), 103–110.

Cortese, C., Truscott, F., Nikidehaghani, M., & Chapple, S. (2021). Hard-to-reach: The NDIS, disability, and socio-economic disadvantage. *Disability & Society*, 36(6), 883–903. https://doi.org/10.1080/09687599.2020.1782173

Cremin, K. (2018). Article 28: Adequate standard of living and social protection. In I. Bantekas, M. A Stein, & D. Anastasiou (Eds.), *The UN Convention on the Rights of Persons with Disabilities: A commentary*, pp. 801–832. Oxford University Press.

Crenshaw, K. (1989). Demarginalising the intersection of race and sex: A black feminist critique of antidiscrimination doctrine, feminist theory and anti-racist politics. *University of Chicago Legal Forum*, 1989(1), 139–168.

Crowley, E. P. (2016). *Preventing abuse and neglect in the lives of children with disabilities*. Springer International.

Cuervo, H., Barakat, N., & Turnbull, M. (2015). *Youth, belonging and transitions: Identifying opportunities and barriers for Indigenous young people in remote communities*. Youth Research Centre. University of Melbourne.

Curtiss, S. L., & Kammes, R. (2020). Understanding the risk of sexual abuse for adults with intellectual and developmental disabilities from an ecological framework. *Journal of Policy and Practice in Intellectual Disabilities*, 17(1), 13–20. https://doi.org/10.1111/jppi.12318

Dammeyer, J., & Chapman, M. (2018). A national survey on violence and discrimination among people with disabilities. *BMC Public Health*, 18(1), 355–364. https://doi.org/10.1186/s12889-018-5277-0

Darragh, J., Reynolds, L., Ellison, C., & Bellon, M. (2017). Let's talk about sex: How people with intellectual disability in Australia engage with online social media and intimate relationships. *Cyberpsychology*, 11(1), 1–9. https://doi.org/10.5817/CP2017-1-9

Davis, A., & Gourdine, R. (2022). Intersectionality and social security age-18 redetermination: Reducing the stress and trauma of transition for black transition-age youth with disabilities. *Child & Adolescent Social Work Journal*. https://doi.org/10.1007/s10560-022-00892-y

DaWalt, L. S. Taylor, J. L., & Mailick, M. R. (2021). The transition to adulthood for individuals with intellectual and developmental disabilities. In L. M. Glidden, L. Abbeduto, L. L. McIntyre, & M. J. Tassé (Eds.), *APA handbook of intellectual and developmental disabilities: Clinical and educational implications: Prevention, intervention, and treatment*, vol. 2, pp. 281–298. American Psychological Association.

de Beco, G., Lord, J. E., & Quinlivan, S. (Eds.). (2018). *The right to inclusive education in international human rights law*. Harvard Law School Project on Disability. Cambridge University Press. https://doi.org/10.1017/9781316392881

Department of Justice and Regulation. (2005). *Victorian implementation review of the recommendations from the Royal Commission into Aboriginal Deaths in Custody*, vol. 1. Victoria State Government.

Dhanda, A. (2012). Universal legal capacity as a universal human right. In M. Dudley, D. Silove, & F. Gale (Eds.), *Mental health and human rights: Vision, praxis, and courage*, pp. 177–188. Oxford University Press.

Dinwoodie, R., Greenhill, B., & Cookson, A. (2020). 'Them two things are what collide together': Understanding the sexual identity experiences of lesbian, gay, bisexual and trans people labelled with intellectual disability. *Journal of Applied Research in Intellectual Disabilities*, 33(1), 3–16. https://doi.org/10.1111/jar.12252

Douglas, H., & Harpur, P. (2016). Intellectual disabilities, domestic violence and legal engagement. *Disability & Society*, 31(3), 305–321. https://doi.org/10.1080/09687599.2016.1167673

Dowse, L., Cumming, T. M., Strnadová, I., Lee, J.-S., & Trofimovs, J. (2014). Young people with complex needs in the criminal justice system. *Research and Practice in Intellectual and Developmental Disabilities*, 1(2), 174–185. https://doi.org/10.1080/23297018.2014.953671

Dowse, L., Rowe, S., Baldry, E., & Baker, M. (2021). Research report: Police responses to people with disability. Royal Commission into Violence, Abuse, Neglect and Exploitation of People with Disability. Commonwealth of Australia. https://disability.royalcommission.gov.au/system/files/2023-05/Research%20Report%20-%20Police%20responses%20to%20people%20with%20disability.pdf

Dowse, L., Soldatic, K., Didi, A., Frohmader, C., & van Toorn, G. (2013). Stop the violence: Addressing violence against women and girls with disabilities in Australia. Background Paper. https://doi.org/10.3316/ielapa.319572534274985

Dowse, L., Soldatic, K., Spangaro, J., & Van Toorn, G. (2016). Mind the gap: The extent of violence against women with disabilities in Australia. *Australian Journal of Social Issues*, 51(3), 341–359.

DRC. (2023). Final report: Executive summary, our vision for an inclusive Australia and recommendations. Royal Commission into Violence, Abuse, Neglect and Exploitation of People with Disability.

(2023A). Voices of people with disability. Final Report: Volume 1. Royal Commission into Violence, Abuse, Neglect and Exploitation of People with Disability.

(2023B). About the Royal Commission. Final Report: Volume 2. Royal Commission into Violence, Abuse, Neglect and Exploitation of People with Disability.

(2023C). Nature and extent of violence, abuse, neglect and exploitation: Final Report Volume 3. Royal Commission into Violence, Abuse, Neglect and Exploitation of People with Disability.

(2023D). Realising the DRC 2023D human rights of people with disability. Final Report: Volume 4. Royal Commission into Violence, Abuse, Neglect and Exploitation of People with Disability.

(2023E). Governing for inclusion. Final Report: Volume 5. Royal Commission into Violence, Abuse, Neglect and Exploitation of People with Disability.

(2023F). Enabling autonomy and access. Final Report: Volume 6. Royal Commission into Violence, Abuse, Neglect and Exploitation of People with Disability.

(2023G). Inclusive education, employment and housing. Final Report: Volume 7. Royal Commission into Violence, Abuse, Neglect and Exploitation of People with Disability.

(2023H). Criminal justice and people with disability. Final Report: Volume 8. Royal Commission into Violence, Abuse, Neglect and Exploitation of People with Disability.

(2023I). First Nations people with disability. Final Report: Volume 9. Royal Commission into Violence, Abuse, Neglect and Exploitation of People with Disability.

(2023J). Disability services. Final Report: Volume 10. Royal Commission into Violence, Abuse, Neglect and Exploitation of People with Disability.

(2023K). Independent oversight and complaint mechanisms. Final Report: Volume 11. Royal Commission into Violence, Abuse, Neglect and Exploitation of People with Disability.

(2023L). Beyond the Royal Commission. Final Report: Volume 12. Royal Commission into Violence, Abuse, Neglect and Exploitation of People with Disability.

Duffy, S., & Gillespie, J. (2009). Personalisation & Safeguarding. www.in-control.org.uk/media/52833/personalisation%20safeguarding%20discussion%20paper%20version%201.0.pdf

Eastgate, G., Scheermeyer, E., van Driel, M. L., & Lennox, N. (2012). Intellectual disability, sexuality and sexual abuse prevention: A study of family members and support workers. *Australian Family Physician*, 41(3), 135–139.

Ellem, K., Baidawi, S., Dowse, L., & Smith, L. (2019). Services to young people with complex support needs in rural and regional Australia: Beyond a metro-centric response. *Children and Youth Services Review*, 99, 97–106. https://doi.org/10.1016/j.childyouth.2019.01.033

Ellem, K., Denton, M., & Davidson, D. (2020). Supporting people with intellectual and developmental disabilities leaving prison. In W. Lindsay, L. Craig, & D. Griffiths (Eds.), *What works for offenders with intellectual and developmental disabilities*, pp. 263–282. Wiley-Blackwell.

Ellem, K., & Richards, K. (2018). Police contact with young people with cognitive disabilities: Perceptions of procedural (in)justice. *Youth Justice*, 18(3), 230–247. https://doi.org/10.1177/1473225418794357

Ellem, K., Smith, L., Baidawi, S., McGhee, A., & Dowse, L. (2020). Transcending the professional-client divide: Supporting young people with complex support needs through transitions. *Child & Adolescent Social Work Journal*, 37(2), 109–122. https://doi.org/10.1007/s10560-020-00651-x

Ellem, K., Wilson, J., & Chenoweth, L. (2016). When families relinquish care of a child with a disability: Perceptions from birthmothers. *Australian Social Work*, 69(1), 39–50.

Eriksson, A., Saunders, B., Lansdell, G., & Bunn, R. (2019). 'Short fuse and no filter': Acquired brain injury – How a medical disability transforms into a social and criminal justice concern. *International Journal of Law, Crime & Justice*, 57, 126–136.

Federation of Ethnic Communities' Councils of Australia, National Ethnic Disability Alliance, Refugee Council of Australia, & Settlement Council of Australia. (2019). Barriers and exclusions: The support needs of newly arrived refugees with a disability. www.amparo.org.au/publications-reports-2/

Fennell, P., & Keeling, A. (2018). Article 16: Freedom from exploitation, violence and abuse. In I. Bantekas, M. A. Stein, & D. Anastasiou (Eds.), *The UN Convention on the Rights of Persons with Disabilities: A commentary*, pp. 466–493. Oxford University Press.

Fiala-Butora, J. (2018). Article 23: Respect for home and the family. In I. Bantekas, M. A. Stein, & D. Anastasiou (Eds.), *The UN Convention on the*

Rights of Persons with Disabilities: A commentary, pp. 628–655. Oxford University Press.

Fisher, K. R., Purcal, C., Jones, A., Lutz, D., Robinson, S., & Kayess, R. (2021). What place is there for shared housing with individualized disability support? *Disability and Rehabilitation: An International, Multidisciplinary Journal*, 43(1), 60–68. https://doi.org/10.1080/09638288.2019.1615562

Fisher, M., Epstein, R. A., Urbano, R. C., Vehorn, A., Cull, M. J., & Warren, Z. (2019). A population-based examination of maltreatment referrals and substantiation for children with autism spectrum disorder. *Autism*, 23(5), 1335–1340. https://doi.org/10.1177/1362361318813998

Fisher, M. H., Baird, J. V., Currey, A. D., & Hodapp, R. M. (2016). Victimisation and social vulnerability of adults with intellectual disability: A review of research extending beyond Wilson and Brewer. *Australian Psychologist*, 51(2), 114–127.

Fisher, M. H., Shivers, C. M., & Josol, C. K. (2020). Psychometric properties and utility of the social vulnerability questionnaire for individuals with intellectual and developmental disabilities. *Journal of Autism and Developmental Disorders*, 50(7), 2348–2359. https://doi.org/10.1007/s10803-018-3636-4

Flynn, S. (2021). Measuring parenting capacity for disabled children using a child protection assessment. *Journal of Social Work*, 21(6), 1489–1511. https://doi.org/10.1177/1468017320957492

Forster, S., & Pearson, A. (2020). 'Bullies tend to be obvious': Autistic adults' perceptions of friendship and the concept of 'mate crime'. *Disability & society*, 35(7), 1103–1123. https://doi.org/10.1080/09687599.2019.1680347

Franklin, A., & Smeaton, E. (2017). Recognising and responding to young people with learning disabilities who experience, or are at risk of, child sexual exploitation in the UK. *Children and Youth Services Review*, 73, 474–481. https://doi.org/10.1016/j.childyouth.2016.11.009

Frohmader, C., Dowse, L., & Didi, A. (2015). *Preventing violence against women and girls with disabilities: Integrating a human rights perspective in domestic violence in Australia. Submission 160*. Women with Disabilities Australia. wwda.org.au/wp-content/uploads/2015/04/Think-Piece_WWD.pdf

Fyson, R., & Kitson, D. (2010). Human rights and social wrongs: Issues in safeguarding adults with learning disabilities. *Practice*, 22(5), 309–320. https://doi.org/10.1080/09503153.2010.517831

Garolera, G. D., Díaz, M. P., & Noell, J. F. (2021). Friendship barriers and supports: Thoughts of young people with intellectual disabilities. *Journal of Youth Studies*, 24(6), 815–83. https://doi.org/10.1080/13676261.2020.1772464

Gibbs, A. (2022). We are not doing enough for children with neuro-disabilities. *Aotearoa New Zealand Social Work*, 34(2), 90–93.

Gibson, M. (2020). There's no safe place at home: Domestic and family violence affecting LGBTIQ+ people. https://search.informit.org/doi/10.3316/cinch.130925997

Gill-Atkinson, L., Devine, A., Zayas, J., Marco, M., Ignacio, R., Marella, R., & UP Center for Women's Studies Foundation. (2018). *Promoting disability inclusion in sexual and reproductive health research and programming: Experiences from W-DARE*. University of Melbourne.

Gilmore, L., & Cuskelly, M. (2014). Vulnerability to loneliness in people with intellectual disability: An explanatory model. *Journal of Policy and Practice in Intellectual Disabilities*, 11(3), 192–199.

Ginn, H. (2021). *Securing sexual justice for people with intellectual disability: A systematic review and critical appraisal of research recommendations. Journal of Applied Research in Intellectual Disabilities*, 1–14. https://doi.org/10.1111/jar.12867

Goffman, E. (1963). *Stigma: Notes on the management of spoiled identity*. Prentice-Hall.

Goodley, D., & Runswick-Cole, K. (2011). The violence of disablism. *Sociology of Health & Illness*, 33(4), 602–617. https://doi.org/10.1111/j.1467-9566.2010.01302.x

Gratton, F. (2021). Neurodiversity. In A. Goldberg & G. Beemyn (Eds.), *The SAGE encyclopedia of trans studies: M–Z*, pp. 564–567. SAGE. https://doi.org/10.4135/9781544393858

Gray, B., & Ridden, G. (1999). *Lifemaps of people with learning disabilities*. Jessica Kingsley.

Gray, M. Hetherington, T. (2013). Indigenization, Indigenous social work and decolonization: Mapping the theoretical terrain. In M. Gray, J. Coates, M. Yellow Bird, & T. Hetherington (Eds.), *Decolonizing social work*, pp. 1–19. Ashgate.

Green, A., Abbott, P., Davidson, P. M., Delaney, P., Delaney, J., Patradoon-Ho, P., & DiGiacomo, M. (2018). Interacting with providers: An intersectional exploration of the experiences of carers of Aboriginal children with a disability. *Qualitative Health Research*, 28(12), 1923–1932. https://doi.org/10.1177/1049732318793416

Hall, P. (2019). Disability hate speech: Interrogating the online/offline distinction. In K. Lumsden & E. Harmer (Eds.), *Online othering: Exploring digital violence and discrimination on the web*, pp. 309–330. Palgrave Macmillan.

Harpur, P. (2010). Rights of persons with disabilities and Australian anti-discrimination laws: What happened to the legal protections for people using guide or assistance dogs? *University of Tasmania Law Review*, 29(1), 49–79.

(2017). Nothing about us without us: The UN Convention on the Rights of Persons with Disabilities. In A. Leithner & K. Libby (Eds.), *Oxford research encyclopedia of politics*, pp. 49–79. Oxford University Press.

(2020). *Ablism at work: Disablement and hierarchies of impairment*. Cambridge University Press.

Harpur, P., Connolly, U., & Blanck, P. (2017). Socially constructed hierarchies of impairments: The case of Australian and Irish workers' access to compensation for injuries. *Journal Occupational Rehability*, 27(4), 507–519. https://doi.org/10.1007/s10926-017-9745-7

Harpur, P., & Douglas, H. (2014). Disability and domestic violence: Protecting survivors' human rights. *Griffith Law Review*, 23(3), 405–433.

Harpur, P., & Stein, M. A. (2018). Indigenous persons with disabilities and the Convention on the Rights of Persons with Disabilities: An identity without a home? *International Human Rights Law Review*, 7(2), 165–200.

(2019). Children with disabilities, human rights, and sustainable development. In C. Fenton-Glynn (Ed.), *Children's rights and sustainable development: Interpreting the UNCRC for future generations*, pp. 139–164). Cambridge University Press. https://doi.org/10.1017/9781108140348.007

(2022). The UN Convention on the Rights of Persons with Disabilities and the global south. *Yale Journal of International Law*, 47(1), 75–117. http://hdl.handle.net/20.500.13051/18064

(2022A). The Convention on the Rights of Persons with Disabilities as a global tipping point for the participation of persons with disabilities. In A. Leithner & K. Libby (Eds.), *Oxford research encyclopedia of politics*, pp. 1–22. Oxford University Press.

Harpur, P., & Szucs, B. (2023). Using the new disability human rights paradigm to create higher education leadership opportunities. *International Journal of Discrimination and the Law*, 23(1–2), 144–162. https://doi.org/10.1177/13582291231169668

Harris, B., & Woodlock, D. (2021). *'For my safety': Experiences of technology-facilitated abuse among women with intellectual disability or cognitive disability.* eSafety Commissioner. www.esafety.gov.au/about-us/research/technology-facilitated-abuse-women-intellectual-or-cognitive-disability

Harwick, R. M., Unruh, D., & Lindstrom, L. (2020). Transition to adulthood for youth with disabilities who experienced foster care: An ecological approach. *Child Abuse & Neglect*, 99, 104–310. https://doi.org/10.1016/j.chiabu.2019.104310

Healy, J. C. (2020). 'It spreads like a creeping disease': Experiences of victims of disability hate crimes in austerity Britain. *Disability & Society*, 35(2), 176–200. https://doi.org/10.1080/09687599.2019.1624151

Henderson, D., & Bigby, C. (2021). Stories from the wild west frontier: The National Disability Insurance Scheme experiences of people with severe and profound intellectual disability. In M. Cowden & C. McCullagh (Eds.), *The National Disability Insurance Scheme: An Australian public policy experiment*, pp. 381–402. Palgrave Macmillan.

Hill, A., Lyons, A., Jones, J., McGowan, I., Carman, M., Parsons, M., Power, J., & Bourne, A. (2021). *Writing themselves in 4: The health and wellbeing of LGBTQA+ young people in Australia.* National report, monograph series 124. La Trobe University.

Hill, L., Baker, C., Kelly, B., & Dowling, S. (2017). Being counted? Examining the prevalence of looked-after disabled children and young people across the UK. *Child & Family Social Work*, 22(1), 287–295. https://doi.org/10.1111/cfs.12239

Hill Collins, P., & Bilge, S. (2016). *Intersectionality*. Polity Press.

Hoffman, L. C. (2013). An employment opportunity or a discrimination dilemma? Sheltered workshops and the employment of the disabled.

University of Pennsylvania Journal of Law and Social Change, 16(2–3). https://scholarship.law.upenn.edu/jlasc/vol16/iss2/3

Holland, L., Reid, N., & Smirnov, A. (2023). Neurodevelopmental disorders in youth justice: A systematic review of screening, assessment and interventions. *Journal of Experimental Criminology*, 19(1), 31–70. https://doi.org/10.1007/s11292-021-09475-w

Hollomotz, A. (2009). Beyond 'vulnerability': An ecological model approach to conceptualizing risk of sexual violence against people with learning difficulties. *British Journal of Social Work*, 39(1), 99–112. https://doi.org/10.1093/bjsw/bcm091

(2012). 'A lad tried to get hold of my boobs, so I kicked him': An examination of attempts by adults with learning difficulties to initiate their own safeguarding. *Disability & Society*, 27(1), 117–129.

Holt-Lunstad, J. (2022). Positive social connection: A key pillar of lifestyle medicine. *Journal of Family Practice*, 71(1), S38–S40. https://doi.org/10.12788/jfp.0245

Holt-Lunstad, J., & Steptoe, A. (2022). Social isolation: An underappreciated determinant of physical health. *Current Opinion in Psychology*, 43, 232–237.

Human Rights Watch. (2020). *'He's never coming back': People with disabilities dying in Western Australia's prisons*. Human Rights Watch.

Hutchison, A., & Kroese, B. (2015). A review of literature exploring the possible causes of abuse and neglect in adult residential care. *Journal of Adult Protection*, 17(4), 216–233. https://doi.org/10.1108/jap-11-2014-0034

Ismail, M., Hussein, S., Stevens, M., Woolham, J., Manthorpe, J., Aspinal, F., Baxter, K., & Samsi, K. (2017). Do personal budgets increase the risk of abuse? Evidence from English national data. *Journal of Social Policy*, 46(2), 291–311. https://doi.org/10.1017/s0047279416000623

Jacobs, P., MacMahon, K., & Quayle, E. (2020). Who decides? Transitions from school to adult services for and with young people with severe intellectual disabilities. *Disability & Society*, 35(7), 1058–1084. https://doi.org/10.1080/09687599.2019.1669435

Jawaid, A., Riby, D. M., Owens, J., White, S. W., Tarar, T., & Schulz, P. E. (2012). 'Too withdrawn' or 'too friendly': Considering social vulnerability in two neuro-developmental disorders. *Journal of Intellectual Disability Research*, 56(4), 335–350. https://doi.org/10.1111/j.1365-2788.2011.01452.x

Jenaro, C., Flores, N., Vega, V., Cruz, M., Pérez, M. C., & Torres, V. A. (2018). Cyberbullying among adults with intellectual disabilities: Some preliminary data. *Research in Developmental Disabilities*, 72, 265–274. https://doi.org/10.1016/j.ridd.2017.12.006

Johnson, B. J. (2020). Daily life in National Disability Insurance Scheme times: Parenting a child with Down syndrome and the disability politics in everyday places. *Qualitative Social Work: Research and Practice*, 19(3), 532–548. https://doi.org/10.1177/1473325020911691

Johnson, H., & Yee, R. (2020). Perceptions of frontline staff to training and communication tools to support adults with intellectual disabilities to report abuse and neglect: 'Something to work with'. *Research and Practice in Intellectual and Developmental Disabilities*, 7(1), 75–86. https://doi.org/10.1080/23297018.2019.1680312

Jorgensen, C. R., Dobson, G., & Perry, T. (2021). Migrant children with special educational needs in European schools: A review of current issues and approaches. *European Journal of Special Needs Education*, 36(3), 438–453. https://doi.org/10.1080/08856257.2020.1762988

Kapp, S. K. (2020). Introduction. In S. K. Kapp (Ed.), *Autistic community and the neurodiversity movement stories from the frontline*. Springer Nature Palgrave Macmillan.

Kappelides P., Bould, E., & Bigby, C. (2021). Barriers to physical activity and sport participation for people with intellectual disabilities from culturally and linguistically diverse backgrounds. *Research and Practice in Intellectual and Developmental Disabilities*, 8(2), 157–169. https://doi.org/10.1080/23297018.2021.1939114

Kendrick, M. (1996). The natural authority of families. *CRUcial Times*, (6), 1–2.

Khalifeh, H., Howard, L. M., Osborn, D., Moran, P., & Johnson, S. (2013). Violence against people with disability in England and Wales: Findings from a national cross-sectional survey. *PLoS ONE*, 8(2), e55952–e55952.

Khawaja, N. G., & Carr, K. (2020). Exploring the factor structure and psychometric properties of an Acculturation and Resilience Scale with culturally and linguistically diverse adolescents. *Australian Psychologist*, 55(1), 26–37. https://doi.org/10.1111/ap.12436

Khawaja, N. G., & Ramirez, E. (2019). Building resilience in transcultural adolescents: An evaluation of a group program. *Journal of Child and Family Studies*, 28(11), 2977–2987. https://doi.org/10.1007/s10826-019-01473-x

Kildahl, A. N., Helverschou, S. B., & Oddli, H. W. (2020). Clinicians' retrospective perceptions of failure to detect sexual abuse in a young man with autism and mild intellectual disability. *Journal of Intellectual and Developmental Disability*, 45(2), 194–202. https://doi.org/10.3109/13668250.2019.1680821

King, M. (2020). Dedifferentiation and difference: People with profound intellectual and multiple disabilities and the National Disability Insurance Scheme (NDIS). *Journal of Intellectual & Developmental Disability*, 45(4), 320–325. https://doi.org/10.3109/13668250.2020.1759246

King, J., Edwards, N., Correa-Velez, I., Darracott, R., & Fordyce, M. (2016). Restrictive practices on refugees in Australia with intellectual disability and challenging behaviours: A family's story. *Advances in Mental Health and Intellectual Disabilities*, 10(4), 222–232. https://doi.org/10.1108/amhid-02-2016-0004

King, J., Edwards, N., Correa-Velez, I., Hair, S., & Fordyce, M. (2016A). Disadvantage and disability: Experiences of people from refugee backgrounds with disability living in Australia. *Disability and the Global South*, 3(1), 843–864.

Korpershoek, H., Canrinus, E. T., Fokkens-Bruinsma, M., & de Boer, H. (2020). The relationships between school belonging and students' motivational, social-emotional, behavioural, and academic outcomes in secondary education: A meta-analytic review. *Research Papers in Education*, 35(6), 641–680. https://doi.org/10.1080/02671522.2019.1615116

Kramer, J. M., Schwartz, A. E., Watkins, D., Peace, M., Luterman, S., Barnhart, B., & Alexander, J. S. (2019). Improving research and practice: Priorities for young adults with intellectual/developmental disabilities and mental health needs. *Journal of Mental Health Research in Intellectual Disabilities*, 12(3–4), 97–125. https://doi.org/10.1080/19315864.2019.1636910

Larkin, P., Jahoda, A., MacMahon, K., & Pert, C. (2012). Interpersonal sources of conflict in young people with and without mild to moderate intellectual disabilities at transition from adolescence to adulthood. *Journal of Applied Research in Intellectual Disability*, 25(1), 29–38. https://doi.org/10.1111/j.1468-3148.2011.00652.x

Lawn, S., & Kaine, C. (2022). *Understanding loneliness and mental health*. Lived Experience Australia Ltd. South Australia. www.livedexperienceaustralia.com.au

Legano, L. A., Desch, L. W., Messner, S. A., Idzerda, S., Flaherty, E. G., & Council on Child Abuse and Neglect, & Council on Children with Disabilities. (2021). Maltreatment of children with disabilities. *Pediatrics*, 147(5), 401–411, Article e2021050920. https://doi.org/10.1542/peds.2021-050920

Levine, A., & Breshears, B. (2019). Discrimination at every turn: An intersectional ecological lens for rehabilitation. *Rehabilitation Psychology*, 64(2), 146–153. https://doi.org/10.1037/rep0000266

Lewis. A. K. (2021). Cultural and linguistic diversity among children and families referred for diagnostic evaluation of developmental delay and disability: Implications for service delivery. *Journal of Policy and Practice in Intellectual Disabilities*, 18(2), 113–119, https://doi.org/10.1111/jppi.12358

Lightfoot, E. (2014). Children and youth with disabilities in the child welfare system: An overview. *Child Welfare*, 93(2), 23–46.

Lines, J., Combes, H., & Richards, R. (2021). Exploring how support workers understand their role in supporting adults with intellectual disabilities to access the Internet for intimate relationships. *Journal of Applied Research in Intellectual Disabilities*, 34(2), 556–566. https://doi.org/10.1111/jar.12822

Ludici, A., Antonello, A., & Turchi, G. (2019). Intimate partner violence against disabled persons: Clinical and health impact, intersections, issues and intervention strategies. *Sexuality & Culture*, 23(2), 684–704.

Maclean, M. J., Sims, S., Bower, C., Leonard, H., Stanley, F. J., & O'Donnell, M. (2017). Maltreatment risk among children with disabilities. *Pediatrics*, 139(4), e20161817.

Mansell, J., Beadle-Brown, J., with members of the Special Interest Research Group on Comparative Policy and Practice (2010). Deinstitutionalisation and community living: Position statement of the comparative policy and practice special interest research group of the International Association for the Scientific Study of Intellectual Disabilities. *Journal of Intellectual Disability Research*, 54(2), 104–112. https://doi.org/10.1111/j.1365-2788.2009.01239.x

Manthorpe, J., Stevens, M., Rapaport, J., Challis, D., Jacobs, S., Netten, A., Jones, K., Knapp, M., Wilberforce, M., & Glendinning, C. (2011). Individual budgets and adult safeguarding: Parallel or converging tracks? Further findings from the evaluation of the Individual Budget pilots. *Journal of Social Work*, 11(4), 422–438. https://doi.org/10.1177/1468017310379452

Marques Garcia Ozemala, L., Ortiz Sosa, D., & Urban, A. M. (2019). Violence against women and girls with disabilities: Latin America and the Caribbean. Inter-American Development Bank. https://publications.iadb.org/en/violence-against-women-and-girls-disabilities-latin-america-and-caribbean

May, T., Roberts, J., Webber, M., Spreckley, M., Scheinberg, A., Forrester, M., & Williams, K. (2018). Brief history and user's guide to the Australian National Disability Insurance Scheme. *Journal Paediatric Child Health*, 54(2), 115–120. https://doi.org/10.1111/jpc.13748

McCallum, R., & Martin, H. (2013). The CRPD and children with disabilities. *Australian International Law Journal*, 3(20), 17–31. https://classic.austlii.edu.au/au/journals/AUIntLawJl/2013/3.html

McCarthy, M. (2017). 'What kind of abuse is him spitting in my food?' Reflections on the similarities between disability hate crime, so-called 'mate' crime and domestic violence against women with intellectual disabilities. *Disability & Society*, 32(4), 595–600. https://doi.org/10.1080/09687599.2017.1301854

McCauley, E. (2021). Differential risks: How disability shapes risk in the transition to adulthood for youth who age out of foster care. *Child Youth Services Review*, 131, 106293. https://doi.org/10.1016/j.childyouth.2021.106293

McCausland, R., & Dowse, L. (2020). The need for a community-led, holistic service response to Aboriginal young people with cognitive disability in remote areas: A case study. *Children Australia*, 45(4), 326–334. https://doi.org/10.1017/cha.2020.49

McLaughlin, J. (2023). Bringing disability studies and youth studies together to enhance understandings of youth transitions. *Journal of Youth Studies*, 27(6), 1–16. https://doi.org/10.1080/13676261.2023.2182674

McNeill, S., & Wilson, G. (2017). Use of direct payments in providing care and support to children with disabilities: Opportunities and concerns. *British Journal of Social Work*, 47(7), 1903–1922. https://doi.org/10.1093/bjsw/bcw159

McVilly, K., McCarthy, M., Day, A., Birgden, A., & Malvaso, C. (2022). Identifying and responding to young people with cognitive disability and neurodiversity in Australian and Aotearoa New Zealand youth justice systems. *Psychiatry, Psychology and Law*, 30(6), 789–811. https://doi.org/10.1080/13218719.2022.2124548

Mendes, P., Johnson, G., & Moslehuddin, B. (2012). Young people transitioning from out-of-home care and relationships with family of origin: An examination of three recent Australian studies. *Child Care in Practice: Northern Ireland Journal of Multi-disciplinary Child Care Practice*, 18(4), 357–370. https://doi.org/10.1080/13575279.2012.713849

Midjo, T., & Aune, K. E. (2018). Identity constructions and transition to adulthood for young people with mild intellectual disabilities. *Journal of Intellectual Disabilities*, 22(1), 33–48. https://doi.org/10.1177/1744629516674066

Mikton, C., Maguire, H., & Shakespeare, T. (2014). A systematic review of the effectiveness of interventions to prevent and respond to violence against persons with disabilities. *Journal of Interpersonal Violence*, 29(17), 3207–3226. https://journals.sagepub.com/doi/abs/10.1177/0886260514534530

Miller, R. A., Dika, S. L., Nguyen, D. J., Woodford, M., & Renn, K. A. (2021). LGBTQ+ college students with disabilities: Demographic profile and perceptions of well-being. *Journal of LGBT Youth*, 18(1), 60–77. https://doi.org/10.1080/19361653.2019.1706686

Minkowitz, T. (2017). CRPD and transformative equality. *International Journal of Law in Context*, 13(1), 77–86. https://doi.org/10.1017/S1744552316000483

Mirfin-Veitch, B., & Conder, J. (2017). *'Institutions are places of abuse': The experiences of disabled children and adults in state care*. Donald Beasley Institute.

Mitchell, L. M., Turbiville, V., & Turnbull Iii, H. R. (1999). Reporting abuse and neglect of children with disabilities: Early childhood service providers' views. *Infants and Young Children*, 11(3), 19–26. https://doi.org/10.1097/00001163-199901000-00006

Mykitiuk, R., & Chadna, E. (2018). Article 6: Women with disabilities. In I. Bantekas, M. A. Stein, & D. Anastasiou (Eds.), *The UN Convention on the Rights of Persons with Disabilities: A commentary*, pp. 171–197. Oxford University Press.

National Disability Insurance Agency. (2022). *Pricing arrangements and price limits 2022–23*. National Disability Insurance Agency.

National Ethnic Disability Alliance. (2023). *Factsheet: An overview of Australia's migration health requirements and how they impact on people with disability and/or health conditions*. National Ethnic Disability Alliance. http://neda.org.au/sites/default/files/fact-sheets/English/migration-disability-factsheet-english.pdf

National Health and Medical Research Council. (2018). *National Statement on Ethical Conduct in Human Research 2007 (Updated 2018)*. National Health and Medical Research Council, the Australian Research Council and Universities Australia. Commonwealth of Australia.

Nelson, R., & Lund, E. (2017). Bronfenbrenner's theoretical framework adapted to women with disabilities experiencing intimate partner violence. In A. Johnson, R. Nelson, & E. Lund (Eds.), *Religion, disability, and interpersonal violence*, pp. 11–23. Springer International.

Nixon, M., Thomas, S. D. M., Daffern, M., & Ogloff, J. R. P. (2017). Estimating the risk of crime and victimisation in people with intellectual disability: A data-linkage study. *Social Psychiatry and Psychiatric Epidemiology*, 52(5), 617–626.

Nyberg, A., Ferm, U., & Bornman, J. (2021). School-based abuse prevention programs for children with disabilities: A qualitative study of components and methods. *Australasian Journal of Special and Inclusive Education*, 45(2), 252–267. https://doi.org/10.1017/jsi.2021.18

O'Brien, W., & Fitz-Gibbon, K. (2018). Can human rights standards counter Australia's punitive youth justice practices? *International Journal of Children's Rights*, 26(2), 197–227. https://doi.org/10.1163/15718182-02602004

Office of the Public Advocate. (2012). *Breaking the cycle: Using advocacy-based referrals to assist people with disabilities in the criminal justice system*. Office of the Public Advocate. www.publicadvocate.vic.gov.au

Oksanen, A., Hawdon, J., Holkeri, E., Näsi, M., & Räsänen, P. (2014). Exposure to online hate among young social media users. In M. N. Warehime (Ed.), *Soul of society: A focus on the lives of children and youth*, pp. 253–273. Emerald Group Publishing.

O'Shea, A., Latham, J. R., McNair, R., Despott, N., Rose, M., Mountford, R., & Frawley, P. (2020). Experiences of LGBTIQA plus people with disability in healthcare and community services: Towards embracing multiple identities. *International Journal of Environmental Research and Public Health*, 17(21), 1–14. https://doi.org/10.3390/ijerph17218080

Ottmann, G., McVilly, K., Anderson, J., Chapman, J., Karlyawasam, I., Roy, A., Satari, N., & Stefano, A. (2017). Barriers and enablers to safeguarding children and adults within a disability services context: Insights from an Australian Delphi Study. *Social Policy & Administration*, 51(3), 488–510. https://doi.org/10.1111/spol.12189

Park, G. R., & Seo, B. K. (2020). Revisiting the relationship among housing tenure, affordability and mental health: Do dwelling conditions matter? *Health & Social Care in the Community*, 28(6), 2225–2232. https://doi.org/10.1111/hsc.13035

Pearson, C., Watson, N., Gangneux, J., & Norberg, I. (2021). Transition to where and to what? Exploring the experiences of transitions to adulthood for young disabled people. *Journal of Youth Studies*, 24(10), 1291–1307. https://doi.org/10.1080/13676261.2020.1820972

Peer, J. W., & Hillman, S. B. (2014). Stress and resilience for parents of children with intellectual and developmental disabilities: A review of key factors and recommendations for practitioners. *Journal of Policy and Practice in Intellectual Disabilities*, 11(2), 92–98. https://doi.org/10.1111/jppi.12072

Pickles, J. (2021). Designing hate crime reporting devices: An exploration of young LGBT+ people's report needs. *Journal of LGBT Youth*, 18(4), 394–420. https://doi.org/10.1080/19361653.2019.1685057

Pillay, Y., Brownlow, C., & March, S. (2021). Transition services for young adults on the autism spectrum in Australia. *Education and Training in Autism and Developmental Disabilities*, 56(1), 101–111.

Platt, L., Powers, L., Leotti, S., Hughes, R. B., Robinson-Whelen, S., Osburn, S., Ashkenazy, E., Beers, L., Lund, E. M., & Nicolaidis, C. (2017). The role of gender in violence experienced by adults with developmental disabilities.

Journal of Interpersonal Violence, 32(1), 101–129. https://doi.org/10.1177/0886260515585534

Plummer, S.-B., & Findley, P. A. (2012). Women with disabilities' experience with physical and sexual abuse: Review of the literature and implications for the field. *Trauma, Violence, & Abuse*, 13(1), 15–29. https://doi.org/10.1177/1524838011426014

Punton, G., Dodd, A. L., & McNeill, A. (2022). 'You're on the waiting list': An interpretive phenomenological analysis of young adults' experiences of waiting lists within mental health services in the UK. *PLoS ONE*, 17(3). https://doi.org/10.1371/journal.pone.0265542

Puyaltó, C., Pallisera, M., Fullana, J., & Díaz-Garolera, G. (2022). Challenges of having a loving partner: The views of adults with intellectual disabilities. *International Journal of Developmental Disabilities*, 68(1), 64–72. https://doi.org/10.1080/20473869.2019.1701786

Pyysiäinen, J., Halpin, D., & Guilfoyle, A. (2017). Neoliberal governance and 'responsibilisation' of agents: Reassessing the mechanisms of responsibility-shift in neoliberal discursive environments. *Distinktion (Aarhus)*, 18(2), 215–235. https://doi.org/10.1080/1600910X.2017.1331858

Ramasamy, V., Rillotta, F., & Alexander, J. (2021). Experiences of adults with intellectual disabilities who identify as lesbian, gay, bisexual, or transgender within mainstream community: A systematic review of qualitative studies. *JBI Evidence Synthesis*, 19(1), 59–154. https://doi.org/10.11124/JBIES-20-00032

Ravenscroft, J., Wazny, K., & Davis, J. M. (2017). Factors associated with successful transition among children with disabilities in eight European countries. *PLoS ONE*, 12(6), e0179904–e0179904. https://doi.org/10.1371/journal.pone.0179904

Rees, P., & Manthorpe, J. (2010). Managers' and staff experiences of adult protection allegations in mental health and learning disability residential services: A qualitative study. *British Journal of Social Work*, 40(2), 513–529.

Reiter, S., Bryen, D., & Shachar, I. (2007). Adolescents with intellectual disabilities as victims of abuse. *Journal of Intellectual Disabilities*, 11(4), 371–387. https://doi.org/10.1177/1744629507084602

Richardson, L., Beadle-Brown, J., Bradshaw, J., Guest, C., Malovic, A., & Himmerich, J. (2016). 'I felt that I deserved it': Experiences and implications of disability hate crime. *Tizard Learning Disability Review*, 21(2), 80–88.

Rigby K. (2003). Consequences of bullying in schools. *Canadian Journal of Psychiatry – In Review* 48(9), 583–590.

Rivara, F., & Le Menestrel, S. (Eds). (2016). *Preventing bullying through science, policy, and practice committee on the biological and psychosocial effects of peer victimization: Lessons for bullying prevention; board on children, youth, and families.* Committee on Law and Justice; Division of Behavioral and Social Sciences and Education; Health and Medicine Division; National Academies of Sciences, Engineering, and Medicine. National Academies Press.

Robinson, S. (2012). Enabling and protecting: Proactive approaches to addressing the abuse and neglect of children and young people with disability. Issues paper for Children with Disability Australia. https://cyda.org.au/enabling-and-protecting-proactive-approaches-to-addressing-the-abuse-and-neglect-of-children-and-young-people-with-disability/

Robinson, S., Frawley, P., & Dyson, S. (2021). Access and accessibility in domestic and family violence services for women with disabilities: Widening the lens. *Violence against Women*, 27(6–7), 918–936. https://doi.org/10.1177/1077801220909890

Robinson, S., & Graham, A. (2021). Feeling safe, avoiding harm: Safety priorities of children and young people with disability and high support needs. *Journal of Intellectual Disability*, 25(4), 583–602. https://doi.org/10.1177/1744629520917496

Royal Commission into Violence, Abuse, Neglect and Exploitation of People with Disability (2021). Overview of responses to experiences of culturally and linguistically diverse people with disability. Issues paper. https://disability.royalcommission.gov.au/system/files/2023-02/Overview%20of%20responses%20to%20the%20Culturally%20and%20linguistically%20diverse%20people%20with%20disability%20Issues%20paper.pdf

Salerno-Ferraro, A. C., & Schuller, R. A. (2020). Perspectives from the ASD community on police interactions: Challenges & recommendations. *Research in Developmental Disabilities*, 105, 103732–103740. https://doi.org/10.1016/j.ridd.2020.103732

Salmon, N., Barry, A., & Hutchins, E. (2018). Inclusive research: An Irish perspective. *British Journal of Learning Disabilities*, 46(4), 268–277. https://doi.org/10.1111/bld.12247

Schalock, R. L., Luckasson, R., & Tassé, M. J. (2021). An overview of intellectual disability: Definition, diagnosis, classification, and systems of supports. *American Journal on Intellectual and Developmental Disabilities*, 126(6), 439–442. https://doi.org/10.1352/1944-7558-126.6.439

Scherer, H., & Reyns, B. (2019). Visible disabilities and risk of interpersonal victimization. In B. Berry (Ed.), *Appearance bias and crime*, pp. 243–255. Cambridge University Press. https://doi.org/10.1017/9781108377683.014

Schmidt, E., Dougherty, M., Robek, N., Weaver, L., & Darragh, A. R. (2021). Sexual experiences and perspectives of adolescents and young adults with intellectual and developmental disabilities. *Journal of Adolescent Research*, 1–26, Article 07435584211028225. https://doi.org/10.1177/07435584211028225

Schwehr, B. (2010). Safeguarding and personalisation. *Journal of Adult Protection*, 12(2), 43–51.

Seale, J., Nind, M., & Simmons, B. (2013). Transforming positive risk-taking practices: The possibilities of creativity and resilience in learning disability contexts. *Scandinavian Journal of Disability Research*, 15(3), 233–248. https://doi.org/10.1080/15017419.2012.703967

Senate Community Affairs Reference Committee. (2015). Violence, abuse and neglect against people with disability in institutional and residential settings, including the gender and age related dimensions, and the particular situation of Aboriginal and Torres Strait Islander people with disability, and culturally and linguistically diverse people with disability. www.aph.gov.au/parliamentary_business/committees/senate/community_affairs/violence_abuse_neglect

Sherry, M. (2010). *Disability hate crimes: Does anyone really hate disabled people?* Ashgate.

Shier, M. L., Turpin, A., Nicholas, D. B., & Graham, J. R. (2019). Dynamics of a culture of workplace safety in human service organizations: A qualitative analysis. *International Social Work*, 62(6), 1561–1574. https://doi.org/10.1177/0020872819858744

Siebers, T. (2013). Disability and the theory of complex embodiment: For identity politics in a new register. In L. Davis (Ed.), *The Disability Studies Reader* (4th ed.), pp. 278–297. Routledge.

Sinclair, J., Hollway, J. A., Sanford, C., Cameto, R., Benson, B., Arnold, L. E., & Seeley, J. R. (2023). Developing the diagnostic interview for adolescents and adults with mild/moderate intellectual disabilities: An interview schedule of mental disorders (DIAAID). *Journal of Mental Health Research in Intellectual Disabilities*, 1–28. https://doi.org/10.1080/19315864.2023.2214089

Smith, L., & Dowse, L. (2019). Times during transition for young people with complex support needs: Entangled critical moments, static liminal periods and contingent meaning making times. *Journal of Youth Studies*, 22(10), 1327–1344. https://doi.org/10.1080/13676261.2019.1575346

Sobsey, R. (1994). *Violence and abuse in the lives of people with disabilities: The end of silent acceptance?* Paul H. Brookes Publishing.

Soldatic, K., van Toorn, G., Dowse, L., & Muir, K. (2014). Intellectual disability and complex intersections: Marginalisation under the National Disability Insurance Scheme. *Research and Practice in Intellectual and Developmental Disabilities*, 1(1), 6–16. https://doi.org/10.1080/23297018.2014.906050

Stalker, K., Taylor, J., Fry, D., & Stewart, A. B. R. (2015). A study of disabled children and child protection in Scotland: A hidden group? *Children and Youth Services Review*, 56, 126–134. https://doi.org/10.1016/j.childyouth.2015.07.012

Stein, M. A., Barnett, P., Harper, P., Porter, B., & O'Cinneide, C. (In press). Strategic litigation and ESCR rights: Education as a case study. In. M. A. Stein & M. Langford (Eds.), *Disability social rights*. Cambridge University Press.

Stein, M. A., & Challenor, B. (In press). Employment in disability social rights. In M. A. Stein & M. Langford (Eds.), *Disability social rights*. Cambridge University Press.

Stein, M. A., & Lord, J. E. (2007). Jacobus tenBroek, participatory justice, and the UN Convention on the Rights of Persons with Disabilities. *Texas Journal on Civil Liberties and Civil Rights*, 13, 167–185.

(2012). Human rights and humanitarian assistance for refugees and internally displaced persons with disabilities in Africa. In I. Grobbelaar-du Plessis & T. van Reenen (Eds.) *Aspects of disability law in Africa,* pp. 31–52. Pretoria University Law Press.

Stein, P. J., & Stein, M. A. (2022). Disability, human rights, and climate justice. *Human Rights Quarterly*, 44(1), 81–110. https://doi.org/10.1353/hrq.2022.0003

Stevens, M., Woolham, J., Manthorpe, J., Aspinall, F., Hussein, S., Baxter, K., Samsi, K., & Ismail, M. (2018). Implementing safeguarding and personalisation in social work: Findings from practice. *Journal of Social Work*, 18(1), 3–22. https://doi.org/10.1177/1468017316652001

Stoffelen, J. M. T., Schaafsma, D., Kok, G., & Curfs, L. M. G. (2018). Women who love: An explorative study on experiences of lesbian and bisexual women with a mild intellectual disability in the Netherlands. *Sex Disability*, 36(3), 249–264. https://doi.org/10.1007/s11195-018-9519-y

Strnadová, I., & Cumming, T. M. (2016). *Lifespan transitions and disability: A holistic perspective*. Routledge.

Strnadová, I., Danker, J., & Carter, A. (2022). Scoping review on sex education for high school-aged students with intellectual disability and/or on the autism spectrum: Parents', teachers' and students' perspectives, attitudes and experiences. *Sex Education*, 22(3), 361–378. https://doi.org/10.1080/14681811.2021.1941842

Strnadová, I., Dowse, L., & Watfern, C. (2020). *Doing research inclusively: Guidelines for co-producing research with people with disability*. UNSW (University of New South Wales) Disability Innovation Institute.

Strnadová, I., Strnadova, I., & Cumming, T. M. (2016). *Lifespan transitions and disability: A holistic perspective*. University of Ottawa Press.

Sutherland, G., Kavanagh, A., Llewellyn, G., Kmjacki, L., Byars, S., & Hargrave, J. (2021). *Nature and extent of violence, abuse, neglect and exploitation against people with disability in Australia*. Report prepared for the Royal Commission into Violence, Neglect and Exploitation of People with Disability. https://disability.royalcommission.gov.au/system/files/2021-03/Research%20Report%20-%20Nature%20and%20extent%20of%20violence%2C%20abuse%2C%20neglect%20and%20exploitation%20against%20people%20with%20disability%20in%20Australia.pdf

Thill, C. (2019). Listening for intersectionality: How disabled persons' organisations have improved recognition of difference in Australia's National Disability Insurance Scheme. In O. Hankivsky & J. S. Jordan-Zachery (Eds.), *The Palgrave handbook of intersectionality in public policy*, pp. 689–704. Palgrave Macmillan.

Thomas, S., & Wolfensberger, W. (1999). An overview of Social Role Valorization. In R. J. Flynn & R. A. Lemay (Eds.), *A quarter-century of normalization and social role valorization: Evolution and impact*, pp. 125–160. University of Ottawa Press. https://doi.org/10.2307/j.ctt1cn6s45.7

Thompson, N. (2006). *Anti-discriminatory practice* (4th ed.). Basingstoke

Thorneycroft, R., & Asquith, N. L. (2015). The dark figure of disablist violence. *Howard Journal of Criminal Justice*, 54(5), 489–507. https://doi.org/10.1111/hojo.12147

Toft, A., Franklin, A., & Langley, E. (2019). Young disabled and LGBTQ+: Negotiating identity. *Journal of LGBT Youth*, 16(2). https://doi.org/10.1080/19361653.2018.1544532

United Nations. (1990). Convention on the Rights of the Child, New York, 20 November 1989, in force 2 September 1990, 1577 UNTS 3.

(2006). Convention on the Rights of Persons with Disabilities. www.ohchr.org/en/instruments-mechanisms/instruments/convention-rights-persons-disabilities

United Nations Committee on the Rights of the Child. (2013). General comment No. 17 on the right of the child to rest, leisure, play, recreational activities, cultural life and the arts, UN Doc CRC/C/GC/17.

United Nations Committee on the Rights of Persons with Disabilities. (2012). Concluding observations on the initial report of Peru, UN doc CRPD/C/PER/CO/1.

(2013). Concluding observations on the initial report of Australia, UN doc CRPD/C/AUS/CO/1.

(2014). General Comment No. 1 on Article 12 on equal recognition before the law, UN Doc CRPD/C/GC/1.

(2014A). General Comment No. 2 on Article 9 on accessibility, UN Doc CRPD/C/GC/2.

(2016). General Comment No. 3 on Article 6 on women and girls with disabilities, UN Doc CRPD/C/GC/3.

(2016A). General Comment No. 4 on Article 24 on the right to inclusive education, UN Doc CRPD/C/GC/4.

(2017). General Comment No. 5 on Article 19 on living independently and being included in the community, UN Doc CRPD/C/GC/5.

(2017A). Concluding observations on the initial report of Canada, UN doc CRPD/C/CAN/CO/1.

(2017B). Concluding observations on the initial report of the United Kingdom of Great Britain and Northern Ireland, UN doc CRPD/C/GBR/CO/1.

(2018). General Comment No. 6 on Article 5 on equality and non-discrimination, UN doc CRPD/C/GC/6.

(2018A). General Comment No. 7. on Articles 4.3 and 33.3 on Participation with persons with disabilities in the implementation and monitoring of the Convention, UN doc CRPD/C/GC/7.

(2018B). Concluding observations on the initial report of Slovenia, UN doc CRPD/C/SVN/CO/1.

(2018C). Observations on the initial report of South Africa, UN doc CRPD/C/ZAF/CO/1.

(2019). Concluding observations on the combined second and third periodic reports of Australia, UN doc CRPD/C/AUS/CO/2-3.

(2019A). Concluding observations on the initial report of India, UN doc CRPD/C/IND/CO/1.

(2019B). Concluding observations on the combined second and third periodic reports of Ecuador, UN doc CRPD/C/ECU/CO/2-3.

(2019C). Concluding observations on the initial report of Niger, UN doc CRPD/C/Ner/CO/1.

(2019D). Concluding observations on the combined second and third periodic reports of Spain, UN doc CRPD/C/ESP/CO/2-3.

(2019E). Concluding observations on the initial report of Iraq, UN doc CRPD/C/IRQ/CO/1.
(2019F). Concluding observations on the initial report of Rwanda, UN doc CRPD/C/Rwa/CO/1.
(2019G). Concluding observations on the initial report of Myanmar, UN doc CRPD/C/MMR/CO/1.
(2021). Concluding observations on the initial report of Djibouti, UN doc CRPD/CDJI/CO1.
(2021A). Concluding observations on the initial report of France, CRPD/C/FRA/CO/1.
(2022). General comment No. 8 on Article 27 on the Right of Persons with Disabilities to Work, UN doc CRPD/C/GC/8.
(2022A). Concluding observations on the combined second and third periodic report of Mexico, UN doc CRPD/C/MEX/CO/2-3.
(2022B). Concluding observations on the combined second and third periodic report of Hungary, UN doc CRPD/C/HUN/CO/2-3.
(2022C). Concluding observations on the combined second and third periodic reports of New Zealand, UN doc CRPD/C/NZL/CO/2-3.
(2022D). Concluding observations on the initial report of Japan, UN doc CRPD/C/JPN/CO/1.
(2022E). Concluding observations on the combined second and third periodic reports of China, UN doc CRPD/C/CHN/CO/2-3.
(2022G). Concluding observations on the initial report of Lao People's Democratic Republic, UN doc CRPD/C/LAO/CO/1.
(2022H). Concluding observations on the initial report of Switzerland, UN doc CRPD/C/CHE/CO/1.
(2022I). Concluding observations on the initial report of Indonesia, UN doc CRPD/C/IDN/CO/1.
(2022J). Concluding observations on the initial report of Bangladesh, UN doc CRPD/C/BGD/CO/1, 11 October 2022.
(2022K). Concluding observations on the initial report of Singapore, UN doc CRPD/C/SGP/1.
(2022L). Observaciones finales sobre el informe inicial de la República Bolivariana de Venezuela, UN doc CRPD/C/VEN/CO/1.
(2023). Concluding observations on the combined second and third periodic reports of Germany, UN doc CRPD/C/DEU/2-3.
(2023A). Concluding observations on the initial report of Georgia, UN doc CRPD/C/GEO/1.
(2023B). Concluding observations on the combined initial and second periodic reports of Malawi, UN doc CRPD/C/MWI/1-2.
(2023C). Concluding observations on the combined second and third periodic reports of Mongolia, UN doc CRPD/C/MNG/2-3.
(2023D). Concluding observations on the initial report of Togo, UN doc CRPD/C/TGO/1.

(2023E). Concluding observations on the initial report of Israel, UN doc CRPD/C/ISR/1.
(2023F). Concluding observations on the initial report of Andorra, UN doc CRPD/C/AND/1.
(2023G). Concluding observations on the initial report of Mauritania, UN doc CRPD/C/MRT/1.
(2023H). Concluding observations on the combined second and third reports of Austria, UN doc CRPD/C/AUT/CO/2-3.

United Nations Department of Economic and Social Affairs, Office of the United Nations Commissioner for Human Rights., & Inter-Parliamentary Union. (2007). Chapter One: Overview – Realising the rights of persons with disabilities: The compelling reasons. In *Handbook for Parliamentarians on the Convention on the Rights of Persons with Disabilities*, pp. 1–9. United Nations.

United Nations General Assembly. (1989). Convention on the Rights of the Child, UN Doc. A/RES/44/25, 20 November 1989. 1577 UNTS 3.
(2006). Convention on the Rights of Persons with Disabilities, UN Doc. A/61/106, 13 December 2006. 2515 UNTS 3.

United Nations Human Rights Office of the High Commissioner. (2018). *Integrating a gender perspective into human rights investigations: Guidance and practice.*

van Schalkwyk, G. I., Marin, C. E., Ortiz, M., Rolison, M., Qayyum, Z., McPartland, J. C., Lebowitz, E. R., Volkmar, F. R., & Silverman, W. K. (2017). Social media use, friendship quality, and the moderating role of anxiety in adolescents with autism spectrum disorder. *Journal of Autism and Developmental Disorders*, 47(9), 2805–2813. https://doi.org/10.1007/s10803-017-3201-6

Velez, G., & Spencer, M. B. (2018). Phenomenology and intersectionality: Using PVEST as a frame for adolescent identity formation amid intersecting ecological systems of inequality. *New Directions for Child and Adolescent Development*, 2018(161), 75–90. https://doi.org/10.1002/cad.20247

Victorian Equal Opportunity and Human Rights Commission. (2013). *Unfinished business: Koori women and the justice system*, Victoria State Government.

Walmsley, J., Tilley, L., Dumbleton, S., & Bardsley, J. (2017). The changing face of parent advocacy: A long view. *Disability & Society*, 32(9), 1366–1386. https://doi.org/10.1080/09687599.2017.1322496

Warr, D., Dickinson, H., Olney, S., Hargrave, J., Karanikolas, A., Kasidis, V., G., K., Ozge, J., Peters, D., Wheeler, J., & Wilcox, M. (2017). *Choice, control and the NDIS: Service users' perspectives on having choice and control in the new National Disability Insurance Scheme.* University of Melbourne. https://socialequity.unimelb.edu.au/__data/assets/pdf_file/0008/2598497/Choice-Control-and-the-NDIS.pdf

West, E. A., Perner, D. E., Laz, L., Murdick, N. L., & Gartin, B. C. (2015). People-first and competence-oriented language. *International Journal of Whole Schooling*, 11(2), 16.

Whitehead, R., Hopkins, L., Hughes, E., Kehoe, M., & Pedwell, G. (2021). 'Everyone on the same team, all working together': Implementing a co-ordinated multi-disciplinary approach to supporting young people with co-occurring intellectual disability and mental health issues. *Journal of Mental Health Research in Intellectual Disabilities*, 14(1), 1–22. https://doi.org/10.1080/19315864.2020.1864689

Whittle, E. L., Fisher, K. R., Reppermund, S., Lenroot, R., & Trollor, J. (2018). Barriers and enablers to accessing mental health services for people with intellectual disability: A scoping review. *Journal of Mental Health Research in Intellectual Disabilities*, 11(1), 69–102. https://doi.org/10.1080/19315864.2017.1408724

Wieland, J., & Zitman, F. G. (2016). It is time to bring borderline intellectual functioning back into the main fold of classification systems. *British Journal of Psychology Bulletin*, 40(4), 204–206. https://doi.org/10.1192/pb.bp.115.051490

Wiesel, I., Whitzman, C., Gleeson, B., & Bigby, C. (2019). The National Disability Insurance Scheme in an urban context: Opportunities and challenges for Australian cities. *Urban Policy and Research*, 37(1), 1–12. https://doi.org/10.1080/08111146.2018.1481026

Wilcox, P., Sullivan, C., Jones, S., & van Gelder, J. (2014). Personality and opportunity: An integrated approach to offending and victimization. *Criminal Justice and Behavior*, 41(7), 880–901. https://doi.org/10.1177/0093854813520603

Wilson, N. J., Macdonald, J., Hayman, B., Bright, A. M., Frawley, P., & Gallego, G. (2016). A narrative review of the literature about people with intellectual disability who identify as lesbian, gay, bisexual, transgender, intersex or questioning. *Journal of Intellectual Disabilities*, 22(2), 171–196. https://doi.org/10.1177/1744629516682681

Wislocki, K. E., & Zalta, A. K. (2023). Assessing the existence of trauma-related diagnostic overshadowing in adult populations. *Psychological Trauma*. https://doi.org/10.1037/tra0001484

Wisner-Carlson, R., Uram, S., & Flis, T. (2020). The transition to adulthood for young people with autism spectrum disorder. *Child and Adolescent Psychiatric Clinics of North America*, 29(2), 345–358. https://doi.org/10.1016/j.chc.2019.12.002

World Health Organisation. (2022). International classification of diseases. www.who.int/standards/classifications/classification-of-diseases

Wyman, J., Lavoie, J., & Talwar, V. (2019). Best practices for interviewing children with intellectual disabilities in maltreatment cases. *Exceptionality*, 27(3), 167–184. https://doi.org/10.1080/09362835.2018.1425623

Wyn, J., Khan, R., & Dadvand, B. (2018). *Multicultural youth Australia census status report 2017/2018*. Youth Research Centre, the University of Melbourne.

Young-Southward, G., Cooper, S.-A., & Philo, C. (2017). Health and wellbeing during transition to adulthood for young people with intellectual disabilities:

A qualitative study. *Research in Developmental Disabilities*, 70, 94–103. https://doi.org/10.1016/j.ridd.2017.09.003

Zhou, Q. (2016). Accessing disability services by people from culturally and linguistically diverse backgrounds in Australia. *Disability and Rehabilitation: An International, Multidisciplinary Journal*, 38(9), 844–852. https://doi.org/10.3109/09638288.2015.1062925

Index

For EU product safety concerns, contact us at Calle de José Abascal, 56–1°,
28003 Madrid, Spain or eugpsr@cambridge.org.

www.ingramcontent.com/pod-product-compliance
Lightning Source LLC
LaVergne TN
LVHW011810200926
848484LV00005B/1131
9781009408707